YESTERDAY'S
FACES

YESTERDAY'S FACES

VOLUME III
From The Dark Side

Robert Sampson

Bowling Green State University
Bowling Green, OH 43403

Acknowledgements

Certain character discussions in this volume have previously appeared, in somewhat different form, as follows: "The Chang Monster," *The Science-Fiction Collector #14* (May 30, 1981); "Peterman From the Old School," *The Mystery Fancier*, Vol. 5, No. 4 (July/August 1981); "Pirates In Candyland," *The Mystery Fancier*, Vol. 6, No. 3 (May/June 1982); and "The Other Spider," *Echoes*, June 1982.

Covers reproduced by permission from the following sources: Blazing Publications, Inc., proprietor and conservator of the respective copyrights and successor-in-interest to Popular Publications, Inc. From *The Black Mask* 1922 and 1923 © by Pro-Distributors Publishing Co., Inc.; © renewed 1950 and 1951 by Popular Publications, Inc. From *Flynn's* 1925, 1926, 1927 © by Red Star News Co.; © renewed 1953, 1954, 1955 by Popular Publications, Inc.
Conde Nast Publications, Inc. for *Detective Story Magazine* 1917, 1921, 1922, 1927, 1928, 1929, 1930, 1931, 1932 © by Street & Smith Corporation; © renewed 1944, 1950, 1955, 1956, 1957, 1958, 1959, 1960. For *The Popular Magazine* 1926 © by Street & Smith Corporation; © renewed 1954.
Dell Publishing Company for *Scotland Yard* © 1931.

Library of Congress Catalogue Card No.: 82-73597

ISBN: 0-87972-362-9 Clothbound
0-87972-363-7 Paperback

To Ed and Jane Keniston—in celebration of dogs and violets and Sunday night musicales, and all those other shining pleasures we shared along the way.

CONTENTS

Acknowledgements   ix

To the Curious Reader   x

Evocation   1

I—Emperors of Evil   4

II—Crime Extraordinary   27

III—The Wicked Brotherhood   63

IV—Four From Edgar Wallace   98

V—In Name Only   123

VI—More Rogues and Bent Heroes   182

Afterword   219

Notes   224

Bibliography   232

Checklists of Series Characters   235

Index   262

ACKNOWLEDGEMENTS

Particular thanks is extended to Paul Bonner, Jr., and the Conde Nast Publications, Inc., for permission to quote from issues of Street & Smith*Detective Story Magazine*; and thanks to Blazing Publications, Inc., for permission to quote from issues of *The Black Mask* and *Flynn's*.

My warmest thanks to Carolyn A. Davis and the George Arents Research Library, Syracuse University, for their patient support and all those xeroxes.

And very special thanks to Penelope Wallace for permission to quote from Edgar Wallace's *The Brigand, Four-Square Jane, The Gaunt Stranger, The Mixer, The Ringer,* and *The Ringer Returns.*

To those friends and collectors who have supported me without complaint, made available copies of their magazines and checklists, and have been accomodating beyond all reason, let me thank:

Dave Arends and Walker Martin for effort beyond the call of duty in reviewing and listing innumerable characters from *Detective Story Magazine.*

Randy Cox, whose comments always made sense, even when my prose didn't.

Ed Keniston, the most amiable of photographers, for all those scalding mornings in the darkroom.

Richard Minter, the Phantom Dealer, who always turned up something useful, no matter how obscure.

Will Murray for his careful ploughing of these endless volumes and all those pages of comment he sent back that had to be checked, every blessed item.

Guy Townsend, whose enthusiasm for fugitive pieces about the past is illogical but gratifying.

And Christopher Lowder, John Hogan, and Pim Koldewyn through whose mutual efforts a massy stream of Edgar Wallace flowed from London and Amsterdam to Huntsville, including books I had waited thirty-five years to read.

TO THE CURIOUS READER

Concealed in the heart of the most devout glimmers a secret belief:
"Were I not a miracle of rectitude, I could be a truly great criminal."

It is a harmless fleck of Auld Hootie, and a testament to the fallibility of us all. For if no man is a hero to his valet, still less is he a criminal genius to his local police.

This realistic assessment is beside the point. The lure of illegal adventure has drawn at man's mind through the ages. Back in antiquity towers Odysseus, glib rogue and pirate. Barely a thousand years later, more or less, Nero and his witty ways demonstrated the joys of wickedness. Still later, ballads were sung of Robin Hood, and penny dreadfuls cried of Spring-heel Jack, and songs ennobled Jesse James.

Even in our own times, the criminal is celebrated. His name enters the newspapers; his exploits enter fiction; and, after his election, his speeches enter *The Congressional Record*.

Our curiosity about the criminal is unslacked. We get a sideways look into his heart by examining our own. For with each pang of our own avarice, each leap of our own libido, each twinge we feel at another's bankroll or pearl necklace or *Spider* magazine collection, we admit our uneasy kinship with those others, the people from the dark side. Their passions reflect our hidden flames.

Fiction tells us that, at the end, a trivial mistake drags the criminal down. His immense plans flake away. His silken women fade. Justice triumphs. We recognize this as an obligatory literary convention. It was a near thing, after all. How obvious that fatal mistake was. How quickly *we* would have seen it.

So fiction whispers of forbidden things. We read, and having vicariously refreshed ourselves, turn again to the lean rewards of virtue.

The appearance of Raffles, gentleman cracksman and thief, in 1899, is usually cited as a benchmark from which later criminal heroes took their bearings. Raffles was magnificent and influential and, above all, popular. But other criminals had occupied series before him. Two years earlier, the face-changing Colonel Clay had begun his activities. And before Colonel Clay, the lively dime novels had offered such wonderful figures as Dr. Quartz, Nick Carter's formidable opponent, in 1891, and Frank and Jesse James in 1881.

If he were not the first of the popular fiction series criminals, Raffles was certainly a key figure, a benchmark, in the development of the type. After him, other criminal heroes stepped forward, their names remembered, if vaguely, even today, including Romney Pringle (1902), Arsene Lupin (1907), Jimmy Valentine (1909), Cleek (The Man of Forty Faces) (1910), the Lone Wolf and The Infallible Godahl (1914). Most of these were discussed in *Glory Figures,* the first volume of this series.

By 1914 the pulp magazines were well launched. At that time, they were all—fiction magazines, mixing western adventure, humor, mystery, crime, and fantasy in a single issue. Editors well knew the public's interest in fictional criminals. As a result, stories of crime emerged vigorously from pulp paper pages. Most criminals were, at first, bit players, appearing only to be foiled in the pages of *The All Story, The Popular Magazine,* and *People's Magazine* of the early 1900s. These publications proved only temporary shelters for criminal leads. The main show under the Big Top began with publication of *Detective Story Magazine,* the first issue dated October 5, 1915. By definition, the magazine was devoted entirely to stories of detection, mystery, and crime. In it, the series criminal (as well as the series detective) appeared almost at once, brazenly flaunting himself in this public place.

For almost a decade, *Detective Story* was the major vehicle for mystery fiction and crime adventure, and a major force in shaping that fiction to the vivid world of the popular magazine.

Detective Story did not long remain the only publication of its kind. Its good example was followed by the slender, little, twice-a-month pamphlet, *Mystery Magazine* (1917). *Black Mask* appeared in 1920 and *Detective Tales,* oversized and thin, in 1922. Later followed *Real Detective Tales* (its contents mainly fiction), *Flynn's* in 1924, and *Mystery Stories* and *Clues* in 1926. Throughout these early years, the offerings of these specialized magazines were supplemented by such general magazines as *Adventure, Argosy, Blue Book,* and *Short Stories,* all regularly publishing stories of detection and crime. In spite of this accumulating competition, *Detective Story Magazine* reigned supreme in its field, never seriously challenged until the mid-Twenties. After that time, the heat in the kitchen became intolerable.

Through these magazines poured a tide of criminals and criminal heroes. Most appeared in a single story, a few in extended series. They spread like a morning glory vine among the double-columned pages. They spread in unexpected directions, hurling out variations. And they contrived to create, week upon week across the years, a succession of distinct character types. In doing so, they drew upon every other popular entertainment form available—hard-bound books and silent movie serials, English magazines and French newspapers, dime novels and stage melodramas and medicine shows. The pulps swallowed it all, molding it to the requirements of popular fiction.

From all this cross-fertilization grew several specific forms of series criminal—the Emperor of Crime, the Mastermind, the Grand Single, the Criminal With a Cause, and the Bent Hero, this last a criminal only by harsh standards.

These characters, criminals and near criminals alike, are the subjects of this volume. They loomed colossal in the thin, bright air of the early mystery magazines. And each, in his own way, added his mite to the crime story as it evolved across the decades.

Robert Sampson
Huntsville, Alabama
1987

EVOCATION

In the half-light of the smoke-choked room, the face of the Great Detective was difficult to discern.

"...as for representatives of the criminal mind in the popular press," he concluded, "we have fallen upon commonplace days, for there is neither originality nor that essential trace of art to inform their fiction with some slight trace of interest. Classification is the solitary joy remaining to us, Watson."

"Who Watson is, I don't know," I cried cheerfully. "Chick is good enough for me. But it's dollars to holes you've struck it, chief. Crooks aren't original."

The Great Detective drew reflectively on his fine cigar. "If you survey the general magazines from about 1915 to 1930, you find them overrun with scoundrels."

"There's something in that, chief."

"Four types of these literary crooks are immediately evident:"
"First are men of great ability. They are genius and fiend in one. They are Emperors of Crime. Dr. Quartz comes immediately to mind."

"He does," I said, "sure as you're a foot high."

"They display endless genius in the accomplishment of vast crimes. They are educated. Their minds are subtle and penetrating, and they possess remarkable administrative abilities. All of them dominate and direct armies of ruthless crooks."

"That's true, chief."

"They plot on an international scale, manipulate national destinies, sway governments. Power is their goal—and all the gold in South Africa. These superlative geniuses are often Anglo-Saxon. More rarely they are French. And frequently they are Oriental, Dr. Fu Manchu being the most brilliant example."

His lean bronze face hardened. He tamped rough-cut tobacco ruthlessly into his short, blackened pipe. "Still another group, Petrie, are criminal masterminds, organizers and planners of immense capability. They employ hundreds for crime and yet they scheme alone, aided only by a few close associates—a dacoit or two, or a singularly beautiful woman. But they strike for millions, for personal wealth. The mastermind would

1

rather loot Ohio than dominate the nation. I have often blundered, Petrie. But never by underestimating geniuses such as these."

"Remarkable," I said, as he tugged thoughtfully at his left ear. "So there are Emperors of Crime and Criminal Masterminds. Still that leaves the rank and file of the criminal legions unaccounted for."

The shadow of a smile flickered across his lips. "That's the crux of the matter, Walter. The crime statistics of New York City, alone, testify to the correctness of your statement. Yeggmen, dips, petermen, con men— all those trades collectively comprising the professional class of criminal— The Grand Singles, the third group of fictional criminals.

"The Meat and Potatoes of Crookdom," I cried. "Gad, that would be an intriguing article for the *Star!*"

"Indeed it would, Walter. Analytical evaluation assures us that 87.6948% of identified crimes are performed by professional criminals. They appear in more modest percentile levels in the magazines. Authors make them cute, too often: small-time thugs, inoffensive leather lifters. Since they are, in a way, modest heroes, the authors make their crimes attractive, allow them to escape punishment to carry their adventures on for protracted periods, an offense to society and a reproach to every decent instinct," he thundered.

I bent forward to turn up the lamp. But a touch of his black-gloved fingers restrained me. In the weird blue light, I could see only two blazing eyes that seemed to penetrate my soul.

"And yet a fourth class, Vincent."

In the silence of the room, his voice was a chilling whisper.

"I have seen the fourth class. Amateurs at crime. Young people gone wrong for a cause. For vengeance reasons, they turn to crime. They are gifted with skill and luck. Some steal to avenge themselves on society. Others to gain stimulation from crime."

"However, they often repent," I said.

A low laugh filled the room with throbbing mockery.

"Yes," hissed that sinister whisper. "Many repent. Some return their spoils. Others donate it to charity. A few prey only on other crooks. An interesting group, Vincent. But men of crime, all."

"Yet I still do not understand," I faltered.

From the darkness shuddered a soft laugh expressive of sympathy and understanding. Emboldened, I stated:

"What if the criminal does repent? If the love of a good woman has opened his eyes to the folly of his course. If he has laid aside his evil and made restitution. Then, if events hound him temporarily back to crime...."

"Then," hissed the sinister whisper from the shadows, "they are termed Bent Heroes and discussed in a later chapter."

The light went out. In the blackness, a spectral laugh rose to a shivering crescendo of mockery. It rang like a knell, then faded in a host of gibing echoes. I was alone in the blackened room.[1]

I—EMPERORS OF EVIL

The emperor of crime emperors was Fu Manchu. Tall, spare, richly marinated in evil, he glided through thirteen books, from *The Insidious Dr. Fu Manchu* (1913) (the original title was *The Mystery of Dr. Fu Manchu*) to *Emperor Fu Manchu* (1959). Much later, in 1976, four additional stories (three of them trifles) were collected in the paperback, *The Wrath of Fu Manchu*, together with eight other stories unrelated to the series. These books were written by Sax Rohmer, the familiar pen name of Arthur Henry Sarsfield Ward.

Fu Manchu is one of the more magnificent characters in fiction. He operates at a high level of the absurd in regions where fiction becomes myth and fortunate choices of image and subject fuse with what seems inevitability. Before Fu Manchu hovered the generalized menace of the Yellow Peril. After Fu Manchu, the general became the specific, and the Yellow Peril modified to endless reiterations of the Devil Doctor, that satanic, lean genius, copied and renamed for a hundred different stories.

The Fu Manchu series, gracefully mad, chases brightly along. Here leers menace incomprehensible, dipped in the drowsy perfume of the Orient. Weird thin keenings of the dacoits rise from the shrubbery. These dainty feminine hands, soft as warm velvet, drip blood. Immense schemes rear, gigantic in conception, netting up whole continents, then dissolve on one man's death or one man's escape. Here complex scientific murder plots fail because of one man's knowledge. And here the searing genius of Fu Manchu, The Devil Doctor, the superb, and his hordes of spiders, stranglers, scorpions, poisons, assassins concentrate against fallible Nayland Smith and his few allies.

But evil fails. And fails again. And repeatedly fails. Leaving Smith ruffled and Dr. Fu Manchu foiled until the next novel.

And, of course, the novel after that.

Through these shining marvels, stalks Dr. Fu Manchu, shoulders high, eyes glittering green. He is the quintessence of genius gone twisted and strange. By our standards, not his.

"I worked for my country," he explains in *The Daughter of Fu Manchu*. "I hoped to awaken China."

4

His actual intentions appear to vary from book to book. In *The Insidious Dr. Fu-Manchu,* he seems to be the agent of powerful, secret forces. On their behalf, he is methodically slaughtering, by centipede and chlorine gas, all those who might impede China's domination over India and the Western world.

Later, he is revealed to be the President of the Si Fan, The Council of Seven (Headquarters in Ho Nan, China). The purpose of the Council is to dominate the world—China controlling all; the Council controlling China; Dr. F—M——————controlling the Council. Neat.

The Si Fan operates in a straight-forward manner: what can't be achieved by threats and torture is handled by murder. Poison, if possible. If not, then by accident, drugs, stabbing, or various devices involving starved rats and compression within wire waist-coats.

In recognition of the Council's bias toward the blood-arts, its representation is drawn from a choice cross-section of the murderous sacred orders—the Dacoits, Thugs, and Hashishin. These represent the more direct philosophies of China, Tibet, Afghanistan, Burma and Syria.

Only the best minds have been recruited to the service of the Si Fan. In addition to hordes of killers, it boasts hordes of scientists intimidated into contributing their services. Most are full of a drug which drops them into a state of living death. Only Fu Manchu has the antidote. This he doles out once a month. They cooperate or down they fall, rigid and lacking all vital signs, and are hauled away and buried by well-meaning friends, who do not realize that inside that deathly exterior, a conscious mind shrieks in vain....

Thus, by such persuasion, Dr. Fu Manchu may rely on an unending flow of advanced inventions. With these (and other products of his own genius) he baffles the police and causes consternation among world governments. In 1929, his manipulations resulted in a world depression. In 1931, he used artificial catalepsy. In 1933, he used a torpedo-firing, submersible yacht; also an artificial plague transmitted by a synthetic insect—half fly and half flea. In 1959, he was served by a living dead thing patched from corpses and had his hand into anti-gravity, flying saucers, and rays that destroyed gold.

All this did not come at once. About 1919, Fu Manchu seemed to have gone into retirement. His position on the Si Fan was filled by Fo-Hi, the Golden Scorpion. In the book of that title, Fu Manchu made a brief appearance, perhaps one page long, and spoke one line. His name was not given.

After 1919, the Si Fan grew inactive. Fu Manchu aged enormously. By 1931, he was old, old, resembling an unwrapped mummy. At that time, his daughter, Fah Lo Suee (in *The Daughter of Fu*

Manchu) reactivated the Si Fan. The moment was not politically expedient and the Devil Doctor reappeared, again taking over the organization.

By some ill-explained process, his youth was renewed. Thereafter, through numerous serials in *Collier's,* he again focused his peculiar genius to the problem of overwhelming the Western world.

Near the end of the series, during the 1950s, his efforts turned to expelling the Communists from China, Evil hating Sin. In a sort of left-handed way, he supported activities in England and America which would aid in freeing China.

Thus Fu Manchu operates on a lofty international scene. He enjoys considerably more scope than his nearest rival, Professor James Moriarty, with whom he shares certain specific similarities.

As Holmes tells us in "The Final Problem," Moriarty is "extremely tall and thin and his forehead domes out in a white curve.... He is a genius, a philosopher, an abstract thinker. He has a brain of the first order...."

His great Chinese doppleganger is as extraordinary. Dr. Fu Manchu stands six-feet tall. He looks taller, since he is lean and long-limbed. His hands are large, bony, long; his chin is pointed, his skull enormous. Rohmer writes that he had a "brow like Shakespeare and a face like Satan." Sparse, neutral-colored hair scatters on his head, is customarily hidden by the little black cap he wears, indicating that he is a mandarin of high rank. As such, his word, once given is inviolable.

Like a cat, he moves in gliding silence. His shoulders hunch high. From him radiates a personal power that is almost physical. It strikes men like a blow. The shine of his eyes is sufficient to stun. Those eyes are narrow and long, brilliant green. Across them, a sort of opaque film flicks and clears. It is probable that he can see in the dark.

His body may be fragile, but the force exerted by his will is brutally strong. His presence fills you with inarticulate horror.

Rarely has a man been so educated. Holding degrees from four universities, he has a PhD and is a doctor of medicine. He speaks every civilized language. In early stories, his voice has a guttural quality, and he stresses the sibilants, emphasizing each syllable. This manner of speaking later smooths away.

Perhaps his only relaxation is opium. Smoking this has seriously stained his teeth. He does not seem to have become an addict, avoiding this unfortunate end by some chemical magic unavailable to lesser mortals.

During the late 1890's, he governed the Province of Ho Nan for the Empress Dowager, Tsze-Hsi. During that period, he had a daughter by a Russian mother. This exquisite girl, Fah Lo Suee, Lily Blossom, served for years as one of his main striking tools. (The story of Fu Manchu is the story of gloriously beautiful women aiding his plans.) In person, Fah Lo Suee is stunning. Her face, long and oval, is the color of ivory. She possesses the brilliant jade-green eyes of her father. Her nose is, perhaps, a trace too long, her perfect lips a fraction too full. Once in her presence, such trifles are not noticed. Her melting silver voice, the glow of her oriental perfume, washes away your caution.

It is doubtful that women like her.

As an agent for world domination, Fah Lo Suee has the serious defect of sudden love flashes. Without warning, she will fall into a numbing Oriental passion for the hero. By attempting to save him—after he has tumbled into various complex traps—she repeatedly, if accidentally, frustrates the Doctor's deep-laid plans.

Her last appearance is in "The Wrath of Fu Manchu," a long short story.[1] In this, she falls in love with Sir Denis Nayland Smith, Fu Manchu's permanent adversary. Through her intervention, Smith is saved. The story takes place about 1948. In it, Fah Lo Suee is as gloriously beautiful as ever. Apparently, she had access to Fu Manchu's youth secrets.

Nayland Smith is the central character in most of the novels. While Fu Manchu appears sparingly, never long in view—thus sharpening your appetite—Smith carries the action of the story. Abrupt, brisk, driving, Smith fends off the murder attempts, falls into traps, is rescued barely in time, deducts where the next murder stroke will fall, fails to prevent it. He fails, also, to put a final end to Fu Manchu, time after time. Yet he never despairs. He is entirely admirable.

A tall, lean, intense man, he has wavy, iron-gray hair. His skin is tanned deep brown; his eyes are described as steely. After some years of serving the English government in Burma, he returned to England, became a department chief at Scotland Yard, then an Assistant Commissioner. Still later he was knighted.

He speaks numerous languages and is hard, tough, shrewd and resolute. Fu Manchu hates him but admires his clarity of mind and tenacity. Throughout the series, he carries a large, dilapidated rubber tobacco pouch, crammed with excessively coarse-cut tobacco. He smokes a charred briar pipe with a big bowl and a very short stem. When in deep thought, he puffs furious at this, while pulling his left ear, a characteristic gesture.

His friend, Dr. Petrie, is an intelligent Dr. Watson. Petrie appears in most stories, either as the narrator or a principal actor. A graduate of Edinburgh University, he practiced for some years in Cairo. He received the medal of the Royal Society for research into tropical diseases. That research saved his life. In *Bride of Fu Manchu,* he contracts the Doctor special plague but is saved by the untested antidote that he, Petrie, has discovered.

On the side, Dr. Petrie writes fiction. Thus he joins the legion of literary secondary heroes. In *The Insidious Fu Manchu*, Petrie meets his future wife, the dainty Karamaneh of incredible beauty, once Fu Manchu's slave. They marry and have a daughter. Immediately, Fu Manchu kidnaps the child and raises her in his company for years.

It is the Devil Doctor's plan (in *Bride of Fu Manchu*) to wed this lovely child or at least to have a son by her but matters turn out otherwise. She is saved, after exhausting adventures, finds her true parents and becomes the wife of a splendid young Englishman.

These events irritate Fu Manchu no end. But he gets over it. No failure frets him long. Perhaps his pet marmoset, seated on his shoulder, whispers patience. After all, patience is essential to sinister Oriental doctors.

There were many sinister Orientals on both sides of the Atlantic. Dr. Fu Manchu was the most prominent, and he shaped the face of Oriental menace in pulp magazines from 1913 to the present.[2] He was not, however, the first. Popular literature prior to 1913 was already packed with menacing Far Eastern types, all representing a threat most dire to Western civilization—the threat of The Yellow Peril.

That captivating phrase, "The Yellow Peril," was the creation of that unlikely phrasemaker, Kaiser Wilhelm. Apprehension darkened his mind. All around he saw evidence of a terrible ripening power among the peoples of the East. "Wilhelm, who dealt in world dynamics, had been brooding over the rise of a new power in Asia. Vividly he saw its yellow hordes overwhelming Europe."[3]

In 1895, as if to confirm the Kaiser's worst fears, Japan's military forces lunged into China, unexpectedly sweeping all before them and gobbling up chunks of territory. Japan's abrupt success sent shudders of anxiety through the Western world: "Die gelbe Gefahr!"—The Yellow Peril!

There it stood hulking among its dragons and bayonets, grinning in ferocious menace, which, in 1900. was affirmed by the terrifying violence of The Boxer Rebellion. At that time, the Dowager Empress of China ordered that all foreigners were to be killed, an ill-advised act of state that resulted in the Western nations carving all sorts of economic sanctions from China.

But worse followed. During 1904-1905, the Russians fought the Japanese and got severely whipped. That disaster did little to relax Western nerves. Nor did a visitation of the Japanese navy to Mexico in 1911, which conjured up in the United States horrid thoughts of an alliance between those countries.

As usual, popular literature leaped enthusiastically upon these events, transforming them into hysterical fiction replete with militant hordes and Oriental war leaders. M.P. Shiel wrote at least three novels on the military menace of China. "The Empress of the Earth" appeared as a serial in *Short Stories,* February 5 through June 18, 1898; this he later published as *The Yellow Danger,* describing the invasion of Europe under warlord Yen How. *The Yellow Wave* followed in 1905, and *The Dragon* in 1913, the latter book reissued in 1929 as *The Yellow Peril.*[4]

Other accounts of crafty Oriental plotting, international and unsettling, surfaced in unexpected places. One of these was the 1912 *Union Jack,* an English boys' paper featuring Sexton Blake. The peril was, in this case, Prince Wu Ling, Chief of the Brotherhood of the Yellow Beetle. His purpose, as usual, was to place "the heel of the East on the West, to carve a path of saffron through a field of white, to raise on high Confucius, Buddah, and Taoism across the world."[5] Just how such passive philosophies as those of Confucius and Buddah informed these blood-thirsty goals is a problem best left to those editing boys' papers.

After the beginning of World War I, tender United States' apprehensions of possible Japanese-Mexican action were violently inflamed. Into Turtle Bay, on the coast of Mexican Lower California, sailed the Japanese battle cruiser, the *Asama.* This promptly went aground in the mud—or so it was claimed—and there it sat, week after week, apparently unable to be freed. At this outrage, the Hearst newspapers shook the sky with clamor. The Yellow Peril was in Mexico and doom impended.

Among the minor consequences of the *Asama's*'s visit was a ten-chapter silent movie serial. This, starring Irene Castle, was produced by Hearst's film company and depicted a joint Japanese-Mexican attempt to conquer the United States and ravage the heroine. Neither effort succeeded, although the invaders swaggered hatefully about for nine chapters, being smashed only in the tenth.[6] Echoes of this film rang for years through the pulps; the idea, reasonably intact, survived to inspire a 1935 fantasy war novel in the *Operator 5* pulp magazine.

The public willingness to subscribe to Oriental menace myths had roots deeper even than silent movies, novels by Shiel and the articulation of Kaiser Wilhelm's memorial phrase. From about 1870 into the early 1900s, the public had been deluged with newspaper and magazine articles about the San Francisco and New York City Chinatowns. The articles, one and all, reveled in those garish ingredients of opium, slave girls, tongs, hatchetmen, secret dens of vice, and other mysterious ways inscrutable, Oriental, strange.

Something over 90% of this was the usual uninformed drool. In part, some Chinese were at fault. They reasoned that, if tourists wanted opium dens, opium dens they should have. Immediately, dens were provided where, for a price, the passing public could gaze on a scene of smoky squalor. The real dens remained safely tucked away together with the gambling rooms, the primary vice of Chinatown.

In the mid-1870s, the San Francisco Chinatown took hold as a tourist attraction. Through the quarters flowed large numbers of visitors, alert for interesting depravity. They wrote brightly colored articles for the New York and Montreal papers. And English correspondents came warily into the Quarter for delicious thrills touring "the labyrinth under the trap doors of Bartlett Alley. This subterranean haunt was so noisome with mould and seeping sewage that it was dubbed the 'Dog Kennel' by the press."[7]

The British correspondents wrote back to London about the sins of Chinatown, so that people half the world away could thrill to scenes duplicating similar squalor down the street in Limehouse. The distant is more deliciously exotic. (In Limehouse, too, myth far outran reality.)

Tong warfare through Chinatown lacquered the legend ever more vividly. To clarify some of the confusions, elaborations, distortions, and sensational passages that filled the dime novel and carried over into the movies and popular fiction, we need to distinguish among the following:

-the Tongs, numbers of which were a combination of trade union and lodge.

-the Six Companies, which, in San Francisco, were separate benevolent and legal-aid type societies. The presidents of each were joined in a sort of loose, super-coordinating body and arbitrated disputes. This group had no real authority, other than moral. A similar loose affiliation in New York gave rise to endless pulp stories of a Supreme Chinatown Arbiter, which garbled the actual situation.

-the Fighting Tongs, which were very loosely organized groups, from 20 to 300 members, equivalent to a criminal gang and dedicated to preserving interests in opium, girls and gambling. The more violent a tong, the more glorious its name. Thus, The Progressive Pure Hearted Brotherhood or the Society As Peaceful As the Placid Sea. Each one boasted numbers of *boo how doy:* hatchet men, killers with pistol, hatchet, knife or lead pipe. These tongs developed from secret political organizations on mainland China, resembling those as the nut resembles the tree. The tong, as we know it, was a New World innovation.[8]

From about 1870 to 1906, the fighting tongs disputed and slaughtered vigorously. In 1900, they were so exceedingly active and visible that the San Francisco *Call* carried, on its front page, a box score of the dead and wounded.

All this kept the wheels of the sensational press whirling. Police raids on gambling houses and houses of prostitution disclosed few culprits but numbers of concealed stairways, trap doors, secret panels and twisting passageways. The 1885 crime report of Alderman Willard B. Farwell went into vast detail concerning crime in San Francisco's Chinatown, complete with maps and detailed descriptions of buildings and escape routes. That these depended upon trap doors and doors faced with iron sheet only thrilled readers more.

As you might expect, the dime novels benefited wonderfully from all this. In the *Nick Carter Library* #26, "Nick Carter in San Francisco; or, Unearthing Crime in Chinatown" (January 30, 1892); and in "The Hip Ling Society; or, A Chinese Infamy Stamped Out," #164 (September 22, 1894), Nick battled the power of the tongs, as Old Cap Collier and the Bradys had done and would do.

In 1898, a San Francisco *Call* reporter, B. Church Williams, claimed to have joined one of the fighting tongs. Whether he did or whether he didn't, the *Call* got a bright purple story. The details of Williams' initiation promptly leaped into popular literature.

These details included mixing members' blood drops in a bowl of vinegar. Each man inserted a finger and sucked the finger clean, thus demonstrating blood brotherhood and a strong stomach. The initiate then walked between two rows of sword-bearing members who hacked ferociously, if non-lethally, at him. All followed by elaborate oaths and the shattering of bowls of chicken blood.[9]

Although not so indicated by the popular press, the New York City Chinatown blossomed later than that of San Francisco, but no less garishly. When Jimmie Dale and Nick Carter walked Gowers Street, the Chinatown scene already flamed in readers' minds:

(Through the mist) glowed lights of sickly yellow, ghastly green and mysterious ruby...mere patches of illumination suspended in space, to burn through all eternity....

For this was Chinatown. And in Chinatown, the dream world of the languid and the economical of movement, time does not exist in the Caucasian sense.

Outside, strangeness. Inside, exotic wonder:

Such a room rightfully belonged in dreamland....furnished so magnificently that luxury fairly dripped from the adornments....It was floored with an enormous blue rug, the color unrelieved except at a far corner, where, in gold, were the three symbols of the man-killing tong.

Gorgeously embroidered black tapestries, in rare colors and bizarre designs, covered the walls. The lights were subdued, coming from pale green and orange globes. They

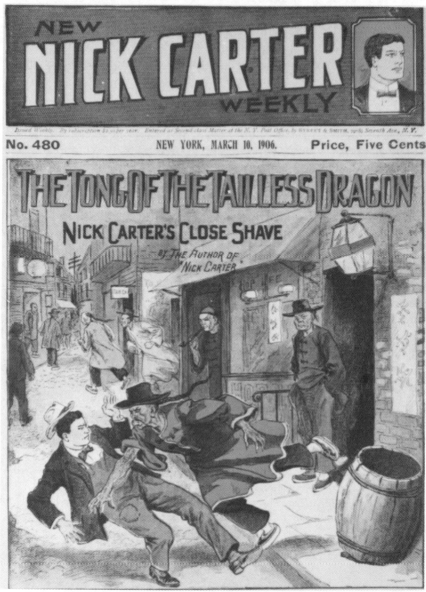

A tall, muscular Mongolian came out of an opium-joint with such precipitation that he collided violently with the detective. Nick went down with the Chinaman on top of him.

Nick Carter Weekly #480 (March 10, 1906). Tong violence and Oriental mystery in the deeps of Chinatown was as popular in the dime novels as in the later pulps.

gleamed on a table of solid silver, on grotesque carvings and porcelains...stolen from some Oriental prince's palace.

This glorious nest glows at the center of a maze:

> The passage was not a straight one. It wound like a corkscrew....Another trip along a cavern; down a ladder; forward again; then up more steps. All this time, they had been in stillness as absolute as the jet blackness. Beyond the walls, Oriental gamblers were sing-songing and cackling, and flutes were playing weird strains to addicts hitting the pipe.

And at the heart of the nest, the spider:

> (The figure) had the straggly white hair of extreme age, matching the mustache that dropped over the sides of his mouth. Very lean, indeed, was this venerable ancient. He stood up, in his robe of imperial yellow, gaunt and foreboding.[10]

Newspaper articles, Thomas Burke's Limehouse nights and a whole lot of Fu Manchu went into the making of those passages. They appeared in 1929, just when reason would tell you that the images would be exhausted. But instead, the Chinese scene would leap, revitalized, from the pages of the single-character pulps—particularly *The Shadow* and *The Spider*. Through the 1930s, Oriental Menaces would direct hordes of gangsters, as well as hatchetmen, and the twisting underground passages would be crammed with concealed devices to slay the intruder: whirling blades, trap doors over pits of boiling acid and poisoned vermin. The 1930s pulps mingled memories of ancient newspaper stories about Chinatown and the tong wars, with details drawn from Sax Rohmer, dime novels and turn of the century Yellow Peril fiction. This somewhat various dish was scrambled well and served forth, a new delight for the reader.

Matters had become complex by the 1930s. Once they had been simpler.

The Oriental Menace combines two distinct themes—that of the War Lord, dealing with military power, and that of the Crime Emperor, dealing with criminal profits. The War Lord theme developed in three branches. The first of these, The Yellow Peril, in which the East menaces the West, was described by M.P. Shiel and followers. Second was the Asian Internal Struggle, in which the East attacks the East, as recorded in many of Harold Lamb's novelettes for the *Adventure* magazine. And, third, Adventures in the Inscrutable East, describe the exploits of Occidental heroes among Far Eastern perils; to this group belong the *Argosy* Peter the Brazen series and the Milton Caniff "Terry and the Pirates" comic strip.

The War Lord fiction usually takes place in the Far East. Stories about Oriental Crime Emperors, however, begin closer to home. They are most usually placed in a Western capital—London, or New York, or Sauk City—where the deadly Oriental genius and his followers are busy demolishing Western civilization. The Crime Emperors vary widely, but there appear to be two general types—the Plotter and the Adventurer. The Plotter spins at the center of the web, while his minions slash wildly about; the Adventurer thrusts himself personally into the action, often leading his men. Much more rarely, he performs on his own.

Most Oriental series characters embodied one or more of these elements, variously weighted. That great original, Fu Manchu, is both a Crime Emperor and a War Lord, a Plotter and a distinguished representative of the Yellow Peril. But such complexity was not the general rule. The usual Oriental Menace drew upon a single facet of Fu Manchu's accomplishments. All, of course, bowed before the joss of the Yellow Peril, but few rendered more than perfunctory homage. Their interests focused elsewhere.

The initial wave of Oriental series villains (1916-1919) were clever brigands—which is to say, slick thieves. The writers of these series had read Sax Rohmer, obviously, but the taste of the times was for criminal adventures and criminal heroes.

A typical Oriental menace from these primitive times may be found in Arthur B. Reeve's 1916 *The Romance of Elaine*. In this book, birthed of a silent movie, that master of evil, Wu Fang, ran the spots off Craig Kennedy. (The characters were discussed in Volume II of this series.) Eventually, Wu Fang died in a Sherlock-Holmes-At-Reichenbach-Falls ending, derivative and inept.

No character in *The Romance of Elaine* is as substantial as cardboard. At best, they are a collection of stereotypes of unsurpassed banality, as if the book had been copied from old carbon paper. The characters do serve an unplanned function as an index to the cliches of the time. Thus we learn that, by 1916, a Chinese villain was malignant, full of murder schemes involving poisons, deadly vermin, and knives; that he consistently out-thought the Occidental hero; that he was assisted by tough Oriental killers waving knives and hatchets; that he wore exotic robes in exotic surroundings; and that, although he commanded faithful hordes of minions, he would personally administer his evil plans, if he had to stand outside the window all night long.

The characteristics that fit Wu Fang also apply, without tailoring, to Li Shoon, another Oriental master of evil.

Li Shoon appeared in 1916-1917 issues of *Detective Story Magazine*. The author, H. Irving Hancock, featured the character in long short stories that are slicked up dime novels with Sax Rohmer overtones.

Li Shoon is a large, stout man who looks like a fiend:

...a round moonlike yellow face, topped by the bulging eyebrows and the sunken eyes that describe Li Shoon.

He behaves like a fiend, too: "He's a wonder at everything wicked—an amazing compound of evil, a marvel of satanic cunning." The description thoroughly butters the cake, although it is true that Li Shoon's path is marked by more corpses than customary in 1916 fiction. Obstruct his will an instant, and down you tumble. If you aren't raddled by the terrible lachesis venom (which bloats you terribly), then you are doomed by arsine gas from his terrible gas gun which kills without a trace, leaving only a slight, terrible abrasion inside your nostril.

Li Shoon commands a mazy force of Malays, Chinese and other deadly types, all murderous. None are more so than the terrible Weng-yu, Li Shoon's lieutenant, and the dreaded Ming, a short little fat Mongol who favors black cigars and is chief torturer and executioner.

Although Li Shoon steals nothing less than millions, he is motivated by noble thoughts:

(He) tried ever to raise countless millions to launch his project of making his society, Ui Kwoon Ah-How, the wealthiest and most powerful body on earth. He dreams of making himself the huge man-power in China (sic), and of waking his country from her centuries of sleep to take over mastery of Asia.[11]

What the Si Fan thought of these plans has not been recorded.

"Under the Ban of Li Shoon" (August 5, 1916, *Detective Story Magazine*) tells how this wily Oriental and a crooked secretary forged away a rich old man's estate. The land is sold for millions; the old fellow is murdered. This foul plot was scotched and the plotters jailed through the superhuman efforts of Donald Carrick, The Human Hound, the force for Good in this series.

Contrary to what you may expect, Carrick is not a detective but a "gentleman adventurer." Wealthy, handsome, something of a snob, he swaggers efficiently around, puffed with self-satisfaction, a glowing pain in the neck.

He is accompanied by the usual Watson. This one is named Dr. John Fleming, and he is a chemist and criminologist, who performs as a mildly scientific assistant when he is not standing there stunned, muttering: "Gad, Carrick!"

Fleming loves Miss Sylvia Dorrance, whose function in the series is to be abducted, to gaze wildly about; and to implore with pitiful eyes. She appears rarely, often in the company of her aunt, and serves principally as the candied marshmallow that keeps Fleming at Carrick's side. Whether Sylvia loves Fleming is a moot point. She does not appear to have the intelligence to love anything.

We left Li Shoon in jail. But by the September 5, 1916, issue of *Detective Story Magazine* (in which all these stories appeared), our marvel of satanic cunning has forged a release from The Tombs for himself and all his pals. Thus begins "Li Shoon's Deadliest Mission." As soon as they detect the escape, the police call Carrick for help, just as they used to do when Nick Carter was practicing.

Off we go. The trail leads to Central Park. There sprawls the faithless secretary, pale and dead, his nostril mysteriously scratched. And beautiful Sylvia has been abducted. In consequence, Fleming panics in a scene displaying no vestige of adult behavior.

Now begins raw drama:

The fleeing criminals are chased in high-powered autos.

The death trap in the country—the poisoned spikes.

Li Shoon escapes by airplane.

Clues lead to Denver, Colorado, But first, the viper in the Pullman berth, the midnight attack of the Stranglers, the Hero-is-dead Deception.

In Denver, Li Shoon is tracked to his grim lair. The loot is concealed in the cellar; Sylvia is concealed upstairs.

Fleming dismantles the basement wall with acid: The search for the secret door—the discovery—the surprise—the police raid.

Li Shoon escapes, littering the world with corpses.

It seems certain that Donald Carrick, The Human Hound, is dead of arsine gas inhalation.

Fleming carries on alone: Gun fire—pursuit by car.

Ding dab this is exciting.

Through the black night—the switched taxi—the frenzied chase.

CARRICK IS NOT DEAD!

Li Shoon and Weng-yu, cornered, hurl themselves over a cliff.

Dead! They are dead at least. You can see their bodies way down there.

Sweet Sylvia is saved and her aunt, also.

It is very, very busy narrative, crisp and packed with dialogue. The sentences crackle with that pleasing electricity that the dime novels often generated, a pleasant, shallow excitement.

Li Shoon speaks two lines in the entire story.

(You noticed that no one went down to inspect the two bodies at the cliff foot? That was to allow for a sequel, if editor and readers desired same. They did and "Li Shoon's Nine Lives" was published January 5, 1917. Li Shoon takes up piracy in the Pacific, stealing and robbing and hiding in an artificial cave, until, cornered, he blows up his ship, crew, and self. Sylvia marries Fleming, and the series ends warmly—

unless a further unexamined story lurks among the stacks of old *Detective Story.)*

Wu Fang and Li Shoon were lesser Oriental menaces, lofty in their own series, but reflecting Fu Manchu's light, rather than shedding their own. But more original figures stalked the columns of the popular magazines, grinning among the verbs and nouns. Soon two series began which offered an alternative to Fu Manchu. Their publication history was erratic, their story sequences fragmentary, but their characters were remarkable.

The first of these, the Peter the Brazen series, concerns the adventures of a young ship's telegrapher in China. Through two groups of stories in *Argosy* (1918-1919 and 1930-1935), Peter faced a succession of bandits, pirates, and major Oriental menaces. His exploits, while endlessly beguiling, will be examined in a later volume.

The second of the 1919 figures was an authentic Emperor of Crime, the great Mr. Chang.

Mr. Chang: "I have no scruples. I am a criminal without a single redeeming virtue. Still, I would rather be that than a man without a single redeeming vice."[12]

Mr. Chang's adventures, written by A.E. Apple, were published in the *Detective Story Magazine* from 1919 to about 1931, twenty-five or thirty stories in all. At least eleven of these were reprinted in *Best Detective Magazine* between 1933 and 1935. Two book collections were made by Chelsea House: *Mr. Chang of Scotland Yard* (1926) and *Mr. Chang's Crime Ray* (1928).

In his own way, Mr. Chang is as spectacular an Oriental fiend as Doctor Fu Manchu. Chang, however, has no top-lofty aspirations. He strikes for immediate gain, and the dream of world domination does not concern him. He is a lone wolf by nature, a thief and murderer by choice. He is an ice-hearted, cold-blooded villain whose pulse never exceeds 50. Unsullied by emotion, he hacks fortune from the round eyes.

Decidedly, he is bad company.

In person, he is a lean man, powerfully muscled. His face, grim, cruel, evil, resembles a parchment mask tightly shrunken over high cheek bones. His teeth are long and white. His voice, usually harsh and throaty, softens to a catlike purr when luring some dupe to destruction.

(He has) boring black eyes with fires smouldering in their depths. An uncanny spirit radiated from him, suggestive of the jungle under ghastly moonlight.

Just why a first-class Oriental menace is described so consistently in animal terms is beyond guessing. To emphasize his inhumanity, likely.

Not being far removed from the jungle beast, and accordingly a nocturnal prowler, by daytime he was usually languid and disinclined to embark upon ventures. It was in the black of night that his senses became alert, his brain highly keyed, his faculties vigilant.[13]

Apple carries this to extremes, as Apple does, He points out, with glaring eyes, that Mr. Chang is not only close to the jungle, but Orientals— deadly Chinese and such— are quite different from other men.

Mr. Chang: "We Chinese have no nervous systems in the Occidental sense....Opium affects me about like a Russian cigarette affects you."[14]

Never does he allow anything to fluster him. He is absolute master of his emotions ("if he really had any"). Comes trouble, and he accepts it placidly, being a fatalist, for "only a fool and a weakling falters when confronted by the inevitable."

For all this, Mr. Chang is much more than a savage *thing*.

Granted his entire heartlessness. Granted that he is motivated entirely by self-interest, and is, therefore, a monster. Still he is that marvel in popular fiction—a man who thinks and has something to say that does not directly advance the plot. Few enough villains, Chinese or otherwise, give the impression that they can handle intellectual work more complex than distinguishing between hot and cold.

Mr. Chang can and does. Moreover, he has few illusions:

"A murder without a motive is the height of stupidity—the utmost emotional folly."
"I have always contended that a beautiful woman is worth her weight in opium, provided that you have her prisoner and know when to sell her as a slave girl."

His business is not sentiment but crime. It is his chosen profession. "He devoted his energies and talents to it as effectively as if...to an honest calling." Millions, he says, have passed through his hands. Much of that has returned to China. More has been gambled away. Frequently he is down to only ten or fifteen thousand dollars pocket money. But such a genius is never long in want. In real life, he would become a senator.

Royal blood fills his veins. His father was "mandarin of the first class, a prince...." In spite of family connections, Mr. Chang found trouble early. He committed his first murder at the age of nine. Years of spectacular crime forced him to flee China to live on his wits—and proceeds of the ruby buttons he cut from his father's robe.

"In my day," Chang remarks, "I was a wild man from Luzon with a wagon show." From that humble first step, he became, according to Mr. Apple, the "archmurderer of the century."

Which stretches matters slightly. But the trick in this series is to pull the reader's leg, gently, gently, and, gently, gently, let the reader know it. The reader responds smiling slyly at this joke shared with Apple. By this arrangement, Apple is free to be serious, to be satirical, to roll in melodrama and fantasy, to have a good old time without ever being called to account for his transgressions. [15]

Thus it is perfectly reasonable that there are warrants out for Mr. Chang in every country and every state in the U.S. Back in China, his name is used to frighten children. In each story, another purple fact is added to the legend—each added with due solemnity that quite obscures the put-on in Mr. Apple's eye.

Biographical data for A. E. Apple are far sketchier than for Mr. Chang. An article on Apple's life was written by C. D. Hubbard in the series "Popular Detective Story Writers." This appeared in the May 12, 1928 issue of *Detective Story Magazine*. The article contains much type, little information. According to Hubbard, Apple was:

...born in Ohio and lived most of his life in boom oil towns. From working in the oil country and serving as shipping clerk in a brass works, to selling advertising on the road, Apple finally arrived at the point where he wanted to write fiction. His first short story was sold when he was but nineteen. Since that time, he has alternated between newspaper work, advertising, and story writing.[16]

In Mort Weisinger's *Pony Express* column, *Writer's Review*, April 1935, appears the remark that Apple "suicided two years ago." The note is abrupt and final. No other reference to Apple has been found.

Information concerning Mr. Chang's career is considerably more extensive. The first story of the series, "Mr. Chang," appeared in the September 9, 1919 issue of *Detective Story Magazine*. The story set the pattern for those stories to follow:

Mr. Chang plans a crime. For the more obvious parts of the plot, he uses a white dupe, who is kept drunk. The crime is successful until the dupe, in blind panic, accidentally spoils it. The loot is lost, but, just as justice closes in, Mr. Chang slips away by a clever trick.

"Mr. Chang" opens in the unlikely vicinity of West Virginia. Mr. Chang's plan is to blackmail a reformed thief named Peter Lunn. To do so, he enlists the aid of Silver Lemoy, a small-time carnival grifter. Lemoy's function is to be framed for Chang's crime.

He will be the first in a long line of dupes and fall guys. All are ensnared by Chang's exquisite lies and quantities of his yellow-bark brandy. This astounding beverage is distilled from wormwood, liquid fire that seems to be the color of iron oxide. It comes in bottles covered by woven grasses. For all its power, yellow-bark brandy leaves no hangover. On the other hand, it seems to temporarily disengage moral sense. Four drinks and you kill the world.

Now Chang's crimes begin. First he murders the lawyer who holds the papers identifying Lunn with his former crime. Lemoy, blanked out on yellow-bark brandy, is easily convinced that he committed the murder.

These elaborate preparations completed, the blackmail plot begins. From this point on, the story resembles a rope of black and white strands. We follow the black plots of Chang and Lemoy for a few chapters. Then we switch to the pitiful Lunn, his lovely darling daughter and her rambunctious fiance. How they do struggle in Chang's web. Black and white alternating.

At length Lemoy's nerve fails. He bolts. The blackmail plot begins to crumble before the stubborness of the fiance. Now Chang is faced with evidence that he murdered the lawyer. It is the inevitable dawn of truth—and, as you know, only a fool or weakling falters when confronted....

Being neither a fool nor weakling, Chang steals a vehicle loaded with nitroglycerine, flees and is apparently vaporized when the load explodes.

Perhaps Apple intended that Chang die at this point. Likely so.

But it's hard to obliterate an insidious Chinese who is not far removed from a jungle beast. Near the end of 1924 (or perhaps earlier, all magazines not having been examined), another story flashes up. And then another. Three stories make a series, and with a series, a writer can surf bravely down the years.[17]

The stories, all interesting, all different, are still all built on the same core.

"Mr. Chang and the Glittering Lady" (May 16, 1925) tells how he plots to steal a show queen's million-dollar diamond-loaded cloak. The scene is Montreal. The press-agent is crooked and full of yellow-bark brandy. Behind him lurks Chang, purring orders, hell in his eyes as he rolls endless wheat-paper cigarettes one-handed, and snaps kitchen matches to flame against his thumb nail.

By this time, Chang has caused so many problems that Scotland Yard has commissioned Operative Eugene Lantana to bring that Oriental Fiend back at any cost. Lantana does not have a lot of luck. The glittering cloak is stolen during a performance, although the audience is 80% police.

But, as usual, the superb crime is spoiled by the dupe. Lantana follows the press agent to Chang's hideout, deep within secret passages. Facing Lantana's pistol, thoroughly trapped, Chang promptly gives up:

"I have played for big stakes.... I have lost.... I fail to see why emotions should enter into it. The inevitable must be accepted."[18]

He escapes in time however, for the June 6 issue.

From A Reader: How any one can admire such a cruel, cold-blooded, even though clever rascal, is beyond my ken.

During 1926, Mr. Chang appeared about once a month. As customary in an extended series, the stories became progressively less complex. The black strand shrank to a lean thread. The focus shifted ever more to Mr. Chang as he slicked along.

June 12, 1926: "Mr. Chang's Blackmail Horde." Chang plots to steal the contents of a lawyer's safe. He assumes that the lawyer, now dying, would be holding papers of highly sensitive information. Through these, he will blackmail wealth.

As usual, matters swim along until the crime is committed. Then, of course all goes wrong. The dupe fumbles. Chang is trapped unarmed in an upper room. The house is surrounded. Outside the door, with drawn gun, hulks Dr. Ling.

Dr. Ling? Oh, he has replaced poor Lantana of the Yard. Ling is a gigantic, moon-faced Oriental genius who has been employed by Chinese businessmen to rid themselves of Mr. Chang.

Again Chang is trapped. For an instant, it appears that he may be forced to use the sacred dagger with the jade handle that he keeps taped to his chest. For suicide, you see, just in case Mr. Apple's ingenuity falters.

But it does not falter—not in this story. Chang escapes in an ending that frankly is a gross cheat.

So many endings are. Mr. Apple seems given to writing himself into impossible holes. In "Blackmail Horde," Chang pretends to be arrested by a fake Dr. Ling and so slips off to freedom. (This solution invalidates the whole last third of the story, since, if Ling was a fake, Chang wasn't trapped.)

In still another story. Chang evades justice by hurling himself from a high window and floating away on a parachute that had been concealed under his coat. That brought howls of reader outrage. As well it should.

"Mr. Chang's Revenge" (January 15, 1927) tells how he is again trapped in a sealed treasure room. No possible exit. Poison gas pours into the room. Can it be the end?

No. Not until "The End of Mr. Chang" (May 28, 1927). By this time, Dr. Ling presses him fiercely. It is harder to rob, now. Harder to hide. Chang is holed up with his dear friend, the witch doctor, Yat, a betal-leaf chewing, ancient scoundrel of engaging evil, who reads dreams and controls an imposing rabble of hunchbacks and hatchetmen.

The Chinese merchants have offered $250,000 for Chang's capture. He vows to steal this. Armed with an inoperative death ray (picked up in a previous story), he slides forth through the maze of tunnels beneath Doctor Yat's establishment. Down there he discovers a secret entrance into those tunnels leading to the tong that has offered the reward.

Alone in the twisting dark, Chang faces one danger after the other. To the center of tong headquarters he penetrates. He is discovered. He flees and then learns that he has been lured into an elaborate trap.

Hordes of armed enemies are ahead of him.

Raging waters foam over him.

Snared in the flooded maze, he almost drowns.

By sheer accident, he escapes. And promptly returns to the tong's headquarters, determined to steal the money, then battle free.

It is an error. A final trap remains. As Chang seizes the cash, an iron cage clanks around him. Gas fizzes in.

Unconscious, Chang is stripped naked, searched. The cage is welded shut. As the story closes, he is to be transported back to China, there to be exhibited and, ultimately, beheaded.

"Thus," murmurs Doctor Ling, "ends the career of the notorious Mr. Chang."

That was January 1927. Thereafter, silence, through the end of The Jazz Age, the beginning of the Depression, (these calamities an inevitable consequence of Mr. Chang's downfall). Until the November 15, 1930 issue of *Detective Story*, which contains "Mr. Chang, Tortured." The story picks up exactly where it left off.

Here stands Mr. Chang, lean, fierce as ever, still in his cage of welded steel rod after more than three years. He watches inscrutably, smoking a wheat-straw cigarette that has been soaked in rum and given an opium sweat. (Don't ask me; I have no idea what it means.) He has been exhibited all over China, admission at a dollar a head. Now preparations are underway for his execution—a national holiday.

His own father sits on the Council for Execution. A gifted torturer, Doctor Hip Yee, has been summoned to supply the artistic finale.

Detective Story Magazine (December 27, 1930). Robber, murderer, artistic fiend, Mr. Chang gradually became a parody of Oriental master criminals.

Inside his cage, Mr. Chang emotionlessly endures it all: the starving leopards clawing at him, the plague-ridden rats swarming over the bars, the electric coils that heat his cage red-hot.

Slowly his cell floods with water. He drowns and goes to Hell, where he immediately begins stealing everything not bolted down.

From this delightful occupation, he is brought back to life by Doctor Hip Yee's art. His coffin waits, a foot-square box. For he is to be reduced to little tiny bits by the "Death of a Thousand Slices."

Doctor Hip Yee gives Chang a pill which will paralyze him without dulling his sensations—Mr. Chang not being informed of this effect. But the Honorable Doctor has over-reached himself. Chang does not take the pill and, when the Doctor's attention wavers, Chang has him, and the Doctor gets the pill stuffed down his craw.

Disguised as the Doctor, Mr. Chang proceeds to carve pieces from the worthy torturer before an approving audience. But before he removes much, he is detected. And escapes.

Returns to America. In "Mr. Chang's Tong War" (December 27, 1930) he has moved 1,000 quarts of nitroglycerine into the basement of Dr. Ling's tong. Before blowing the place to electrons, Chang proceeds to rob it. Now follow many spirited adventures. These center about a gigantic elephant statue with a mouthful of currency and electrified teeth.

Poor old Doctor Hip Yee, freshly arrived from China and lacking various personal parts, dies in high-amperage flame. Chang misses killing Dr. Ling; Ling misses Chang, who again escapes.

Old business generally out of the way, Mr. Chang now strikes at a new opponent—Rafferty, the master criminal, another of A. E. Apple's series characters.

Rafferty is a pleasantly engaging genius whose career of amiable crime paralleled that of Mr. Chang's in 1920's-1930's *Detective Story Magazine*. Aided by a wonderously gluttonous German scientist, Rafferty amused himself by stealing large items. No killing. But he stole houses, and trains, and museums and towns. In a well-concealed headquarters, Rafferty has collected about 39 trillion dollars in stolen stuff.

This headquarters, Mr. Chang now breaks into (January 31, 1931). Once inside, he spends most of the story dodging gas and electrical traps. He makes his escape—pockets bulging with Rafferty's diamonds—by smashing all the lights with gold nuggets. Alas, at the end, Mr. Chang is left swimming in the middle of the ocean, far far from land.

"He was intent on the probability that he was doomed to drown."

Not only doesn't he drown, he returns, February 28, 1931, in "Mr. Chang cages Rafferty." It is now Rafferty's turn to escape, and he does so. And leaves Chang apparently shot dead. But no.

The bullet only knocked him out and left a furrow on the right side of his forehead and a wicked scar. Annoying. Electing to ignore Rafferty for the nonce, Chang now concentrates upon a certain Dr. Barcelona, an ill-omened fellow who believes himself to be the Devil. "Mr. Chang Meets the Devil" (May 23, 1931) describes the stirring events after Chang strolls to the Devil's door and knocks for admission.

Thereafter, it is in, out, up and down. Chang is trapped. He escapes. He captures Dr. Barcelona, who then escapes.

Chang is caged in a corridor which fills with flame.

Since he is wearing asbestos clothing, he is unharmed.

He dreams that he is in Hell (in consequence of being gassed) and has a merry time there. He wakes to discover that he is being attacked by gigantic streptococci germs.

He kills one with his fingernails, an admirable feat—even considering that the germ is really an octopus.

After that achievement, he rips loose some steel bars with his bare hands. He places the doctor in an electric furnace set at 5,000 degrees, and leaves with a bag full of money. Remarking, as he exits:

"If he really is Satan, he will survive."

A blandly biting exit line for Mr. Chang's last story.

"Mr. Chang, of course, was an emperor of crime," says Mr. Apple. But not really. Not an emperor in the Fu Manchu sense. Chang was a loner at heart, an extraordinary single who worked his craft in solitary diligence. He was (says Mr. Apple, bland-faced) the greatest, most outstanding murderer in the whole entire world. By that gigantic thunder, he softly parodies all stories about master criminals and all series featuring sinister Chinese emperors of crime.

The true crime emperor, like Fu Manchu, administers a vast organization. Society groans beneath his schemes. He shakes capitols and horrifies governments as he strikes for power. Immediately beneath the crime emperor, in the hierarchy of fictional villains, appears a swarm of lesser figures. Call these Masterminds. They perform at less lofty levels than Fu Manchu or Dr. Mortiarty. Their schemes are a blush more modest, their gangs a fraction less immense, and their immediate concerns are less for power than for riches. They steal enthusiastically on a large scale, like politicians.

Examples range from Fantomas, a spectacular criminal genius, disguise master, and murdering fiend, to Ravenswood, a gang leader in transition from the dime novels. They include Black Star, a costumed terror pillaging society; The Spider, a deadly plotter lurking; and Rafferty, a blithe master who added new dimensions to crime.

Among these illustrious talents should also be included Anthony Trent (The Master Criminal), The White Rook, and The Joker. But these gentlemen are special cases, each of them reforming at last and turning their supple intellects to fields less asocial. A true Mastermind never reforms. Never, at least, until the ultimate period of his series. So Mr. Trent and the others will be examined elsewhere. For the present our subject is crime, unrelieved, unrepentant, deeply satisfying.

II—CRIME EXTRAORDINARY

1-

The Fantomas series is represented in the United States by about five books, none in print. Originally the series appeared as weekly, paper-backed pamphlets which swarmed over 1913 French news-stands. The adventures were co-authored by Pierre Souvestre and Marcel Allain until Souvester's death in 1914. Thereafter they were continued by Allain. It is not known how long publication continued at the rate of a weekly novel, but the series itself lasted into the 1920s, with hardback reprints being issued as late as 1927.

A novel a week sounds like a stunning load, but it is really a matter of nomenclature. It would be more accurate to call these stories novelettes. The New York dime novelists had long since demonstrated that one man and a quire of paper could equal 20,000-25,000 words a week. Surely they could do as well in France.

And surely they did.

The basic situation of the series is this: Detective Juve of the Paris police and the journalist Fandor struggle through endless dangers to capture that arch criminal, Fantomas.

Fantomas is a master disguise artist, a genius among the disguise masters of that remote time. His real face permanently concealed, Fantomas may appear as two, possibly three, people during a story. At least one of these is a major character and part of the game is to guess which face conceals the fiend. In this series, "fiend" is the exact word. Fantomas differs from other disguise-prone criminals such as Colonel Clay and Arsene Lupin. These were nice boys, both of them, who appreciated a joke. But there is no humor in Fantomas; he is all melodrama and blood.

When not looking exactly like someone else, Fantomas appears in traditional costume:

(He was) enveloped from head to foot in a dark cloak. All (the girl) could see of him was his profile: his features were concealed by a soft felt hat with turned down brim, which showed at intervals against the sky when the lightning flashed and flickered.[1]

We are in the presence of the mystery figure, a dark-clad unknown who glides by night, menacing and terrible, out of *Wuthering Heights* and *The Castle of Otranto*. When he hurls off the cape, he is revealed as a man "upright, young, vigorous, superbly muscular. He was sheathed from head to foot in a tight-fitting garment, black as Erebus!"

(She could not) see his face, a black hood covered it: two gleaming eyes alone were visible, eyes that to the distraught girl seemed lit by fires from hell!
This vision, the vision of a man without a face, resembling no other man, this apparition with nameless mask, its body like some statue cut from solid darkness, was yet so definite in its mystery that (she), uttering the indescribable cry of some inhuman thing, articulated: "Fantomas! You are Fantomas!"

She is correct. It is the terror in person. And, as usual with mystery figures, he freezes her with a burst of laughter, soulless and frigid.

He laughed because the body of this woman, huddled in the mud, crushed to the earth, was a pleasing thing, because Fantomas was happy when he made human creatures suffer, when he tortured, when he wrought sweet vengeance....

A monster without bowels, declaiming in the swooping rhetoric of mania:

"I am Fantomas.... I am he for whom the entire world is searching, whom none has ever seen, whom none can recognize! I am Crime incarnated! I am Night! ...No human sees my face, because Crime and Night are featureless! I am illimitable Power! I am he who mocks at all the powers, at all the efforts, at all the forces! I am master of all, of everything; of all times and seasons... I am Death! ...thou hast said it—I am Fantomas!"

Thunder and scarlet lightning rumbling among the exclamation points. Some part of this mad orating is intended to scare the girl to death. It is a vintage Fantomas tactic, for he is endlessly clever and understands more about the human soul than a madman should.

In most activities, he is the essence of calculation. Each of his innumerable murders has a double object—to get rid of an enemy and to settle blame for the crimes of Fantomas or associates upon the dead man.

He has many associates: Apaches, white-collar crooks, once innocent girls led into Sin, legions of blackmailed folk, eminent Frenchmen with ringing titles and an insatiable itch for francs.

All these he manipulates with inexhaustible guile. He works beyond sight and hearing. His dupes do not know their employer, although he moves smoothly among them. He is the famous noble, the broken-down musician, the cab-driver, his own lieutenant, the old man in the cafe, the menacing whisper in the darkness. He is Crime, Night, Death!

And very rarely does he appear in his black garb.

The authorities rather doubt that he exists. They treat Detective Juve coldly, for he is known to have a bee in his bonnet about Fantomas.

Juve is a brisk, heavy-set man, whose mustache is barely turning gray. Agile as a teen-ager, as astute as a sage, he is as celebrated throughout France as (say) a great wine. Two or three times, Fantomas has framed him into prison, and once he came within a whisper of being executed. It is Juve's destiny to pursue that murderous will-o-wisp, Fantomas, for 300 pages and lose him on page 301.

Jerome Fandor, the journalist, has also had his problems with Fantomas. Their destinies seem bound together, for reasons obscure and dark. When only 18, Fandor (then named Charles Rambert) was accused by his own father of committing a murder. Fantomas had done it, but Rambert/Fandor became a fugitive. His mother then went insane. Detective Juve, however, believed the boy innocent, protected him, renamed him Fandor, started him in newspaper work and on a ten-year pursuit of "The Genius of Crime."

In the course of his adventures, Fandor fell in love with the beautiful, blonde Elizabeth Dollon, her brother murdered by Fantomas. After harsh adventure, she accomplished the near impossible for a heroine: she dies, accidentally shot. Perhaps she was too close to marrying Fandor for, as you know, marriage to the hero is a death warrant.

Now one adventure leaps from another. Endings smear into beginnings, The endless serial pulses like a paper heart, thrusting along its charge of melodrama.

Fantomas leads an Apache gang.

He steals military secrets for Germany, the crime of crimes. Then he kidnaps a French statesman and demands 1,000,000 francs to terminate his operations and disappear.

Hard for authorities not to believe in him now. He murders the Minister of Justice. He steals a gigantic collection of Russian jewelry. He steals a secret artillery component, tosses a girl into a bear cage, devises an exploding lake for the mortification of his enemies.... It is a glorious record. The stories are steeplechases through a carnival. Even if your heart is hardened against criminal geniuses and disguise artists, the sheer activity leaves you with the urge to applaud.

Fantomas towers distinct among a welter of cowled, cloaked mystery figures lurking disguised by night, their ways unknowable. The mystery figure itself, garbed in black, gliding silently among the shadows, was a convention of visual menace established firmly in the gothic novels and later exploited by fifty years of dime novels and story papers. After Fantomas, such a master as Edgar Wallace would use similar figures in his 1920 *Jack O'Judgement* and the 1923 *The Clue of the New Pin*.

In 1931, Walter Gibson would draw upon a tradition of almost two hundred years, when he used the mystery figure to give concrete form to that mysterious radio voice, The Shadow.[2]

Fantomas was unique, but, like The Shadow, he was visualized within the context of a well-worn convention. He provides a useful checkpoint in the history of the mystery figure. You read the novels and know that, in pre-World War I popular fiction, the figure looked so, radiated menace so, ranted so. In this perspective, Fantomas becomes one wave tall in a black sea.

2-

While Fantomas raised hob in France, a less spectacular figure stretched at ease in his suite at the New York City Waldron Hotel. His face is familiar. Clean-cut, resolute, firm, it has appeared a hundred times in fiction, variously named. Usually the features belong to decent, hard-working members of the community. But not in this case. For this gentleman is Mr. Richard Ravenswood, master criminal, leader of a secret gang known as The Red Ravens.

The thinness of his lips should have exposed the secret.

Lounging with Ravenswood is a wiry little man of about thirty, his face "remarkably shrewd and expressive." This is Kenneth Nolan, Ravenswood's valet. Valet within the hotel. Outside in the naughty world, the valet becomes the Chief Lieutenant and his name changes to Paddy. Then, indeed, he is resourceful and clever.

He is no match for Ravenswood, you understand. Ravenswood is the audacious master, the disguise genius whose ingenious raids baffle the police. He wears on his third finger a bloodstone set into a ring; the blood-red spots form an almost perfect outline of a bird—a raven. Thus the title of the series, "The Red Raven Stories," which ran in *Detective Story Magazine* from November 20, 1915, to March 20, 1916, nine adventures in all. A second series of ten stories, "The Return of Red Raven," ran from December 5, 1916 through April 20, 1917 in the same magazine.

Ravenswood and his Red Ravens are direct from the land of dime novels. These stories are simple, almost fragmentary, patched with wonderful passages in the boys' literature style.

As in this scene, where the members of the Red Raven gang are gathering for instructions:

...At the weather-beaten back door of a gloomy old building in the East Side, where each, when he arrived, pressed the head of one of several nails in the faded casing.

Black Mask (June 1922). Following Raffles' good example, the master criminal moved through the highest levels of society, reforming only when softened by love.

Then, without waiting, he put his mouth near a knot hole in the wall, uttering a peculiar, guttural noise, twice repeated.

It sounded very like—the croaking of a raven.

Through a hidden tube from within came a sharply whispered question:

"What noise is that?"

"The croak of a night bird."

"His name?"

"A Red Raven"

"Croaking for what?"

"Admission to the rookery."

"What word admits one?"

"Nevermore."

All this just to get into the hideout. You can imagine the boredom of the doorkeeper, for there are at least twelve members of the gang.

The first story of the series is titled "A String of Beads." Ravenswood, disguised as an Englishman, drugs everyone in a wealthy New York household, cracks the safe and steals all the jewels, taking care that the crime appears to be an outside job. His gang is scattered all over the grounds, serving no more useful purpose than watching.

Detected by the butler, Ravenswood makes him a member of the Red Ravens, rather than killing him. ("I have never killed a man...and never will, unless in self-defense," he says.) He gives the butler a string of amber beads from the loot, which the butler dons under his shirt. Amber beads (you see) are a specific for a sore throat. And the butler has such a sore throat, you wouldn't believe.

Off the crooks glide into the night. Ravenswood stays on at the mansion, hopefully unsuspected. At least until the arrival of Detective Joe Glidden, "a serious, grizzled man of fifty, broad and compact, tending to corpulency, but strong as a bull and tough as a pine knot." He is also taciturn, smart and quick.

The classical situation has now been established: The master criminal and his good lieutenant oppose the dangerous detective. This is a primary structure that will shape the bulk of series crook stories for decades to come.

It was a structure hardly new even in 1915, for the same arrangement supports half the Old Sleuth and Nick Carter stories and three-quarters of Jesse James. But particularly Nick Carter. For the author of The Red Raven stories, Scott Campbell, was Frederick W. Davis, who wrote a substantial percentage of the *Nick Carter Stories*. He had also written serials for the *New York Weekly* and contributed detective series to the early *Popular Magazine*.

Detective Glidden quickly discovers that the crime was an inside job. (He observes, as did Sherlock Holmes, that the dog did not bark in the night—although, with twelve people lurking out there among the bushes, the dog ought to have noticed something.) The butler confesses and Glidden organizes a raid against the Red Raven's secret headquarters.

He has no luck. They all escape. Ravenswood, however, does return a valuable necklace of diamonds and sapphires to its owner because it was a gift from her lost love. The Raven is given to sentimental gestures.

In "Gold Plate" (February 5, 1916), Ravenswood gasses everyone in a mansion and steals a fabulous collection of gold plate. Once again, Glidden and company arrive too late. But Ravenswood's luck is soon to run out.

His distinctive ring is recognized. His cover is blown. His final coup fails. Following a deadly fight with the police, the gang is captured. Ravenswood, alone, wounded, desperate, clings to the rigging of a balloon that reels crazily away into the storm, amid a hail of police bullets. Now the balloon staggers out over the Atlantic, blown toward inevitable doom.

The Red Raven gang is slapped into Sing Sing.

Two years pass, fictional time.

Comes the December 5, 1916, issue of *Detective Story Magazine*, and "The Opening Wedge" introduces a new series of Ravenswood adventures. The editorial procedure of the period was to publish groups of short stories, identified as a "series," in bursts of five or six. All stories contained the same lead characters. Often a weak narrative continuity held the series together, but each story was complete and followed chronologically.

Successful series could be extended incrementally to ten or even twenty stories. If, after a reasonable time, readers demanded more, an additional series could be launched—"The Further Adventures of...."

As "The Return of Red Raven" begins, Nolan and another gang member have escaped from Sing Sing. Hot for loot, they kidnap the glowing Englishman, Lord Rockdale, just off the boat, come to marry a New York beauty.

Amazement and awe! The Lord is Ravenswood, himself, impeccably disguised. He has already abducted the Lord and has him concealed aboard the ship.

And where has Ravenswood been?

Safe and merry, preserved by the luck of the popular series character. The balloon dropped him near a ship. Rescued, he sailed around the world and settled in England to plot and scheme. Now he has returned to the States with the declared intention of busting his boys out of Sing Sing—just as soon as he collects that ransom for Lord Rockdale.

But Glidden, too, has returned to the series. Thorough as ever, he has the ransom secured in a mansion, guarded by close-packed police.

No respectable Mastermind, however, is daunted by police. To lure them all outside the mansion is simple. To whisk up the money and flee is elementary. And afterward, Glidden roars: "Only one man on earth could have turned this trick.... Dick Ravenswood and his Red Ravens."

From this good beginning springs a long series of crimes. Most are successful. The gang is together again and into their pockets flow currency, gold, jewelry, silver, the wages of crime, pleasingly ample. Glidden fails and again fails. During one encounter, he shoots Ravenswood, but not fatally. From that evil comes good. Ravenswood is able to save the detective from death. A magnificent gesture. Beneath the grime of crime glows gold of richest hue, as you might put it.

The game continues until terrible failure during the Suburban Bank robbery. Once more the gang is arrested. Only Ravenswood and Paddy escape, warned by a timely telephone call from that lovely, young, wealthy, socially-prominent widow, Mrs. Stella Morton. Once she had been befriended by Ravenswood, a deed winning her gratitude and her heart.

As for Ravenswood—love gusts its refreshing currents through the chambers of his heart.

Crime seems repugnant to him now.

He resolves to reform.

He will make his way in the world, becoming worthy of her.

He renounces crime. Goodbye, Paddy. Goodbye, dear friend.

Then away to bid Stella a temporary farewell, nobility and bathos mingling in a drench of sentiment:

Stella: "I could not live without your love, nor with a world between us. Even though they 'get you,' as you term it, I will not forsake you. Where you go I will go, and though all the world turns against you and reviles you, I will cleave closer to you, a loyal wife, whether in adversity and sorrow or in the full realization of your newborn hopes and lofty aspirations."

Ravenswood (his eyes glowing with such a light as never shone on land or sea): "You have turned me from the darkness to the light. You have shown me the straight road, from which I never again will turn. I will, in so far as I can, repair past evil with future good."

Standing back in the darkness, listening to these sentiments, is Glidden. For weeks he has watched Stella, knowing that Ravenswood would come to her. He hesitates.

Suddenly a shot rings out.

Down in the street, Glidden finds a dead man. All evidence identifies the murderer as—can it be?—Stella's brother.

But no. Ravenswood steps forward, his hard face luminous with self sacrifice. "I alone killed him."

But no.

As the lead characters pose at stage center, Act III, Scene 4, locked in giddy drama, Paddy appears, pistol in hand. He hurls a signed confession at Glidden. While lurking about, Paddy witnessed the murder. It was done by a political rival of Stella's brother. Paddy caught the rascal in the act, forced him to scribble down a signed confession.

Here 'tis.

With this glad news, Paddy escapes. Forevermore.

And will Ravenswood go to prison?

Not likely, It is the final story of an extended series. Glidden owes Ravenswood his life and he knows, positively, that the man intends to go straight. "I'll quit even with you, if it costs me my badge.... Go straight, and good luck to you!"

So ends "The Green Curtain," number 10 of the second and final series. Proving that you may enjoy a life of crime and never suffer for it. Or not much.

All this is the concentrated essence of the dime novel at its most mannered. The dialogue pulsates with that bombast peculiar to 4th of July orations, stage language rolling out the cadenced sentences: No Man is accountable for his actions, only for his intentions. A woman's love redeems all. If I orate gloriously enough, all is excused. How clear and bright the improbable rings. Within the cloistered world of *Detective Story Magazine,* it all seems possible.

The kiss of the dime novels still glowed on the forehead of *Detective Story.* In the first issue, October 5, 1915, appeared the *second* part of a four-part Nick Carter serial, "The Yellow Label." This had begun in the final issue of *Nick Carter Stories,* #160. The serial bridged that potentially lethal gap between the ex-dime novel and the new magazine, and confirmed Nick Carter readers arrived painlessly in the New Canaan, bemused but soothed.

Like the early *Popular Magazine, Detective Story Magazine* contained fiction aimed at several different age groups, a traditional Street & Smith technique of hedging its bets. Ormond Smith (head of the publishing company) wished the magazine to appeal both to adults and young readers—particularly those young males who no longer seemed so eager to buy every issue of Nick Carter and Frank Merriwell.[3]

This view of its audience strongly colored *Detective Story's* first years and explains the strong juvenile tone of such offerings as The Red Raven series. During the first eighteen months of its life, about 20% of the fiction in *Detective Story* was slanted toward the young reader. But that percentage soon changed. The magazine swiftly established itself and, by the time its twice-a-month issuance increased to weekly (with the September 4, 1917 issue) Street & Smith had discovered that most of the readers were adults.

Youngsters read it, all right, but most of the letters which came in (every one of which was carefully studied) made it evident that youngsters just didn't have ten cents each week to spend on a magazine.[4]

As a result of this change in readership (assuming that there had really been a change, market research being then even more a branch of voodoo than now), the magazine contents were quietly readjusted. The Tom Sawyerish flavor of the dime-novel based fiction was reduced and diluted. But the dime novel bones remained quite visible. Nick Carter, himself, edited the new magazine for its first several years. His name stood on the masthead, although Frank E. Blackwell did the work. Aside from Nick Carter's presence, the dime novels continued to be represented by such sturdy old house names as Harrison Keith, Douglas Gray, and, of course, Scott Campbell. All these kept the spirit of dime novels days bright in the new, improved, modern, adult-oriented, 160-page magazine.

In addition to its dime-novel strain, *Detective Story Magazine* offered two other forms of detective and mystery fiction. One of these was the formal mystery problem story, full of clues and intelligent detectives, and often strongly seasoned with the manners and atmosphere of England. The other form was that of crook stories—Chinese crime emperors and American Masterminds and all manner of lesser criminals, ranging from geniuses to klutzes, gang leaders, swindlers, pick-pockets, con men and meek, absconding bank tellers. The fiction focused on the crime. It showed the criminal in the act, all covered with fine sweat, then followed him to capture and belated remorse.

Dime novel, English-style mystery, American crook story—it was a satisfying mixture. But perhaps the crook story predominated. Through *Detective Story* ranged a dazzling array of criminals. With vast relish they compounded their crimes, artful as a chef adding the ultimate rose to a wedding cake. Eagerly they varied blackmail with robbery and kidnapping. Rarely did they murder—for that skated close to forbidden territory. In 1917, a man must be a French or Chinese monster to kill. Deadly violence was not permissible—even for such picaresque villains as Black Star.

3-

Black Star, that genius of crime, that subtle master, that hooded and caped titan in black, led his avaricious hordes through *Detective Story Magazine* from 1916 to 1930.

"He never stoops to murder," we are told, "and does not allow his men to murder."

Stealing is different. Black Star would steal the sky. He delights in mass kidnapping and revels in impossible crimes. Like Fantomas, his mind sparkles with tricks. And, like Fantomas, his identity is concealed. He wears a black hood ornamented by a star of blazing jet on the front. For that extra touch of mystery, the face beneath the hood is masked. His figure is robed in black.

A hand-picked gang serves him—men and women skilled in the professions and trades—lawyers and electricians, actresses and safe crackers. All are appropriately hooded, masked, mysterious.

Black Star and his horde were created by one of the great shapers of pulp magazine fiction, Johnston McCulley. Born in Ottawa, Illinois, in 1883, McCulley became a newspaperman, wrote plays in his spare time and soon switched to short fiction for the popular magazines. His first book was published in 1908 and was followed by one or two books a year until about 1947. Most of these first appeared as serials or series stories in *Argosy All-Story Weekly* and *Detective Story Magazine,* markets avid for the adventures of mysterious criminals and justice figures trampling on the letter of the law. McCulley industriously churned out fiction to meet these needs, as well as western, adventure, and, it is suspected, love stories. He used his own name and a variety of pseudonyms, among them Raley Brien, George Drayne, Fredrick Phelps, Rowena Raley, and Harrington Strong.

Over three decades of professional work, McCulley created a variety of series characters. Of these, the most widely known are Zorro and Thubway Tham, both first appearing in 1919. Other prominent characters included many costumed heroes: Black Star was followed by The Thunderbolt, The Man In Purple, and The Crimson Clown, all strangely dressed, all hotly sought by the police for robbing respectable thieves that the Law could not touch. McCulley's costumed extraordinaries are, in fact, justice figures, although much diluted samples of that strong wine. They are justice figures simplified to blandness, with all the deadliness strained out. But they are recognizably part of that honorable tradition founded by Edgar Wallace's Just Men. McCulley's series characters solidly established the costumed figure in 1920s mystery-adventure fiction and in the decade following, when that figure became a staple of the mystery-adventure pulps. Costumed detective-adventurers became an exceedingly visible sub-genre, and The Black Hood, the Red Hood, the Ghost Detective, The Black Bat, The Crimson Mask, The Shadow and the Spider would each, in his own way, carry the fire that

McCulley had scattered through *Detective Story Magazine.*

During the 1930s, McCulley turned increasingly to western and historical fiction, including serials featuring Zorro and Zorro-like characters for *Argosy.* This fiction he intermixed with radio and motion picture scripts. From 1944-1951 he published a series of Zorro short stories for the magazine *West,* and later, in 1957-1958, he scripted the Zorro television series for Walt Disney.

He died in California, November 28, 1958.

The Black Star adventures appeared early in McCulley's career and were his first popular series. They were slight beguilements, increasingly done to formula, but softened by humor and the courtliness of the villain. In common with other McCulley characters, Black Star is neither particularly substantial nor particularly consistent. But he has a highly developed sense of honor: he keeps his word. He is touchy of his reputation. He enjoys challenges and no stuffy sentiments drag at his darting mind.

"I am a genuine criminal," he writes (he is forever writing notes), "and proud of it."

His activities begin in the novelette, "Rogue for a Day," published in the March 5, 1916 *Detective Story Magazine.* The series opens in the bedroom of Roger Verbeck, who represents the forces for Good in the series. Verbeck is that familiar figure, a tall, good-looking young millionaire, who dabbles in criminology. He is assisted by his servant and personal friend, Muggs, a small, tough man who seems to be "going through the process of drying up." He was formerly a small-time crook, saved from suicide by Verbeck's kindness. They are the first of several Master and Man teams McCulley will present to readers of the magazine.

Verbeck has remarked slightingly, at a small private party, that although the police are unable to capture Black Star, he could do so. This remark immediately brings a minion to Verbeck's apartment in the middle of the night, for Black Star is touchy about his honor and reputation, and responds promptly to a slur. He has written a letter to Verbeck—the first of many, for Black Star is filled with words and pours them bravely forth on the page:

...To show you how useless it would be for you to pit your brains and skill against mine, I am putting this letter on your desk while you sleep.... I am even leaving a Black Star on your bed.... After this exhibition, either admit that the Black Star is clever, or do as you boasted you could do—catch me.[5]

The minion is captured as he plants the letter, but is allowed to escape and shadowed to Black Star's secret headquarters. There, Verbeck and Muggs watch the henchman report to Black Star. No words are spoken. Each has a small blackboard and they write on these. "...thus they conversed, each writing on his blackboard and erasing after the other had read."

Minion (writing on blackboard his ID number): "Number Six."
Black Star (writing): "Countersign."
Minion: "Florida."
Black Star: "Report."

It is all brisk business here. None of that Red Raven tra-la. Or not much. This is, after all, still volume 2, Number 5, of *Detective Story Magazine,* and the young readers crave excitement.

They get it. Verbeck captures Black Star. Black Star drops Verbeck down a trap door. Muggs knocks Black Star out and saves Verbeck, They promptly remove Black Star's mask:

There was revealed the not unhandsome face of a man about forty-five.... It was one (Verbeck) never had seen before. ...Verbeck had been half of a mind that the master crook was some one known to the city in general as a respectable man, a sort of Jekyll and Hyde.[6]

But not so. That sort of subtle masquerade would do for the later pulps in which all costumed master criminals were respectable businessmen by day. In 1915, Black Star was only what he claimed to be—a professional criminal out to loot the city down to its curbs and traffic lights.

Verbeck now decides to impersonate Black Star and round up the gang. After stashing Black Star away in the old Verbeck mansion, Roger goes forth to meet a member of the gang. But the meeting is a failure. He sees no one but Howard Wendell, brother of Roger's fiancee who is, perhaps unfortunately, named....

Well, she is a dear gentle girl, very sweet. Pretty and loyal. Roger makes new plans. He returns to Black Star's headquarters....You see, about Howard Wendell's sister, Roger loves her and the engagement has been announced. So it really doesn't matter all that much about her name, you see.

Disguised as Black Star, Roger arranges for the gang to converge on the Charity Ball that very evening.

Her name is really not essential to this discussion. She will shortly marry Roger and will then be called Mrs. Verbeck. Very satisfactory.

All arrangements are made and the police informed to prepare for a mass arrest. Then—disaster. Black Star reveals that he has just blackmailed a new recruit into his organization—Howard Wendell's sister, Roger Verbeck's fiancee. And when the police trap closes on the Black Star gang, Faustina will....

Well, if you must know, her name is Faustina Wendell. But she is really charming, after you get to know her.

Thereafter, the story peaks as Roger races to save Faustina from the police trap, and Black Star escapes from Muggs, and Roger secures all those otherwise innocent notes and checks incriminating the Wendells from Black Star's archives, and everyone races about in a blind fury, hurling themselves this way and that.

Finally the police are evaded, the Wendells freed, Black Star recaptured, and all ends gloriously.

"Rogue for a Day" was signed John Mack Stone, a pseudonym that remained attached to "Rogue" when the story was reprinted in the June 1930 issue of *Best Detective Magazine*.

After the initial adventure, the Black Star mills began to grind, if slowly. Over the following two years, about ten novelettes and at least one serial were published. They were brisk, loosely chronological, and resembled each other rather closely. Black Star escapes to capture Roger, who escapes capturing Black Star, who escapes to steal gigantically, although never with loss of life.

To assist Black Star during these bloodless coups, McCulley has introduced a fine new device. His criminal is now equipped with vapor bombs and vapor guns, these spewing forth an instantaneous sleeping gas. One whiff and down you sprawl, jaw loose and breathing thickly, while Black Star's men paste small black stars on your forehead.

The sleep gas is a sublime device that deftly solves two narrative needs. It eliminates any possible necessity for murder, thus assuring that the fiction could be read by the faintest heart. And it provided an acceptable (if feebly) realistic method of eliminating opposition wholesale. That in itself simplified narrative logistics, for an insensible opponent does not have to be tied up.

Gas weapons permitted audacious plans and vast accomplishments. It also mildly intensified suspense, since you could depend upon Roger and Muggs to be gassed, or almost gassed, or threatened by gas at least twice a story. Gas proved such a useful device that it was borrowed for several later series. In the *Doc Savage Magazine* (1933-1949) gas is one of the hero's primary weapons in his battles against criminal legions; similar gas devices are used in *The Avenger*, (1939-1942), a spin-off from the Doc Savage series. Both Secret Agent X and The Crimson Clown used vapor guns which seemed to have been built from the Black Star specifications. And most other 1930s avengers, in and out of the single-character magazines, employed a gas weapon at least occasionally. It was too useful a device to be ignored.

Throughout 1917, Black Star pursues the fascinating career of master criminal. In "Black Star's Mistake" (two-part serial, February 5 and 20, 1917), he plans to humiliate Roger and Muggs for interfering with his plans and, incidentally, to steal 300,000 dollars from the bank. He does, but ends up in jail, after some complicated racing about.

"Black Star's Return" (October 2, 1917) finds him in a cell, divested of hood and mask but still master of his vast gang. He promptly escapes, kidnapping the District Attorney, judge, and jury which were trying him, and scooping up Roger as an afterthought. Aided by the brilliant feminine criminal, The Princess, he then proceeds to rob the city hollow. (The city's name is never specified but it was certainly no place for your valuables.)

One elaborate robbery follows another. The Black Star crew kidnaps forty wealthy men from a dance. ("Black Star's Rebuke," October 23, 1917); he follows this by stealing the golden automobile from the auto show and abducts a famous opera singer, The Princess appearing in her place ("Black Star's Serenade," November 27, 1917). No longer does it seem possible to capture him. Away he slides with his shifty crew, leaving Verbeck and the police gritting their teeth among the ruins.

"Black Star's Raid" (December 11, 1917): Grown irritated at the petty swindler, James Larnton, Black Star writes him a letter:

"Slay your worthless self and I'll see that your victims recover through your insurance."

Unwilling to die, Larnton calls in Roger and Muggs. From this point, it is all the old familiar mixture. Our heroes trail a Black Star henchman to an old barn and creep inside. There, in a lavishly furnished room, bright with expensive tapestries and rugs, stands Black Star, writing instructions on a blackboard.

At that moment, Roger and Muggs are captured. By a tremendous coincidence, they are imprisoned in a room where Verbeck used to play as a boy. The room has a movable floor board and so they escape; leaving the reader to scowl and grumble as he will.

Now Verbeck calls the police and they all raid Larnton's office, where the gang is cleaning out the safe. And sure enough, there looms Black Star and men amid a cloud of sleeping gas. They escape, since the story is barely half over and ever more wonderments beckon us.

The following day, Black Star appears at the City Hall, where he holds up the Grand Jury and presents it with the incriminating ledgers from Larnton's office. With some urging, the Jury returns an indictment against Larnton. Having performed as a responsible citizen, Black Star puts the jury to sleep and ambles out, pausing only to rob City Hall down to its echoes.

The adventure is capped by a hysterical automobile chase through the city. The police and Verbeck shoot and shoot. To no avail. Black Star, disguised, melts away.

Larnton, by the way, commits suicide.

"Black Star's Hobby" (January 29, 1918) is gambling—so he claims. His gang takes over a gambling house, so that Black Star can gamble in peace. He pays his losses in counterfeit money, takes his winnings in bundles of cash and has a disreputable good time, and vanishes when the police come swarming in. During the course of the resultant chasing back and forth, Black Star finds time to write to the City Fathers that he has stolen about everything of value in the city. He plans to leave in another week—and if Roger Verbeck wishes to catch him, he had better hurry up.

Which leads grandly to "Black Star's Defeat" (February 26, 1918), a story concentrating a years' action into an hour and a half. Between twelve noon and quarter of one, an army of black-hooded thieves descends upon the city to rob a bank, steal a military relief donation, rescue gang members from jail, black-out all town power plants, and raid the railroad station express office.

That last crime proves their undoing. The express office is defended by determined men. A bloody battle occurs—for Black Star becomes so desperate to enter the office that he authorizes the use of guns. By the time that the gang blasts into the office, police ring the station. Most of the gang is captured. Black Star vanishes, is finally discovered by Verbeck, who deducts that the master of crime is concealed inside a piano case ticketed to be shipped out on the 1 o'clock train.

This is so feeble an excuse for the fight at the express office that you can only grin in embarrassment and look away. Very young readers have been known to toss down the magazine, remarking, in their innocent voices: "That's awful dumb."

Off Black Star goes to jail.

And there he stays for almost a year, until "Black Star's Campaign" (six-part serial, January 14 through February 18, 1919). From this point, the Black Star adventures convert from novelettes to serials spaced at widening intervals.[7] Story content remains unchanged. In "Campaign," the sheriff is tricked into raiding a gambling joint where he arrests forty men. After these are tossed into jail, they turn out to be Black Star's boys, loaded down with vapor bombs. And so Black Star is again free. He has his face changed and vows vengeance: "We are going to loot the city more thoroughly than we did before."

After many thrilling scenes, Verbeck again foils Black Star in the final chapters and the series is placed in hibernation for about two years. The silence is interrupted by "Black Star Comes Back" (three-part serial, January 8 through 22, 1921), after which the series is again suspended, this time for seven years. Such an extended period should have obliterated Black Star from memory, young readers inexorably transforming to young parents and wage-earners as the years grind along. But Black Star continued to be remembered and asked for in the letters published in the "Headquarters Chat" department of *Detective Story*. One day he returned.

He returned far more bloodthirsty than he left, suggesting deep psychological change or altered editorial requirements. In "Black Star on the Air" (three-part serial, March 3 through 17, 1928), he announces over the radio that, unless he is paid half a million dollars, he will explode bombs throughout the city.

Immediately, Verbeck and Muggs give chase. Seven years has not altered them in the slightest. Muggs is still drying up and Roger, tall, handsome, and rich, has not yet got around to marrying Faustina.

Almost at once, Verbeck is captured, his customary fate. While Black Star is writing on the blackboard, Roger gets loose, captures him, leaves him bound, gagged, and handcuffed in another room. That does no good, since the handcuff key has been left in Black Star's pocket. Muggs comes rushing in to join Roger and they are almost blown up together.

Barely escaping, they rush off, with all of the police in town, to descend upon the radio station. There a violent battle is fought with Black Star's mob. Most are captured. As for the hooded master:

...the car whirled around the nearest corner and was gone. And back to them came the mocking laugh of the Black Star.

On that unresolved chord, the series melts away until late in 1930.[8]

Then, "Black Star Back—and How!" (three-part serial, November 1 through 15, 1930). Foolish young embezzler, Lawrence Delair, is blackmailed into Black Star's new-formed gang. As his first assignment, Delair must accompany another gang member to Roger's home. There both Roger and Muggs are gassed and liberally decorated with small black stars. This indicates to the most obtuse that Black Star is back— and how! But Roger has recognized Delair by his fancy finger ring and (echoes of the remote past) shadows him to Black Star's hideout. The same old hoods and masks and blackboard are again in use. The hideout is crammed with criminals and you would think that a police raid should capture someone. But the police raid and, as usual, flop.

Subsequent chapters continue the endless captures and escapes, a technique for using narrative movement to conceal lack of narrative content. In the fullness of time, we learn that Black Star intends wholesale robbery of the social elite at a masquerade party.

Roger and Muggs manage to trap the gang at the party, but not, as you may have suspected, Black Star. Once more he vanishes with all the jewels amid a confusion of gas and mocking laughter.

Exit Black Star. Exit series. No further appearances have been noted.

These innocent entertainments float through the magazine as bonelessly as wraiths, beguiling, active and empty. It is a series of one story repeated with a minimum of variation. Within each story, a few basic scenes repeat: The Capture of Roger and Muggs, Black Star at the blackboard, the Escape, the Partial Success, the Grand Plot, the Inconclusive Victory. How (you wonder) can McCulley dare to repeat himself again? But he does dare.

The pages brim with crime that has the substance of a daydream. It is crime purged of sting. Not actual crime, with spines and painful bones, where people get hurt (although not by gas guns), and lose possessions they value (although they are all wealthy and can afford it) and are endangered by armed robbery, an act of violence against society (although presented as a game of wits).

In the Raffles series, crime was decriminalized by declaring the victims more guilty than the thief. In the Black Star series, the crime is simply trivialized: it is an exciting sport. It is all a game and expressed in terms of a game. After the characters have robbed and raced about and shouted and scuffled and got sweaty, then Mother McCulley will call all back home for nice hot soup.

It is all play in Black Star's world. The neighborhood boys choose sides after school. Some are crooks and some are not and so they run. As a result, no one in the series is particularly competent. There is no need. Roger and Muggs are amiable light-weights with the same degree of foresight as a pithed frog. The police are genial boobs, unable to find their feet in their shoes. The Black Star henchmen seem ferocious until you strip off their black robes, when they become as genially incompetent as the police. Black Star, himself, for all his organizational and administrative ability, and a certain skill at mocking laughter during a retreat, never learns from his mistakes and seems never to profit from his enormous robberies; he spends those millions on nothing more substantial than a newly furnished hideout, a few more black hoods and another box of chalk. In all the series, the only able figure is that of The Princess, and she is not a real character but a convenience to Black Star in working out his plots.

Under this juvenile play hide a few concepts of how the Master Criminal performs in fiction. He administers and directs a large group of criminals, all unknown, who prey on society. His gang is carefully organized in hierarchies, each small group reporting to a leader who reports to a higher leader, who reports upward until, at last, a few selected lieutenants report to Black Star. (As Black Star explains to Roger Verbeck in "Rogue for a Day," this structure minimizes the dangers of a single arrest and makes it almost impossible to penetrate deeply into the organization.) The Black Star gang crudely parallels the structure of the Anarchist groups which lurked through the early 1900s.

The Master Criminal, moreover, plans audaciously and is content only with major crimes. To commit these, he uses pseudo-scientific devices which make easy the most difficult problems. In the familiar tradition of the criminal hero, Black Star first advises the victims and the police that he is about to strike, then appears in a haze of sleeping gas and tactical misdirection to keep his word.

Before the Master Criminal's brilliance, the police wilt haplessly. Unimaginative and inflexible, their only effective role is in support of the hero, an amateur who has joined the chase as a game. Working either alone or with a single friend, he relies on cleverness, insight, and quantities of coincidences to follow the trail to the Master Criminal.

Even in such filmy play-acting, crime must receive some token punishment. For that reason, most of the gang is always captured. Occasionally the Master Criminal is arrested in the last chapter and jailed, so that he will be ready to escape at the beginning of the next story. In those cases where he escapes, he contrives to carry off a substantial portion of his spoils. He bears Verbeck no ill will. It is, after all, only a game, a light entertainment, no more. They are friendly enemies, the pursuer adding spice to the activity.

Let a few weeks pass. It will all begin again. More enormous plots. A newly recruited gang. Another secret hideaway and more teasing letters to the police, fresh hoods and new gas guns, and an outstanding plan to embarrass Mr. Verbeck in the eyes of the community. The Master Criminal, secure in his own abilities, stands scribbling once more on his blackboard, laughing in that provoking way, the very shape and figure of a superior man gone wrong.

4-

After the February 26, 1918, "The Defeat of Black Star," occurs almost a year's gap in the record of that gentleman's activities. The void is filled by another Johnston McCulley master criminal. From April 16, 1918, to April 29, 1919, McCulley published in *Detective Story* a series of novelettes about that remarkable supercriminal, The Spider. Much later, the stories were collected in three Chelsea House hardbacks: *The Spider's Den* (1925), *The Spider's Fury* (1930), and *The Spider's Debt* (1930).

...the man was not ordinary. He was squat, wonderously fat. His head was gigantic, his neck thick. He had a mass of white hair that was unkempt. His eyes were tiny and black and piercing. His thick lips twitched continually. His cheeks were flabby and white, ghastly looking. His fat, wrinkled hands were spread on the desk before him and the fingers seemed never to be still.[9]

We are in the presence of a gross, menacing intellect that hovers at the center of dark matters, weaving a web of intrigue. Gives you a weird feeling, doesn't it? Sort of an icy tingle.

Worse is to come: He is a cripple, confined to a chair. Wicked cripples are the worst of all. And when you add to that, a horrible smile that twists his fat mouth...

As a superior master criminal, the Spider controls a sprawling organization. Members are kept separated, as good web-strands must be. But they are all over the place—under the bed, peering from the cookie jar.... Each pours in intelligence. Each commits the most dreadful deeds.

The Spider, himself, sits in a large room in a large mansion surrounded by large lawns. The room—The Spider's Den—is large but ordinary. At its center squats a huge, flat mahogany desk with a swivel chair. A book rack stands in the corner. The walls are lined with filing cabinets, each stuffed with information of value to The Spider—data on criminals and rich men, policemen and poor men, yard after yard of it.

To protect this room, the windows are small and barred with steel. Within lurks The Spider, twitching and plotting. Outside bubbles his organization, endlessly skulking.

It is curious. This vast organization, this flow of information, this sleek criminal mind — and nothing really criminal ever happens. True, The Spider prefers to work outside the law. House-breaking means nothing to him. His men will point a pistol with the most desperate. But what small criminal activities these are. How circumscribed. Black Star loots whole towns. Zorro keeps an entire area stirred up. But The Spider, lurking, listening, spends his time punishing traitors and frustrating the plans of other crooks.

It is as if he has created an international crime organization to steal apples from the corner store.

Before the war, in Paris, when he was young and blithe, The Spider headed a gang of spies and thieves. One of his people — one Bertram Blaine — betrayed him to the police. Trapped in a flaming building after a fierce gun fight, The Spider was severely burned. He was rescued by his own men, but the injuries to his legs were permanent.

Escaping to America, he slowly rebuilt the organization. It is secret. So entirely secret that his niece, Silvia Rodney, lives with him but does not realize that he is a crook. She thinks that he is the agent of a foreign power. All those strange people bustling in and out, she believes to be "laboring for the good of humanity."

As you might suppose, Silvia is "young, fresh looking, innocent looking" and has a fresh, innocent mind. She does not wear powder or rouge and is hardly more than twenty. If that description gives you sophisticated women of the world a twinge of guilt, that is too bad.

So far we have a vacant girl and a fat fellow in a chair. How can you get three books out of that material? But how easily it is done. The main character in the Spider stories is not The Spider but a fellow named John Warwick. We follow his adventures, while The Spider lurks ponderously behind the paragraphs, often in a terrible temper.

Warwick is that commonplace of the 1920s—a bored, young rich man. Tall, handsome, thirty-five, with hair already silvering at the temples, he has been an athlete, big-game hunter, explorer and a social favorite. Also, he is bored.

Warwick: "Nothing new in all the world. Every sensation is old. Scenery, buildings, country, city, men, women—I've seen 'em all— what? Adventure, romance, intrigue, big-game hunting, exploration—I've done 'em all! Eternally hoping something new will crop up to make a fellow think life's worth living.... Upon my word!"[10]

Warwick is addicted, don't you know, to an atrocious pseudo-English slanginess—all that sort of thing. Gives you the pip, so to speak. It's a fiddling idle levity that he cultivates—all that sort of rot. You know, old top, like Bertie Wooster, quite so, my word!

As the series flounces on, his affected speech becomes progessively more elaborate and more painful. Other than this, he is reasonably efficient.

His efficiency is highly improved by the presence of his man Togo— my "gentleman Jap," Warwick says. Togo admires this fine young fool and, since he, too, is a member of The Spider's band, is always ready to pull Warwick out of various fires. Not the least of Togo's abilities is a knowledge of pressure points. Let him seize your throat, press with his thumbs, and out you go—cold as an IRS regulation.

All this window dressing is familiar stuff. Throat pressure points, copious information files, socially prominent young man with a double life—these are established data points from the 1930s pulps, particularly those published by Street & Smith. Why bits of business from 1918 continued to be used in the 1930s is hard to explain, but the continuity of editorial personnel at Street & Smith seems to have assured that no fragment of business was forgotten.

As for The Spider series, it goes its blithe way. No two stories are quite consistent. In "The Spider's Den," *(Detective Story Magazine,* April 16, 1918), The Spider is a bad, wicked fellow. And Warwick, the semi-hero, has "no moral scruples." Well, things change; and they do.

But first, Warwick's impending criminal activities must be glazed over. We learn that his society friends have been methodically swindling him. He is almost penniless. Only $5,000 stands between him and ejection from his club, a dreaded fate.

Lured to The Spider's mansion, Warwick learns the truth about his unlucky investments. He agrees to serve The Spider and take revenge on those who cheated him. His boredom is relieved, too. And The Spider is aided in various little enterprises.

Warwick's first assignment is to steal an arrangement of jewels called "The Three Triangles." Off he trots to a social function. At that glittering affair, he discovers another batch of crooks preparing to steal away the same prize. Three of these set upon him. Since he is a Street & Smith hero, he whips them handily. They flee to their hideout, Warwick trailing behind. A series of unusual coincidences permit him to steal back the Three Triangles from those wicked criminals. You can hardly consider that a crime.

As matters turn out, the criminals are playing an elaborate triple-cross on The Spider. The betrayal is foiled by Warwick's wonderful exploits. All this thrust and counter-thrust occurs because a secret code has been engraved on the back of the jewels. The Spider intends to sell this secret to a certain government, so that it can translate coded papers of another government that the certain government has secured. Matters are almost too complicated to explain. At any rate, Warwick has accomplished wonders.

Now the adventures reel out, peril and joy, action enough to ease the worst case of boredom. Best of all, Warwick is falling in love with Silvia, and she, sweet thing, with him.

He rises in The Spider's service. He becomes the right-hand man.

More than once he is almost exposed as a criminal. (Strangely enough, he hardly commits a crime. Merely has exciting adventures, you understand.) Each time he is saved. His cover remains intact and no harm is done.

For a moment in "The Spider's Venom" (September 10, 1918), it seems that Warwick may be involved in a murder. The Spider has located another traitor, a fellow who did him bad in Europe. At that time, The Spider was using a subtle poison "that baffles your chemists, your medical experts." Stuff came from South American sources. I cannot be more exact. This secret, this terrible venom, The Spider used only on traitors. He must have had traitors as other people have cats.

An antidote exists for the venom. The plot requires that the traitor, Chadwick, possess a few drops of antidote which he keeps in a jeweled canteen (just a tiny thing) hanging from a chain around his neck. In case The Spider poisons him, he's all prepared.

As the story opens, The Spider has finally located Chadwick. Warwick is given the job of stealing the jeweled canteen. Then vengeance vengeance vengeance vengeance.

After 25 or 30 pages of failure, Warwick and Togo catch Chadwick— the man's an utter cad, by Jove—while he is driving a car in a cross-country automobile race. The antidote is carried off while Chadwick gawks.

And does Chadwick's slaughter follow?

Oh, no. Not at all. You wouldn't want the hero to be responsible for a murder, would you?

Instead, The Spider will merely allow Chadwick to suffer agonies of anticipation for the rest of his days, constantly surrounded by little black paper spiders stuck mysteriously to his possessions (not unlike the black stars used by another terrible criminal), constantly waiting for the first effects of the poison, any day, any hour, perhaps even now. . . . It is no sweet fate, come to think of it.

You will be pleased to learn that Warwick is no longer suffering from boredom. Quite the reverse. Now he itches for tranquility and the lovely Silvia.

By this time, Silvia has finally discovered that the sun rises and water is wet and her beloved fat uncle is a crook and Warwick is his helper. This knowledge has little effect on her. Warwick, however, is confronted by that perplexity usual to heroes of fiction published in inexpensive magazines—he wants to marry but can't because he may be arrested at any moment.

Since this is popular fiction, a painless way out presents itself. Warwick will do one or two more jobs for The Spider, who will then free him from the gang. And marriage will follow and the good life, financed entirely by profits from crime (although not much is made of this fact).

This, then, is the situation at the opening of "The Spider's Reward" (April 29, 1919).

To begin with, the story has a major structural defect. It plunges off in one direction, then reverses itself violently. Boiling double-talk plasters over the crack. The core story is that Warwick is to go to the mansion of Bertram Blaine—the traitor responsible for The Spider's crippling in Paris, if you remember that far back—and hold Blaine at gun-point until The Spider is carried in by gang members for a final showdown.

The story that develops is rather different. Two tough characters lure Togo to a deserted cabin, knock him on the head and tie him up. He has a terrible time escaping. The purpose is to keep him from helping Warwick, even now held captive in his room by two gunmen. He squirts them with a seltzer bottle and they flee.

Warwick then goes to Blaine's mansion, a spooky place filled with snares and traps and concealed bells. Within minutes, Blaine has dropped our hero down a trap door. When Togo arrives, Blaine is busy pumping gas into the trap.

Warwick is rescued and Blaine tied to a chair. Now The Spider is carried in. He plans (he says) to fire the house and toast Blaine. Remember Paris! Remember your crimes!

At this very moment, the gunmen who had previously menaced Warwick make a sudden reappearance. They are beaten off with about the same difficulty you would experience in licking frosting from a pan. These gunmen (we now learn) are minions of still another supercriminal—name not disclosed—who wanted to get the loot he believed The Spider sought in Blaine's mansion.

That explanation is worse than none at all. The plain fact is that the gunmen were in the pay of Johnston McCulley and were sent to fatten out a story that has almost no content and little suspense. After the gunmen serve their purpose—which is to provide menace and excitement in the first part of the story—they then become liabilities and must be explained away. McCulley tries. If you are half asleep, you might accept what he says. Otherwise, you are inclined to tear the story in half and stamp about on the fragments.

To continue.

Preparations to fire the mansion are complete. Matters have come to a point of high tension. Is The Spider, after all, going to murder? Is Warwick, after all, to lose face with the reader?

Blaine, gone bone white with terror, begs to write a note.

His writing portfolio is brought to him. None of these seasoned supercriminals examine the portfolio, of course, since to do so might introduce that single beam of reason which would dispel the lunacy of these proceedings.

But you have suspected the truth. The portfolio contains a gas bomb. Blaine explodes this, inhales, dies.

The Spider is gratified. Blaine is dead of his own nostril. Revenge is sweet and The Spider was required to do nothing to lower himself in the readers' esteem.

Not that he had planned to do anything. It was all window-dressing, all bluff. He was merely trying to terrify Blaine, The Spider explains. He wasn't going to hurt the man, not really.

The vengeance trail is over. The Spider has decided to retire and pay off the troops.

"I am The Spider no longer, you know—I'm just a crippled old man who wants to see his niece happy. I've a fortune...and I am going to use it in doing good. Perhaps that will be atonement in part for the life of crime I have led."[11]

And the series closes in this sentimental gush of moral felicities.

What a good old man The Spider turned out to be, even if he did have a menacing smile.

The Spider was McCulley's major attempt to create a colossus of crime whose achievements could be compared to those of Professor Moriarty. The remarks of Sherlock Holmes concerning that distinguished man provide a blueprint of McCulley's effort:

Holmes: "He is the Napoleon of crime, Watson. He is the organizer of half that is evil and of nearly all that is undetected in this great city. He is a genius, a philosopher, an abstract thinker. He has a brain of the first order. He sits motionless, like a spider in the centre of its web, but that web has a thousand radiations, and he knows well every quiver of each of them. He does little himself. He only plans. But his agents are numerous and splendidly organized."[12]

McCulley's Spider appears to be a positive print of the Moriarty negative, with the more obvious personal characteristics reversed. Thus Moriarty is thin, The Spider fat; Moriarty has a distinctive movement of the head; The Spider's fingers shake and creep. Beyond these planned dissimilarities, the relationship is reasonably clear and the line between the two Napoleons of Crime is direct. The Spider, however, never achieves the heights of a living character; he remains a device which serves to initiate and unify the casual adventures of Mr. Warwick. Although his name is on the marquee, The Spider is no more than a supporting actor in his own series.

This niggling deficiency is not found in later McCulley series. These feature a title villain (or bent hero) standing boldly at the action's front, gnashing his schemes. Nor did the later master criminals who reveled through *Detective Story Magazine* huddle in the background, silently weaving plots. They were all as busy as Robin Hood. Of the entire group, however, A.E. Apple's Rafferty, the master rogue, was the most active and the most adventure prone. The story focuses tightly on him. It is his series and he makes the best of it.

5-

Rafferty was introduced to *Detective Story* about five months after the presumed termination of Mr. Chang and his series. While Rafferty is also a hero-villain, he is carefully sugared to avoid Chang's negative points, for readers had complained of that latter gentleman's bloodthirstiness and the ethnic glow surrounding him. In the Rafferty series, murder is forbidden and all the ethnic negatives are cleverly shoveled off on his right-hand man, Herr Heinie—Germans still being considered a murderous sub-species, for it was less than ten years since the Armistice. To make the stories even more palatable, Rafferty's crimes are of such magnititude that they transcend crime, *per se.* A man who thought so enormously could almost be considered a statesman.

The series begins in late 1927. "Rafferty, Master Rogue" (October 1, 1927) tells how our hero assembled an intrepid band of criminals, tricked a bank into trusting him with $20,000,000, and escaped with it after a reeling chase. In "The Diamond Pirate" (October 22, 1927), the gang descends upon the jewelry district, gases several city blocks, and methodically strips the area of treasure.

These activities have the sniff of Black Star about them, although no dime novel costumes are evident. If, however, you care to overlook the lavish use of gas, that sublime compound which smooths away all tactical difficulties in Mr. Rafferty's adventures, and accept a level of knavery at levels unattainable until our present day, then you will recognize that Rafferty is only, gently, flexing his intellectual muscles. Soon he will do better, Soon he:

—kidnaps twenty young ladies of towering social rank. These fluttering lovelies he holds aboard a rented yacht, entertaining them lavishly until a five-million dollar ransom can be paid. Then his better instincts intrude and he releases them all, foregoing the ransom, because no gentleman will prey upon women. ("Rafferty Steals a Harem," November 26, 1927)
—cleans out a museum of paintings and art treasures, these to furnish his underground hideout ("Rafferty Pursues Art," December 17, 1927)

—robs a Chinese fence, Mr. Ning, of an enormous horde of jewels ("Rafferty Loots Chinatown," May 12, 1928)
—mounts an elaborate attack against an enormous gambling casino, stripping it thoroughly ("Tied to His Enemy," October 20, 1928)

The young man grinning at us from among these crimes is tall, dark and athletic. He is "slender without being slim. He (has) the sinewy build and lithe ease of a long-distance runner." Hair and eyes are intensely black. He dresses with that immaculate correctness which comes so easily to a character in fiction, although his tie pin, a bit of jade carved as a skull and crossbones, is a tad more facetious than is entirely acceptable to the purest taste.

We recognize that he is the handsome young man who is usually cast as the astute amateur criminologist in those trashy detective stories. He is very like you, could you strike off the shackles of respectability: which is to say, intelligent, audacious, irresistible to women, so forceful that men beg for your leadership.

No man becomes a supercriminal at once. As did the Lone Wolf before him, Rafferty subjected himself to an extended technical apprenticeship in crime. In college, he "specialized in chemistry, physics, psychology and other subjects that would aid a top-notch outlaw. He had been reading law in spare time, for the primary purpose of discovering loopholes."[13] During these years, he also practiced burglary and counterfeiting—not for gain but for experience, sharpening his skills. Short-term profits meant nothing to him.

Rafferty: "Where crooks now plan and arrange for weeks or even months to cop off, say, a hundred thousand dollars, theft on a bigger scale would simply require years of build-up. I'll go further than that. I'll say that if a man in his youth conceived the necessary clever idea, and devoted his whole life to realizing it, just as the average man does to reach success in his chosen field, the sky itself would be the limit of plunder that might be obtained."[14]

Even at this stage of his career, his goals towered. Never, he vowed, would he commit a crime which would net less than a quarter of a million dollars. And there must be no death involved; murder was barbaric, an action unworthy of a man of wit.

After graduation from college, he extended his education by positions with a lock company and a manufacturer of bank doors and vaults. He studied in even less obvious ways:

Every spare minute was devoted to storing away information that might be of possible use to a criminal. He studied timetables and railroad and highway maps as though he were a general soon to direct the attack of an army. He flew in airplanes on every available occasion. He never missed a chance to take a boat trip and note the safe channels.

Detective Story Magazine (October 1, 1927). The amazing Rafferty (seated) converted the master criminal to a lone wolf adventurer who struck for billions.

Nor did he neglect to plan against evil days. He made a thorough study of prisons, visiting these methodically and talking with the officials. Then, after these years of preparation, he resigned his position with the safe company, announcing that he planned to become a detective. "He was reversing the career of the celebrated Vidcoq. Where the Frenchman had been a crook and turned detective, Rafferty was starting as a detective and using that as a stepping stone to crime."

His success was immediate. As the respectable owner of a detective agency, Rafferty found renown within a paragraph. As protective cover, he developed a habit of speech rich in those conversational amenities that distinguished Babbitt and his fellows of the Zenith Booster Club. It was as a detective, supervising a transfer of bank funds, that he accomplished his first major crime. Twenty million in cash and negotiable securities melted away and Rafferty formally entered his true career.

For the purpose of these stories, Rafferty has no real faults—unless an inclination to steal things can be classified as a fault. However, his friend and companion—Herr Heinie—has faults enough for two

Herr Heinie appears in the second story of the series, "The Diamond Pirate." Even a master criminal cannot know all things and do all things. For this reason, Rafferty decided to supplement his awesome abilities with those of a major scientific genius. Herr Heinie, his selection, is a stubby, thick-necked, big paunched scientist and ex-anarchist. He is also a full-time glutton. About him strong odors cling, for distributed through his clothing are dried herring, cheese, onions, sausages and bread. He travels stocked, for hunger might smite him at any moment.

These treats he washes down with beer—black beer—black Munchener beer. This he gulps by the keg, improving its kick by adding a glass of rum to each half-gallon mug.

As with Nero Wolfe, beer only emphasizes Herr Heinie's genius. His function is to provide Rafferty with the necessary technical support to crime about the world. More than this, he is essential to the story, which relies on scientific gadgets to make the crimes work and to accomplish wonderful escapes.

In "The Diamond Pirate," (October 22, 1927) Herr Heinie is lured away to Rafferty's underwater hideout and offered two hundred thousand dollars a year to support our hero's little schemes. After an abortive attempt to poison Rafferty, Herr Heinie is converted to the cause. Thereafter he mixes narcotic gases, builds infra-red searchlights and clever trap doors—all those devices required by a successful master criminal.

Herr Heinie enjoys such challenges. His green-blue eyes glitter. He tosses his straggling yellow hair, crams his mouth with eel pie and potato pancakes. This is the way things shall be done. He swallows. First, we must...

These characters are drawn with vivid colors and easily remembered traits. They are literary cartoons, flickering brightly across the page. Casual fictions, weighing 600 to the pound.

They must be presented in this way, blithe and light. For the subject is the adventures of a successful thief, and Rafferty has none of that unctuous charm that oozes from Raffles. The light tone of the prose is sufficient to excuse all crimes—it is only a story; wouldn't it be dazzling if something like this could really happen?

Those who pursue the critic's high calling, seeing into granite and conjuring up relationships from glowing braziers, will note that Rafferty and Herr Heinie gradually evolve to a double lead. This suggests exciting possibilities. Could this be a case of personality disassociation, the totality of Rafferty's negative personality traits splitting away and coalescing as the hard-boiled, blood-thirsty, violent-minded Heinie, awash in food and drink?

Possibly; possibly. Such delightful tricks have been practiced by Poe and Stevenson and are a standard literary technique, providing spiritual insight and symbolic rigor pleasing to those in search of meaning, rather than narrative movement. In the case of Rafferty and Herr Heine, these interpretations must be their own reward. The truth of the matter is somewhat more banal: in popular fiction, two strong characters do not duplicate traits but contrast them. If one is tall, dark and reserved, the other is short, red-headed and outgoing. Or fat, greedy, yellow-haired and German. Such character building is rather mechanical. It has the unanticipated effect of assigning more negative personality qualities to the second, contrasting character. This is because the first character is normally the one with whom the reader identifies and stands large with positive qualities, even when he is a thief on a huge scale. And so it goes. Character building is implicit in the mechanics of composition. At least, Mr. Apple found it so.

The Rafferty series contains at least one contrast clearly intended by Apple and set into place in the first story. No master criminal can feel entirely complete unless he is pursued by a master detective. Moriarty had Holmes, Fu Manchu had Smith, and Rafferty has Bradley.

Bradley is in his late 20s, a thick-set man with blue eyes and a general appearance suggesting that he is amiable and slow. He is not. A nationally-famous detective, he heads an organization of 3400 men, all dedicated to the purpose of tracking down Rafferty. For Bradley has experienced a string of public defeats at Rafferty's hands and thirsts for revenge. High-blood pressure reddens his face. His sandy hair, already graying, is worn long and parted in the middle (in the style of H.L. Mencken) to conceal a scar where a horse kicked him years before.

Long ago, Bradley attended college with Rafferty. They knew each other well. Their relationship, by that inverted emphasis in 1920s crook stories, is rather complex—not the good detective chasing the bad thief, but the good-hearted thief being menaced by the tainted detective. Rafferty is a model of young manhood in spite of his odd choice of profession. Bradley, representing justice and virtue, is shown to be disgracefully opportunistic. He means to trap Rafferty by tricks or bribes or violated confidences. Any ruse is acceptable.

If he catches Rafferty, "it would make him such a celebrated sleuth that his services would be sought by the mighty—and he could name his own price."

Having clearly established that all the main characters are knaves, Apple at length gives Bradley his chance. He captures Rafferty at the end of "Tied to His Enemy" (October 20, 1928). At the climax of this story, Rafferty and friends have looted a gambling casino and are briskly transferring their bags of gold through an underground tunnel. They are interrupted by Bradley and his foppish assistant, Operative No. 44. Bradley shoots Rafferty in the leg; Operative No. 44 blows up the tunnel with a hand grenade, preventing Rafferty's rescue.

Success is wonderfully sweet. Bradley is widely acclaimed. Rafferty is jailed in a solitary, escape-proof cell, watched day and night by scowling warders ("Rafferty, Gentleman Jailbird," November 10, 1928).But Bradley does not sleep well at night. Outside those stone walls, the huge Rafferty organization whispers untouched and Herr Heinie stokes himself on beer and rum, plotting and cursing. On the day of the trial, rescue comes. Rafferty is conducted to a sealed courtroom, packed with men and guns. No gas masks, however. Herr Heine simply gasses everyone in the room by pouring gas into the ventilation system, and off he goes, the sleeping Rafferty slung over his shoulder. Gas is a splendid solution to all problems.

In no way does this experience diminish Rafferty's enthusiasm for crime. Through 1929, he strikes for stakes even larger than before. In these later stories, the Rafferty organization (which includes thousands of talented criminals) recedes gently into the background. The adventures focus on Rafferty and Herr Heine, doing the best they can, while Bradley snuffles omniously in the rear.

First, an international blackmail ring is robbed to ruin ("Rafferty and the Hush Money King," December 22, 1928). Then, in "Rafferty Invents a New Crime" (January 19, 1929), our smiling genius immobilizes an entire city, taking over police stations, newspapers, airport, train station, telegraph offices. All these are gassed thoroughly and manned with armies of Rafferty men. This being done, the city is competently stripped of valuables. Half a billion dollars in loot vanishes. Law and order sprawls in confusion. And Rafferty, pulled from a tight situation by Herr Heinie's technical genius, vanishes back to his submarine.

Submarine? Yes, he acquired that vessel (stealing it from an unnamed government) before the opening of "The Diamond Pirate." He uses the submarine for a temporary headquarters, keeping it right to hand down at the dock, concealed by a scow or tipsy tub boat, or floating just inside a large warehouse whose doors open to the water. While pursuers bay, while victims squeal, Rafferty and Herr Heinie glide into the ocean and so away, slipping secretly to that anchorage in the underground cavern where Rafferty Headquarters Central is situated. In this unorthodox place are stored the billions in art treasures, antiques, jewels, rugs, tapestries stolen during the series. You would think an underground cave an uncommonly damp place to store art treasures, but no mould, moisture, or mildew stains the pretties. Likely enough, Herr Heinie has constructed a wonderful new ventilation system...

After concocting his new crime (scientific pillage of a city was invented by Black Star years before, although no one seems to have remembered that), Rafferty settles down to lesser activities. After you have stolen half a billion dollars, everything is of lesser scale. His ideas change. No longer is society the primary target of his raids. Instead, he turns his abilities upon individual criminals, it being easier to identify with a criminal who robs other criminals than one who might carry off the $41 in your savings account.

"Rafferty and the Count of Five" (February 16, 1929) describes how he brings a rum-running syndicate to justice, their wealth sticking to his own pocket. In "Rafferty's Phantom Plunder" (August 31, 1929) he destroys the operation of a fake spirit-medium; so far along the ways to respectability has he gone, that he restores much of the wealth carried off to "the widows and similar dupes who could not afford to lose."

Rafferty: "We've stolen phantom plunder—the hoards of dead men, bequeathed to heirs too dumb or ignorant to take care of it. I'm not keeping the swag...in cases where the loss will mean suffering. As for the still-rich victims—they can whistle for their jack. The (medium's) clique preyed on gullible, griefstricken relatives. That's primarily why I wanted to smash the ring. Money was secondary. We already have more millions than we can use."[16]

This mild attack of social consciousness continues in "Rafferty and the Chinese Eight" (September 14, 1929). For reasons that make little sense to either Herr Heinie or the reader, Rafferty proposes to rob the mansion of a wealthy collector. He marches off to do this unaided by his organization, sleeping gas, or much of anything but the loving assistance of Mr. Apple. As Rafferty explains:

"I haven't any plans. In fact, I haven't the slightest idea, what we are going to do to-night. Whether we succeed or fail will depend on whether we can think faster than our enemies—outguess them.

"We need a change now and again. Military tactics become boresome to me. Too cut-and-dried, like having bacon and eggs every morning for breakfast, or being a tradesman. An expedition such as to-night's is an adventure. It stirs us from stagnation—acts as a splendid tonic to our imagination."[17]

His imagination is severely strained. For the mansion is owned by a crooked lunatic, further assisted by eight lethal Chinese. The mansion, itself, is a crazy-quilt of trapdoors, descending nooses, secret passages, red-hot banisters, and collapsing stairs. It revives devices that had lain fallow since the days of Nick Carter. Within a few chapters, Rafferty lies crumpled in the escape-proof basement, and Herr Heinie hangs by his neck in the attic, his fat face blackening.

Yet they escape thanks to a razor blade in Heinie's belt, strips of piano wire in his fake inner soles, and a neat dagger strapped to Rafferty's right calf. (These devices would later appear in such later Street & Smith magazines as *Doc Savage* and *The Avenger,* some years after 1929.) Not only do they escape, but they hi-jack the moving van load of art treasures stolen by the Chinese after they had killed the master of the mansion. Then off to the submarine and away.

"Rafferty Joins the Police" (November 1, 1929) to lecture on how to capture himself. To stimulate the police, and increase the pleasure of the game, he offers $150,000 reward for his own capture. The police come close, and Bradley comes closer, but Rafferty slides cheerfully away.

He returns in the November 1, 1930 issue, "Rafferty Steals 200 Dicks," to accomplish another terrific robbery. He contrives to steal $20,000,000 in gold, the train carrying it, and all the detectives on the train. By this time, his exploits have attracted national attention and Mr. Chang (now uncaged and running amok once more) plans to rob him.

They meet twice. In "Mr. Chang vs Rafferty" (January 31, 1931), Mr. Chang stows himself inside a barrel once containing Herr Heinie's prized black beer. Carried aboard the submarine, he is conveyed to Rafferty's underground headquarters—only to discover that Rafferty has deliberately baited and trapped him. Mr. Chang does not remain trapped. After capturing Herr Heinie and tieing him to some beer barrels, Mr. Chang goes looting through this underground treasure box. He faces Rafferty but fails to kill him, then darts off, escaping to the submarine and is trapped there. Before Herr Heinie can catch him—with the intention of firing him from a torpedo tube 600 feet down—Chang escapes from the submarine and discovers himself miles and miles at sea, obviously about to drown.

But he doesn't. He returns, full of zeal, in "Mr. Chang Cages Rafferty" (February 28, 1931). Now it is Rafferty's turn to be trapped, and so he is. But he escapes and leaves Mr. Chang presumed dead, shot in the head. But he isn't. The honors are approximately equal, and on this rousing draw, the Rafferty series closes. Mr. Chang, as elsewhere noted, continues his career in one more story.

Unless you are determined to probe for meaning, the Rafferty series need not detain you long. The characters are high comic book, the stories amiable fluff. Forty to fifty pages long, they dart gaily forward, brightly innocent tales of high crime. The wages of theft are lavish, indeed. The series is as engagingly amoral as a cat, in that respect. Intelligent crime, aided by science and wonderful gasses, is incredibly profitable, and you have such a good time while getting rich.

These sunny pastures are carefully shorn of thorns. The more usual concerns of daily life are neatly tucked away. No mildew clings in Rafferty's cave, and no annoying detective sets himself to tracking the spare submarine parts which must be purchased. No personnel problems crop up in all that giant organization, which grows dimmer and dimmer as the stories continue. No man suffers from toothache or hangover or family problems. Few human emotions are expressed for few are required.

At the center of Rafferty's world lies a cold stillness. He nests in the heart of his millions, charming, genial, isolated from mankind. His one close friend is Herr Heine. No other comes close. He dare not let them close, for he is a wanted man, with several hundred thousand dollars in rewards posted against him. He writes no books and thinks no poetry. No woman trembles silently in his heart. Not even Miss Sabonn found lodging there: she was the young woman who persuaded him to return the kidnapped girls in "Rafferty Steals a Harem" and who attended his trial in "Gentleman Jailbird." In her presence, he feels uncertain and abashed; momentarily, the possibilities of the past tease him. But he is a realist: now is now. What might have been is a dream. And, anyhow, tomorrow we steal Alaska.

You would think that a successful master criminal would make a more successful accommodation with joy.

However you look at him, the master criminal is clearly a superior fellow. His mind blazes and his schemes stand like sequoias above the sapling plots of his competitors. It is this expansiveness of purpose which sets him apart. He measures by the mile, not the inch. And his joy is not the rattle of gold into his vaults, but the solemn pleasure of seeing a plan run out in all its intricate detail, his people moving in their pre-planned routines, events sequencing along the plan his mind made, his enemies disheveled, and, at the end, the tangible prize of wealth, solid evidence of his power to shape reality with the soft tool of thought.

If, during the 1920s, the master criminal was a gamester, criming for self expression, during the 1930s he performed in other ways for other purposes. Throughout the 1930s magazines, the master criminal was vulgarized and coarsened. Black Star's modest hood and cloak were altered to costumes of scarlet and garish green. The mild gas gun transformed to terror weapons that disintegrated, spouted flame and jetted lightning bolts. Those well-mannered criminals who supported Rafferty and The Spider hardened to machine-gun clutching thugs, grinning in soiled pink shirts and orange ties.

Soon the master criminal, himself, was to grow murderous, eager for indiscriminate slaughters in the hateful idiom of our present urban terrorists. IIis channels of scxuality, long clogged by 1920s propriety, flamed to a horrid form of public sadism.

Other ways for other purposes. Time and readers' taste altered the bland 1920s fiction to stuff that burned the tongue. Perhaps every fictional form contains the seeds of its own vulgarization. Although, admittedly, the master criminal grew shallow and vicious more rapidly than even Mr. Chang might have predicted.

Although the master criminal was a popular fellow, he was a relatively rare figure in the magazines. Through the 'Teens and 'Twenties, far more column space was spent on the slippery feats of confidence men and criminal adventurers, safe crackers, thieves, strong-arm thugs, blackmailers, card cheats and pick pockets. They came swarming out of the dime novels like hornets from a broken nest. At first they conducted business in the general magazines—*Blue Book* and *Popular, Short Stories* and *People's*. Readers relished criminal adventure, particularly when it was circumscribed by those delicate conventions of fiction dictating that criminals prey on the greedy, the dishonest, and the rich. And only those.

Detective Story Magazine promptly filled with crook stories, series crook stories, exploiting these into the early 1930s. *Black Mask* followed rather reluctantly, as did *Detective Tales*, but *Flynn's* and *Clues*, in the mid-1920s, leaped joyously upon the fad and fattened their columns with criminals of both sexes and all degrees of competence. The characters of this wicked brotherhood are beyond counting. Many remain interesting today. A few of them had such vitality they left a small, permanent mark on crime fiction and peer out impishly from the pages of today's mystery magazines, their names forgotten, their contributions long assimilated by the literature.

Let us begin with the nobility of crime. Here stands a crowd of swindlers and confidence men waiting for us. They have many remarkable stories to tell.

Flynn's (December 4, 1926). The hardboiled gang leader, operating from a flossy gambling hell, became a standard figure in late 1920s mystery-adventure fiction.

III—THE WICKED BROTHERHOOD

1-

   The classic picture of the journeyman swindler can be found in O. Henry's *The Gentle Grafter* (1908). Through seven stories, smooth as jade, Jeff Peters and his associate, Andy Tucker, travel across 1900 America, converting chicanery to cash.[1]

Jeff Peters, the Gentle Grafter, is an amusing rogue...whose lineage goes back in the tradition of the picaresque fiction to Lazarillo de Tormes and to Robin Hood.... Jeff carries the narrative forward, chiefly in dialogue form. (He uses) free-wheeling colloquial speech, full of outrageous puns and malapropisms, usually couched in a pseudo-erudite style.[2]

   The small-time grifter, living precariously on other men's dreams, was familiar American folklore—although not limited to this continent; the type is universal. Mark Twain had stuck a pin through the *genus* Peters in *Huckleberry Finn* and the dime novels—particularly the western dime novels—early captured the figure, converting it to a cliche and a figure of fun. Less accessible was Herman Melville's *The Confidence Man* (1857), the story scene a Mississippi riverboat, the action a series of dialogues between the confidence man, in various guises, and his potential victims. When, some fifty years later, the general fiction pulp magazines were established, the confidence man promptly appeared in their pages. The stories did not much resemble those of Melville.

   One of the earliest series noted, "Mr. Simpson's Transgressions," appeared as a six-story sequence in *People's Magazine* (June through November 1907). Written by Campbell MacCulloch, the adventures prance along as brightly as little ponies.

   Mr. Simpson is a fat old trickster who slumps slangily, drinking sherry, in his Riverside Drive apartment. Amid bursts of humorous patois, he plans ever more startling ways of separating the wicked from their gold backs:

Simpson:...to a righteous man like myself,. there's somethin' powerful allurin' in takin' change away from them sharks that steals it from suckers... Th' smooth party that puts up these here bucket-shop jobs, he sure does hate to git stung. Why, son, th' silence that comes off when one o' them guys gets trimmed is just th' same as when a waiter falls down iron stairs with a tray o' dishes. Yeh kin hear him two miles.[3]

In the story, "Bankers and Brokers," *People's Magazine* (October 1907), Mr. Simpson is planning a surprise for an old friend. Once, long ago, that friend glided into the night with $1,300 belonging to Mr. Simpson. The friend, now a respectable broker, is ripe for punishment.

Since Mr. Simpson is a thinker, moving no more than is urgently required, the active part of the sting is conducted by Mr. Larry Kingsley. He is Simpson's right-hand man, trainee, and pal. Kingsley is younger and speaks a grandiose tongue that seems rooted in English:

Kingsley: Why this sudden advocacy of the subjunctive stunt? What phenomenon has broken in upon your objective mind and jerked you up into such a sudden enthusiasm as this?[4]

In spite of his vocabulary, Kingsley is as a babe in guile when compared with Mr. Simpson.

The plan involves tapping the broker's telephone, feeding spurious information to his ticker tape, and presenting him with an innocent rich lamb (Mr. Kingsley in disguise) to gull. The broker gets nipped for $25,000 and Mr. Simpson, sipping a sherry, feels ten years younger.

Already in 1907, a year before *The Gentle Grafter*, the classical ingredients had been mixed for the confidence man story. We have the sly veteran, his young protege, a great deal of "free-wheeling colloquial speech," and a series of dishonest wretches ripely ready to be trimmed. The formula lasted brilliantly.

Of all the confidence men to grace the pulps, the longest lived was Mr. Amos Clackworthy (a name of subtle charm), who appeared in *Detective Story Magazine* from 1920 to 1930. His exploits were published in at least two Chelsea House books, *Mr. Clackworthy* (1926) and *Mr. Clackworthy, Con Man* (1928). At least a dozen stories were later reprinted in Street & Smith's *Best Detective Magazine* from 1933 through 1937.

Mr. Clackworthy elated his fans with theatrical descents upon the world's wicked. If they were evil-hearted, if they oppressed their fellow man, and, particularly, if they had quantities of money, they drew Mr. Clackworthy's attention. If they were evil and relatively poor, he didn't bother them, it is true. But understand—it was business first, sentiment later.

In appearance elegant, solid, substantial, Clackworthy has the imagination of a theatrical producer. His external person brings nods of approval from sedate mid-western bankers. The internal man thinks in melodrama and fantastic flashes. And he stings mercilessly.

As a concession to human needs, he enjoys highballs and fine cigars. Frequently he may be found idling in the Lakeshore Apartments of Chicago, surveying Lake Michigan with qualified approval.

"A sucker is a sucker," says Mr. Clackworthy, "for one reason and one reason only— because he's trying to get something for nothing. We've demonstrated it many times..."

"We" includes Clackworthy's worthy friend, aide and general assistant, James Early, known to the police as The Early Bird because of his fondness for being abroad at 2:00 a.m. Mr. Early is a thin, sharp-faced pessimist, given to predictions of disaster. Not that he really believes in disaster, as far as the commendable Mr. Clackworthy is concerned. Still, it seems appropriate to predict disaster and hope that the heavens will take pity and rain gold.

These stories were written by Christopher B. Booth who contributed a weighty mass of novels, novelettes, serials and short stories to *Detective Story* and other Street & Smith magazines. Born in Centralia, Missouri, around 1890, Booth sold his first piece to *The Popular Magazine* when he was fifteen years old. Five or six other pieces were quickly sold, after which "he lost the touch and received nothing but rejections for the next fourteen years." After graduation from the William Jewel College, he worked on a series of newspapers, including the St. Louis *Globe Democrat* and the Chicago *Daily News*. While on the *News,* he sold his first story to *Detective Story,* and found that his fiction touch had revived itself.[5]

The Mr. Amos Clackworthy who appeared in these initial stories was not as slickly refined as he later became, nor as careful about his targets. And Mr. Early talks a variation of yegg argot that makes your toes curl.

Mr. Early: "Yeh! She's a dinger. Who yuh goin' thuh put the stinger on?"

His later speech is somewhat more sophisticated. Somewhat. The swindles are gloriously elaborate. Thus:

On a farm in southern Michigan live a farmer and wife. They hold shares in a valuable copper mine that, any day, is likely to explode with value. Unwilling to sell, they are talked into it only after some trouble and at a cost higher than foreseen. Now, says Clackworthy, I have only $30,000 immediately available, but I can get the additional $20,000 you want tomorrow morning when the bank opens. This sounds a pretty good offer in cold blood, and much better when you have been built up to it so smoothly and agreeably that your narrow little eyes glint and your hard mouth softens and, possibly, your bitter little soul feels a momentary brush of warmth. Later, after money and stock have vanished, you feel a different set of emotions.

The story is titled "The Feminine Touch" and was published in *Detective Story Magazine,* February 3-10-17, 1920—this odd date because labor problems loused up the printing schedule and this issue was symbolic of three in sequence. The magazine is 160 pages only, however, not 480.

As another example of Clackworthy's art:

A Chicago detective stops by your hardware store and shows a poster for a wanted bank robber. He took a bank for $163,000 that was never recovered. The detective suspects that the funds are concealed close by. A few days later, the bank robber, himself, stops in the store and buys two shovels. You trail him, hear him exclaim in a fury that some *#&$%#(@* has built a barn over where he buried the money. The barn is on property that a young man just bought from you for $18,000 down (he made his pile in Chicago; shady business likely); which makes it funny—the property used to belong to the young man, until you slicked him out of it for $500. Then he wanted to buy it back and, oh, weren't you able to squeeze him.

But that's business.

He's discouraged now. You talk with him again. He wants to go back to Chicago. Yes, he'll sell you the land (with the $163,000 buried under the barn), except that he'll be damned if you'll make another profit off him. He wants $60,000. You pay.

There is a money box under the barn. It contains eleven pounds of nuts and bolts and a Christmas card. All this is related in the story, "Mr. Clackworthy's Christmas Present" (December 25, 1926).

At times, the con makes money for them. Other times are tough. And quite unexpected matters interrupt the smooth flow of rhetoric and cash. In "The Feminine Touch," the young lady on whom the operation depends turns out to be the daughter of a man Clackworthy swindled a few years earlier. She gets $50,000 from them and leaves The Early Bird with a sore head where she hit him with a flat iron.

The three-part serial, "Thubway Tham and Mr. Clackworthy," published February 18 through March 4, 1922, tells of the complexities developing when Tham snares Clackworthy's wallet. Mr. C. determines to make Tham pay for this professional slur by enmeshing him in a confidence web. Elaborate arrangements rear up, difficulties and police follow and events race along. A piece of this serial was later published as a short story, same title, in the December 1934 *Best Detective Magazine.*

After 1923, Clackworthy's adventures appeared less frequently, a natural consequence of writer strain. Each story required Booth to devise a new deception, complicate it to the required length and provide a neat little twist at the end, a double sting, in which Clackworthy either won after he had lost, or lost after he had won. For success did not always come.

During the late 1920s, Clackworthy faded gently from sight, apparently retiring to his highballs and cigars. A late story, "Mr. Clackworthy's Return" (June 14, 1930), shows him able as ever. He has been wiped out in the Depression, so it is out of retirement and back to work—work being the skinning of that iron-souled virago, the widow Prindivale.

Widows are not usually fair game, the sterotype being an elderly lady of considerable mental fluffiness. Reader morality requires that the con man's victim be as repellent as possible, so that the blame for the crime may be shifted from the criminal to the victim. Thus the widow of this story is not fluffy but of steel-ribbed acquisitiveness. Her greed leads her into error: she sells The Early Bird a farm that contains more rocks than dirt.

Worse, she fingers through the baggage of that distinguished scientist from Chicago, a fellow named Clackworthy...

Her prying reveals a secret: The scientist wants that rocky farm because it scintillates with radium, pure ore, dig it with a shovel. She can hardly restrain herself. She must buy it back. At any price...

She pays just $35,000. Mr. Early and Mr. Clackworthy leave the joys of the country to those deserving them and melt away into the city where, we assume, they practiced through the years, unrecorded in fiction but constantly busy. As you know, a con man's clientage is born at the rate of one each minute.

Around 1928, during the period in which Mr. Clackworthy lounged beside Lake Michigan, Stewart Robertson introduced that chocolate-candy con man, Mr. Charles "One Eye" Brannigan to readers of the *Popular Magazine.* "One Eye" because Mr. Brannigan sported a monocle and dressed as richly as a pitchman for male cosmetics, magnificently stylish. He was a tall, aristocratically thin man with greying temples "and sensitive hands." His clothing and deportment were superb.

Alas, his judgment falters, and failure gnaws him. "Mr. Brannigan Stubs His Toe" (May 5, 1928) tells how he comes to Hollywood, eager to sell a reclusive star an imitation diamond necklace for $25,000. By error he sells the necklace to her double who then vanishes, managing not to pay.

This is Brannigan's fate—to be victimized by circumstance. In "Mr. Brannigan Sees Red" (August 1931), he works a swindle in rubies on a western oil man living in Chicago. Too late he discovers that the oil man was once a con man, himself, and recognized the grift.

Mr. Brannigan was a close contemporary, in time and style, of Mr. Edward Farthindale, known as Elegant Edward. This gentleman practiced the sale of disenchanted stock to enchanted people. His recorded activities were collected in *Elegant Edward* (1928), a small red book of short stories, lacy with gold ornamentation and written by Edgar Wallace. Seven stories are included in the book. These had previously been published in the English weekly newspaper, *The Sunday Post,* July 20 through August 31, 1924. The first five stories deal with Elegant Edward Farthindale; the last two, with different characters. In putting the book together, the first story of the series is printed as the fourth; the fifth appears as the second. You hardly notice.[6]

Bibliographic deviations to the side, Elegant Edward is a vision of splendor. He wears a gold monocle, waxed mustache, morning coat, striped trousers and silk hat. "He was a man of middle height, slightly thin. His features, unevenly disposed, had a somewhat worn appearance."

There is a reason why he looks worn. His professional activities are lashed by the jests of Scotland Yard men. They are not sympathetic to his efforts and are amazingly free with information about the departure time for the next train. You wonder why they bothered. Edward is not only grandly dressed, but grandly inept. His schemes, fragile as petals, dissolve in his indiscretions. He is the most put-upon of criminals.

In "Papinico for the Scot," his pockets are looted by Aberdeen Annie, a charming, dear-looking girl. When he rushes boiling off to foil her, in "The Amateur Detective," he foils only himself and ends, again, with pockets rifled. "The Rum Runner" sees him defrauded by his partner in crime. And in "Mr. Macmillan Shares His Possessions," he collects only the measles from an infected automobile. By "A Fortune in Tin," Edward is so demoralized, he sees police instead of lovers and accidentally gives away a batch of worthless shares which become suddenly valuable.

He is a man of deep misfortune. Mr. Brannigan follows the same unlucky path, although Edward has seniority in failure.

By 1928, the con man theme had been used in magazines until it turned itself inside out. Melville's rapacious horror, undulating his character to match each victim's private reality, has himself become a victim. That predatory angel, the confidence man, that being lethal to economic security, had matured to a figure of fun. Time shriveled him to a popinjay in striped pants.

And what of Simpson, Peters, Mr. Clackworthy watching from the past? Could they explain what had happened to their craft during the late 1920s?

Very likely. Minds like theirs could sense so simple a thing as the movement of popular themes through popular magazines, one successful character producing waves of others, variations creating further variations, until the massy wave of 1908 laps weakly on 1930s beaches.

The dwindling of the wave means little. There will be other waves, Larger ones, Wait awhile.

2-

While waiting, consider thieves.

Their adventures stained the magazines long ago, before America marched to war and sauerkraut fell into disrepute. We have already met many of them—gentlemen burglars following the example of Raffles; oriental menaces who rob and worse; disguise artists stealing in the mode of Colonel Clay and Romney Pringle; master criminals, Black Star and Rafferty, directing the sack of cities.

Even in fiction, however, few thieves were as successful as these. Most occupied smaller ponds. The larger number of fictional criminals were only marginally successful and they radiated no glory. Among them you found yeggs, strong-arm men and small-time street criminals. Most appeared only in single stories in *Popular, Top Notch, Short Stories* and that bastion of little crime, *Detective Story Magazine*. The dignity of a series eluded the likes of these, for it is hard to establish a popular series about a thief. His crimes remind the reader of his own vulnerability.

Yet series were written, and readers, unaware of their danger, followed them eagerly.

Among these stories were the celebrated crimes of Mr. Barton Edgeworth. Barton Edgeworth is an all-around criminal whose adventures, once exciting, have tarnished in time until they seem innocent, even simple-minded. He first appeared in the *Detective Story Magazine*, 1917, under the series title, "The Exploits of Barton Edgeworth," nine stories in all. The series was written by Frederick W. Davis, using the pseudonym of Scott Campbell.

Edgeworth is a variant of the Red Raven, lacking the gang and most of the personal polish. At heart, he is an angry man. His ferocity rages to break free:

The savage, brutal instincts in the man could be as fierce as in the mastiff.
(His face was) grim and sinister in the dim light.

He was standing grim and motionless on the rear platform.... Only an omnious gleam and glitter in his dark eyes evidenced his thoughts and feelings.

These descriptions owe a great deal to the dime novel habit of increasing the voltage of every emotion, so that each hiccup becomes a grimace of rage.

For all his described fierceness, Edgeworth is as sentimental as a six-dollar valentine.

Edgeworth: "I'm bad enough, but I draw the line when it comes to harming a woman. I've never done that...nor robbed a man whose need was greater than my own."

The girl he loved (you see) died in his arms. Whenever he is reminded of her—about once a story—he goes all gentle and loses that keen thrust for advantage.

In person, Edgeworth is dark-dark, wavy hair, dark skin, dark eyes, even white teeth. He is, the author tells us, crafty, foresighted and versatile, in addition to being ferocious.

His Irish assistant, Connie Curran, talks to Edgeworth in about the way Chick Carter used to talk to Nick. Curran is a round-faced, florid young man who shares all troubles and some profits.

When two crooks join to make a series, you may be sure that a pursuing police officer is not far behind. His name, in this case, is Clyde Kelsey, a strange policeman, a suavely polite fashion-plate who looks as much like a cop as the floor walker at Saks. Under that glossy exterior, he is all resolution and toughness. He presses Edgeworth and Connie hard; they spend much of the series in flight.

Edgeworth: "I've not been a crook for love of crime, but because it looked like the easiest way to get what I needed."

If the ethics sound a little lumpy, they are no more so than the justifications usual to the crook story. All tell us about the same thing: This criminal isn't such a bad guy; he only steals because he doesn't like to work.

The accompanying assumption, which has passed right down the generations as a solid popular belief, is that it is all right to steal if you steal from a criminal.

Which happens in "Double and Quits" (July 20, 1917). Edgeworth goes after the reward posted for certain stolen heirlooms. Heavily disguised, he offers his services to the robbery victim and Kelsey.

It is not really altruism. Edgeworth has a grudge against the thief. He plays both ends against the middle, leads the police to the robber's hideout and, as the cops smash in the door, he grabs all the money in sight and melts into the night.

Edgeworth: "Take it from me, Connie, the wages of sin is not always what the parson predicts or the doctor orders."

"Unexpected Loot" (September 4, 1917) tells how Edgeworth and Connie accidentally discover an heiress locked away in a hidden room. They free her, foil the plans of a sour old crab and evade Kelsey by a hair.

They are fortunate. After eight stories, they steal pearls so valuable that they can retire. Or they would if Edgeworth did not feel it sporting to give Kelsey one more chance to capture him.

This occurs in "Silhouette or Shadow" (October 23, 1917).

Enter Wanda Kossuth, a lovely Polish national, who is being victimized by her naughty cousin, Boris. Edgeworth is able to prevent her abduction, but the secret papers are still concealed in the hotel suite, where Kelsey squints about, investigating. And the papers must be secured *now!*

Edgeworth grips Connie's hand. In a replay of a similar scene from the last of the Ravenswood series, Edgeworth tells his good friend that the game is over, forever they must part.

Then, densely disguised, he collects the papers from the suite under Kelsey's very nose, locks that unfortunate detective in the bathroom and escapes to happiness and life with Wanda in Paris under his real name, which is not Barton Edgeworth.

The guns in Europe had not yet quenched the sentimental strain endemic to crook fiction of the period. The lachrymose effusions of the 1880s still dripped. A criminal's actions could still be justified by love lost or love gained. That view of human motivation, although thoroughly shopworn, still served casual fictions in equally casual monthly magazines. The explanation was convenient; its triviality in no way deterred the quick, bright ripple of the story.

Among these stylistic relics of the past elbowed more modern fictional styles. Many of these were presented in a different tone, being jaunty and unrepentant, often touched with humor, their sheen undimmed by sentimentality or overmuch realism. And occasionally they offered a character of such vigor that he appeared in chains of stories over a period of years.

One of these long-lived characters was a lanky, long, loose-jointed old scoundrel who had been:

a peterman, a penny weighter, scratch man, steerer, pratt digger, gorilla, slough worker, notch cutter and booze runner.

"Hair well streaked with gray," says the police report. "Large and prominent nose, with coarse pores, gray eyes, several gold teeth. Six feet high."

The report will add that he is a graduate of various institutions, including "Sleepy Holler, the Copper John, Charlie Adams, the Pork Dump at Clinton, and some more."

These comprise the credentials of Big-Nose Charlie, an engaging fellow whose career extended from 1917 to 1934 in the *S&S Detective Story Magazine* and *Best Detective Magazine*—the latter reprinting material from the former. The series was written by Charles W. Tyler, a newspaper man whose work filled *Railroad Stories* and *Detective Story Magazine* during the 'Teens and 'Twenties. Not all the Big-Nose Charlie stories have been tabulated, but it's estimated that between 50 and 75 were published. More maybe. Charlie was an engaging fellow and readers gobbled his adventures.

He is formerly of Kerry Village, Boston. You might tell it in his speech—a peculiar patois that is part transcription from the American, part 1917 thug talk, both parts well stewed in a vaudeville-based Boston accent. Thus:

"Yuh look forward t'keep fr'm lammin' int' trouble, but yuh flicker yuh glim behint so's trouble won't run yuh down."

At times his manner can be formal, or even courtly:

"If yuh will puddin' meh f'r bein' so bold."

At other times he is vaporously vague:

Detective: "Wad you doin' in Florida?"
Charlie: "Oh, I wuz j'st lookin' around." Big-Nose Charlie indicated the world at large with an airy, little movement of his hand. He then cocked an eye at a cloud that hung low on the eastern sky. "Ut looks like rain," he suggested amicably.[7]

The police look upon him coolly. "Watch out for that dumb-looking old goat who's dressed up like a birthday cake," they warn. They always warn too late. That dumb-looking old goat strikes fast, with a grand mixture of sly indirection and direct assault.

His crimes are simple as a line between two points. Only his amazing gyrations before and after the event are dazzling. If his hauls are relatively small—he thinks no higher then $2,000-3,000—still his gall is immense.

To demonstrate: "Big-Nose Charlie At the Policeman's Ball" (April 16, 1921: *Detective Story Magazine*). An evil jeweler has substituted glass for the diamond in Charlie's ring. Much annoyed, Charles marches back to the shop. There he whacks the jeweler firmly, robs him, exits. After that, while the police whiz about on his trail, he attends the policeman's ball and dances with the Commissioner's wife. When the first hue and cry dies down, he steps grandly off into the night.

Very direct action. It is characteristic.

In the story "Big-Nose Charlie's Florida Front" (March 24, 1928), he arrives in Palm Springs to find himself regarded without sympathy by Detective J.B. Firebolt. To occupy Firebolt's mind, Charlie hires a beach bum to wear his clothing. He, himself, slips off to a hotel where a real estate swindler is displaying a roll of $2,000.

This roll, Charlie secures in the simplest possible way. He requests a private interview, yanks the swindler's hat over his eyes, grabs his wallet and leaves. Firebolt never sees him going.

Like most old-line crooks, Charlie has police officers glowering after him in every city. Up in Boston, Inspectors Borsey and Morrison give thanks that the "old shyster" is not around. In Los Angeles, Detectives South and Cornell deplore his presence.

It is Inspector Morrison, however, who runs across Charlie in El Paso. Out hero stands grandly in a Mexican bar, where he has met Mr. Arbielhide of Boston. Mr. A. Has a pocket fat with cash. He has been using the mails to defraud.

As usual, Charlie is direct. He lures Mr. A. to a taxi, whops him over the head, pulls the hat down over his eyes and departs. Mr. A's howls, after waking, attract Morrison, who is in town to pick up a prisoner and his host, an El Paso detective.

All together, they cross the river into Mexico to fetch Charlie back. Which is illegal, sure enough. But Charlie has greased the palms of everybody at the jail and everybody lounging around outside it. The U.S. police get arrested. Charlie, smiling gently, glides out the back door, a respected friend of Mexico. ("Big-Nose Charlie's Ha-Ha," January 10, 1931.)

From Mexico he moves to Los Angeles ("Big-Nose Charlie, Racketeer," August 15, 1931). Once there, he talks himself into the presence of an L.A. gangster and robs him in his own car of $7,000. This time he escapes through the studied indifference of some police officers. They are not overly fond of politically-connected gangsters.

Charlie's technique never loses its direct freshness. Hundreds of warrants must have waited for him. In February 13, 1932 (still *Detective Story Magazine*) he returns to Boston. "Big-Nose Charlie's Safe" tells how he lured away a diamond merchant and tied him up in a hotel room. (All the while, Inspector Morrison haunts Charlie's every move.) Charlie then arranges for the jeweler's safe to be moved out of his office. While this is being done, Charlie feeds peanuts to a squirrel. When the safe is delivered to its new address, he cleans it out and vanishes. The whole thing occupies one restful afternoon.

Well, yes, you're right. But these are comic stories. Not heavy on grim reality, but charming and insubstantial. The stories bubble and froth with light-headed foolery, like very light wine, highly carbonated.

That comic touch explains how Charlie can commit his modest crimes through the years and still please readers. His victims are all unpleasant—mainly crooks, themselves. You don't mind seeing a crook get stung do you? You don't mind seeing the police bump into things and fall down? Of course not.

That's the way it was in *Detective Story Magazine*—crook diddles crook and the police bobble around, and so the years slip by. There have been worse formulas.

The Boston Betty series tries for a similar lightness. But it lacks the self-parody of the Big-nose Charlie saga and manages to project only a rude pertness.

Betty appeared in *Detective Story Magazine* in early 1918. The series was written by Anna Alice Chapin, a busy contributor to the magazine. She specialized in sentimental crook stories in which the hero was a heroine and very lovely. Perhaps she dabbled in crime, but only because she was annoyed. Or seemed to be. It is hard to tell precisely what motivates a Chapin heroine, whose sense lessens in direct proportion to the length of the story.

No matter how dim-witted she is, things come right at the end. The wicked will drop dead on cue, and the lovers forsake crime, or the tissue-paper copy of it described by Madame Chapin, and reform in a shower of cupids and girlish tears.

Such an agreeable formula informed much of Chapin's work. You are faintly astonished to find that her Boston Betty series departs considerably from these well-trod fields. Remarkable as it is, Miss Elizabeth Buxter, Aggie Pelton, Mary Beale (all facets of the Boston Betty diamond) are carefully unsentimental and fettered by no love interest.

"She was a dark, calm-faced young woman, with a fine air of self-possession, but a most winning smile on occasion." Her mouth is rather large. Her hair hangs dark and heavy. Her manner is mild and polite. She has been a pick-pocket, shop-lifter, mail robber, forger and thief, plain and fancy.

Once she fell into the hands of the New York City police. From this arrest—the only time it happened to her—the Law gained a smudgy photograph. Unjailed, Betty marched off to the West for five years. When she returned, our series opens and the crime wave is underway.

No doubt that Betty is at the bottom of it. At the scene of each crime, she leaves a white card, her name signed at the bottom in big, bold writing. She also provides her address, a boarding house in the East 20s.

The address is checked out by poor, old, slow, fat Detective Daniel Lonsdell, who is unable to find the hand on his arm. You wonder how Betty would have fared against sterner investigators. We will never know. In 1918, it was customary practice for an authoress to contrast dull, grey detectives against the glittering gem of the heroine. So sorry if that made Pinkertons scowl.

Lonsdell, at any rate, finds nothing at the boarding house but two shop girls and a dancer. None of these resembles Betty's picture. Hair is the wrong color.

He also finds a landlady of monumental stupidity. She is an outsized tub of flab, with a permanent cold and an inability to grapple with matters more complex than light and dark.

No, none of the girls could be Betty. Two of them were boarding there while Betty was swindling her way across Sacramento. The dancer couldn't be Betty because she practices constantly at night, the house shaking with her thumpings.

Lonsdell trudges dispiritedly away, thinking gray thoughts.

"...look a little lively," Betty writes to the police. (She is constantly penning them little notes.)

After Lonsdell looks long enough, he discovers. . . . It is embarrassing to reveal what he discovers. He discovers that the dancer is out doing Lord Knows What every night. The thumpings in her room are made by a brown and white fox terrier leaping for a bone tied to a light fixture.

Gee whiz, you're right. And it's sixty years too late for us to do anything about it.

Lonsdell is also too late. Betty has long vanished, temporarily leaving behind her mother (the landlady, a fine character actress) and the fox terrier (named "Alibi"). The story is titled "Boston Betty's 'Alibi'," January 1, 1918.

"With 'Alibi's' Aid," January 29, 1918, tells how Betty steals the cash box of a bad-natured theatre operator. She is aided by Alibi, who runs barking through the theatre, and her mother, who waddles haplessly through the theatre. All other characters are singularly foolish.

Betty uses "Ali" as a decoy again during "The Dog In the Machine" (March 26). First she steals an old grouch's good-luck charm, then writes him letters explaining how to get it back: Follow the cab with the dog in it. He does so. So does Lonsdell. While they vapor about, Betty breaks into the grouch's home and cleans him out.

In " 'Baby Jane's' Revenge" (April 23, 1918), an envious rival tips the squeal that Betty has filched four diamonds. But before Lonsdell can nab her, she conceals the diamonds in the hollow of Ali's largest bone. Lonsdell at fault; Betty glows.

The stories are not much for content. For all her little feminine tricks, Betty does not crystallize as an appealing character. She is competent, adequate and remote. The fat mother, dog, and dumb cop become routine almost at once and the series dies, stark and stiff, in the unyielding clutch of its own formula. But nowhere else in mystery fiction will you find a criminal fox terrier.

The stories we have examined so far are nearly weightless confections built around an enticing central character. Success of the series is directly tied to the appeal of that character. Even story content is secondary.

As, for example, the Thubway Tham stories. These have about as little content as the law allows, but they brim with character appeal.

Tham was one of Johnston McCulley's most happily-formulated characters. The lisping little pickpocket appeared in well over one hundred stories, scattered through *Detective story Magazine* (1918-1938), *Best Detective Magazine* (1929-1936), and in such other representative publications as *Clues* and *Detective Fiction Weekly* (1937) and *Black Book Detective* (1948).[8]

The stories are dead-pan comedy played in the manner of the silent movies. The characters are supremely intent on their business. It is humorous, often hilarious to the spectator. To those engaged in the activity of the story, it is serious and often grim.

The marvel is that McCulley wrote so very many stories with such a restricted cast and subject. It is like painting water colors using only three shades of green. Except that the Tham cast consists of only two regulars.

Here slouches the irascible little pickpocket on his sun-touched bench in Madison Square, smoking a roll-your-own. Enter his ancient opponent, Detective Craddock, in good humor or ill.

"Tho I thee your ugly fathe again, do I?" says Tham, a remark equivalent to that one about the game being afoot.

He blisters Detective Craddock with scorn. Detective Craddock issues a stern warning about getting caught in the subway with fingers in inappropriate pockets. They part, glowering. Tham will soon be bumped, hooked, shoved, heaved and pushed into contact with an unpleasant fellow carrying a fat wallet in his hip pocket. The fellow is so unpleasant, we feel that Tham will never get his wallet. But he does, at last.

Thus the outline of a hundred stories.

How skillfully this shanty skeleton is silvered with humor. How neatly suspense is built. Will Tham be able to punish the leering lout by theal, er, stealing his wallet? Is it possible that Craddock will triumph this time?

Tham does not often fail. His victims deserve the punishment they receive, a modest financial blow; for in his own way, Tham is a minor justice figure. It would never do to press this figure of speech too far. During the course of a story, he may casually appropriate three or four other wallets. Even then, his bare-faced stealing is so casually slipped over, you hardly notice that he is, after all, a professional street crook. It is a curious situation.

As the series begins ("Thubway Tham," June 4, 1918), Tham is forced to discard a stolen wallet and watch, fearing Craddock will search him. Returning later for the loot, he discovers that the dishonest saloon keeper has latched on to them. An opportune raid by Craddock and the boys in blue permits Tham to grab the booty and flee, leaving the saloon keeper all up in the air.

And there you are—crime pays if the character is appealing.

The second story of the series, "Thubway Tham's Rival" (June 11, 1918), is an extended wild chase, like the story line of a silent movie. An amateur pickpocket lifts the wallet Tham had marked for himself. Craddock is hot on Tham's trail. ("Thtruth around like a printhe and talkth like a book. He maketh me thick.") Tham is hot on the amateur's trail. Onward through the streets the chase reels, the wallet flying from this pocket to that. But Tham snares it at the last second and leaves Craddock stuck in a crowded subway train.

For a continuing hero, Tham hardly looks appealing. He is a little man "of no particular strength," with a right hand containing genius and left hand almost equally talented. He has a sort of raw, dull appearance—so much so that in "Thubway Tham—Model" (*Clues*, November 1937), a photographer uses him as a model of a country jake.

Thith ith a vile canard; Tham is a full-time city boy, now and forever. It is only that he looks—well, in "Thubway Tham Shakes A Star" (*Detective Story Magazine*, March 31, 1928), his appearance is remarked upon in this way:

"Note his shiftless manner, his furtive glance, the lack of ambition in his face."

A man of Tham's profession does not seek to be noticeable. Already he has had one bout in jail, which left him far too visible to the police. He wishes merely to glide along, anonymous, overlooked, through the subway, his chosen work area, skillfully transferring wealth from one pocket to another, the trickle-down theory in full operation. He is not greedy. He wants only enough to suit his current needs. No more. He does not believe in large accumulation of wealth. It tempts fate, and he doubts that fate is on his side.

(Tham had an) ingrown pessimism against which he fought continually. He looked upon most things with keen suspicion and at times his face was sour.[9]

Pessimism does not prevent him from being a devoted, if not very successful, poker player. If poker is not available, there is always a horse race or a dice game. Lots of ways to lose your roll, other than having it lifted on the subway.

His associates are petty criminals. He lives in a rented room at the lodging house of "Nosey" Moore, a partially-reformed crook. Tham rents a bed, a chair, a dresser and owns two suits, one of which is darker than the other. When funds are plentiful and time hangs heavy, he goes to the movies, preferring good, solid, obvious comedies to love stories. To tell the truth, women abash him and he keeps away from them.

His life, in fact, is highly circumscribed. How on earth could McCulley write so many pages about this shabby petty criminal and keep readers asking for more stories and more?

Perhaps it is Tham's peppery personality that tickles the page. A small-time thief he may be, but he stands solid on his feet. No mere detective can daunt him. No man may insult him without getting ripped off with magician-like deftness. He has little but pride. He lisps hugely— his career began in the days when dialect was popular—and in Tham, this ancient characteristic survived to the late 1930s.

As mentioned, the stories are thin to the point of transparency. "Thubway Tham Reformth" (Detective Story, February 11, 1922) tells how he loses all in a poker game and swears off gambling. For a few pages he turns down opportunities to play cards, bet on horses, but a dice game finally lures him back to scarlet ways. "Thubway Than, Good Thamaritan" (Detective Story, March 27, 1926) finds him accused of lifting a stroke victim's wallet. He didn't; it wouldn't be professional. Nor will he tell the police who did it, although he knows. This moral quandary is resolved when the thief cheats Tham at cards. Tham, in turn, picks the scoundrel's pocket of the gambling winnings and is able to return the stolen money, retaining a healthy profit for himself.

"Thubway Tham's Ides of March" (Detective Story, March 24, 1928) begins with Craddock warning him against that evil day. Scorning this good advice, Tham goes forth to the streets, is promptly knocked down by a truck. He is not hurt but his clothing is wrecked. By appropriate bleats he is able to escalate the damage settlement from $30 to $500, proving that the Ides are not as unfortunate as they might be.

As usual in crook stories, McCulley relies on ethical legerdemain to keep sympathy solidly with the hero. It is the same technique used in confidence-man fiction—the victim is drawn as being exceedingly disagreeable; he deserves punishment. The method is clearly demonstrated in "Thubway Tham's Jewelry Haul" *(Clues,* October 1937). It is a huge haul. Tham lifts a wallet that is filled with jewels and the feat terrifies him. He doesn't know what to do with them. Finally he gets Craddock to take him to the home office of the jewelry company (address is printed on the wallet). He hopes for a modest reward. Alas, the jewels are of glass, and he receives only a dollar for his honest deed. And, as you expected, the wallet of the snooty man in charge.

Yes, it is expected. Part of the story interest is the wait until Tham snaffles the wallet. You feel an unmistakable surge of relief when he finally pulls it off.

"Thubway Tham Buys Buttons" *(Clues,* December 1937) features the punishment of another offensive victim. By a series of elaborate coincidences, Tham is mistaken for a popular comedian who is visiting a movie theatre. Women mob him. Craddock, convulsed with merriment, helps Tham escape to the box office. There they meet the real comedian, an ego-manic, richly arrogant. You will hate him. He sneers loftily and Tham exits with a damage payment for his clothing. It does not reveal the ending and spoil the special effect toward which the entire piece has been structured, to remark that the comedian's wallet also exits with Tham. You expect this, given the formality of McCulley's art.

Excluding Tham's criminal activities, the stories tingle with humor. It all seems highly amusing—unless you were the fat man who lost his wallet in the subway. By contrast, the Simon Trapp series, written by Roy W. Hinds, is graver by far and the humor is subdued. It leaves you with an uplifted but sobered feeling, as if there were nothing on the television but Handel oratorios.

Simon Trapp is a pawnbroker. And also a conniver with criminals and the unsuspected brain behind many a criminal coup. He sits inside a grimy little shop in a feckless part of New York City. His face is wrinkled. A beard hangs long from his chin. At any moment, you expect him to articulate that legendary cry: "Oy, oy, oy!"

He is a man of many parts. For reasonable pay, he will arrange that your safe be blown to diddle the insurance company. Or the safe of your rich neighbor, for more direct gain. Or he can provide for the extraction of your friend's pearl necklace from the secret place beneath the fifth board.

Whatever the crime (short of murder), Simon will know a good man to handle it. He will work out the entry, think out the twists of the getaway. He'll even handle the sale of the goods for you. He is a most useful old fellow.

The police have not suspected his activities for twenty-five years. The people of the district think him admirable. He takes care of his boys—and it is at least possible that he knows both Larry the Bat and Smarlinghue from the Jimmie Dale series. The location and time frame are about right.

Simon Trapp's career in *Detective Story Magazine* ran from 1921 through 1928, with reprints in *Best Detective Magazine* appearing from 1933 through 1937. Roy Hinds, author of the series, was an experienced Street & Smith contributor, whose work also appeared in *The Popular Magazine, Short Stories, Argosy, Flynn's Weekly* and *Wild West Weekly*, among other titles, during the first twenty-five years of the pulps. Compared to Hinds' other work, the Simon Trapp stories are slight. You feel that they may turn to mist and blow from the page.

"Simon Trapp and the Irony of Mercy" (August 20, 1921) tells how the old sinner conspires to railroad his own assistant, Puggie Rooks, into prison. Once there, Puggie is to discover where $60,000 stolen bank funds have been hidden. At Puggie's trial, Simon puts on such a show of being the poor old, broken-hearted guardian of this wayward boy that the judge suspends sentence and paroles Puggie in Simon's custody.

"Simon Trapp Pays a Doctor Bill" (February 11, 1922) demonstrates Simon's habit of making one crime accomplish two different purposes. Two safecrackers have bungled one of Simon's jobs. The first has broken his leg and lies helplessly at the scene of the crime; the second, in panic, flies to Simon, babbling the bad news. Thoroughly disgusted, the old man goes to the relief of the injured man, gets him away before the police come clumping in, and stands the cost of his doctor bill.

Months later, Simon is approached by a friend who needs his safe robbed. There are reasons. He promises to leave the fee inside the safe. Trapp arranges that the crook who broke his leg open the safe, get the money and close it up again. Then he arranges that the second crook blow the safe with nitro, not knowing that it has been emptied.

This is done. The second crook blasts the box, finds only 26 cents inside and flees unrewarded. It is, you see, his punishment for abandoning a man with a broken leg—and also for costing Trapp a doctor bill.

In the December 16, 1922 "Simon Trapp Goes to Sing Sing," he visits that prison with some friends to secure a safe combination from a prisoner. Simon has a horror of seeing the inside of a prison and wears glasses with the lens obscured all during the visit.

"Simon Trapp Brings Midnight Cheer" (December 13, 1924) is full of moral positions, rather obliquely demonstrated. To show a boy, who is veering toward crime, just how bad cracking safes really is, Trapp busts the boy's safecracker father out of jail to have a little talk with his son. "Simon Trapp, Padlocked" (July 9, 1927) describes how he takes revenge on a pair of Chicago crooks who try to blackmail him.

Slender stories, indeed. Dimly through the pedestrian prose you can make out the old pawnshop on Broome Street. Faint echoes of crooks' argot sound in the prose. That vivid, sordid, sharp-edged social scene through which passed Nick Carter and Jimmie Dale and the Lone Wolf is gray now, gone flat and pale. The October 31, 1925 "Simon Trapp Takes a Bus Ride" carries us all over New York City—the underworld, Washington Square, Grant's Tomb. They come and go, words only. No images disturb the drab prose. It is a landscape of nouns, hushed and immobile, through which the characters move without emotion, acting out the synthetic story until Mr. Hinds places the final period. Followers of this series, it might be noted, do not seem to agree with this judgment and continued to clamor for more and still more Simon Trapp adventures. The series obviously contained excellences of some kind. They have grown invisible over the decades.

3-

In all of the series examined, humor is used to soften the criminality of the lead character. By contrast, the Big Scar Guffman series contains no humor and very little of that redeeming content which makes a crook story acceptable to the tender palates of critics. It is, instead, tough, grim and melodramatic. The characters slouching through the stories leave the impression of being unwashed for long periods. They are hard, laconic men, the majority of them ex-cons, as was the writer of the series, Henry Leverage. According to Harold Hersey, a long-time pulp magazine editor who visited Leverage in Sing-Sing:

I never did ask him what had gone awry with his life. He told me when we first met that it was distinctly the wrong thing to interrogate a prisoner concerning his past.... I suspected that Henry Leverage had had a most exciting career. Now and again he let fall hints about experiences in China and Europe, anecdotes of sailing before the mast and adventures in the far West.[10]

Whatever his past, Leverage was a thoroughly professional writer.

Early he published in the *Saturday Evening Post*, a short story, "Whispering Wires," which later became a successful play. He sold short fiction to the slick magazine markets, including *Cosmopolitan*, while, at the same time, filling the pulp magazines with material. He appeared in *Flynn's, Prison Stories, Detective Story Magazine, Argosy All-Story,*

Clues and *Black Mask*, among the more prominent, continuing to write until his death, probably in the early 1930s. At the time Hersey met him in 1916, he was editor of Sing-Sing's magazine, *The Star of Hope*. In his cell,

He had pictures of Joseph Conrad, Kipling, and other well-known authors on the walls. There was a small library on a shelf over a tiny table where he kept his typewriter.... He was turning out thousands of words a week. Like so many experts, he seldom revised a page once it left his machine.... Nervous, wiry, energetic, with eyes sunk deep in his head and a habit of restlessly moving his legs and arms as he talked, he soon convinced me that he was a serious author....[11]

Released from prison in 1919, Leverage continued to produce non-series crook fiction until 1925. In the January 10 issue of *Flynn's*, that year, he introduced his main series character, Big Scar Guffman, as a bit player in the short story, "The Warden's Watch." Big Scar is a gigantic, hulking, iron-hard con serving a life sentence plus fifteen years. Across his cheek runs a deep gash, later described as a "V." It is, in the October 30, 1926 "The Old Clam," a "terrific gash that ran from the point of his chin to the upper lobe of his right ear. Big Scar had earned that mark when two railroad brakemen had thrown him from a freight train. It turned him against society and railroads in general..."[12]

In other stories, the scar appears to be on his scalp. He is, at any rate, marked by society.

Big Scar's cellmate, Sweeney Pike (the semi-hero of "The Warden's Watch"), amuses himself by detecting small crimes within the prison. When the warden's prized watch is stolen, Pike attempts to locate it. He eventually discovers that Big Scar lifted the watch and is using the mainspring to cut the cell bars. Big Scar escapes, leaving Pike with the watch remains.

In "The Old Clam" *(Flynn's Weekly*, October 30, 1926) Big Scar holds up the cashier of a small bank and learns that the cashier (a charming young man) has embezzled bank funds. His uncle from the West is arriving tomorrow to make up the funds, but the bank examiner is due today. As Big Scar is making off with $400 from the bank, he meets, by a remarkable coincidence, the bank examiner and leaves him stranded on a mud bar in the Susquehanna River—where he will remain until the bank shortage is covered.

As "The New Warden" (November 20, 1926) opens, Big Scar is hiking across the desert for reasons unexplained. Perhaps it is because of all those warrants out against him back East.

The price on Big Scar's head for safe-blowing and stick-ups was enough to pay one country's debts. He was wanted in the East by every post office inspector.[13]

While holding up a man to steal his horse, Big Scar discovers that he has caught the new warden of the Querida Penitentiary, just reporting for duty. As no one knows the warden, Big Scar takes his place and saves an old friend from being hanged for a crime that he did not commit.

That is a staple situation in the series. The Law is constantly punishing the wrong individual. It is up to the hardened criminal to correct these errors. Obviously, the side of justice and right is not exactly where we believe it to be. The Law is not only blind but stubborn and rigid in error. It is a malignant cloud hurling out punishment.

The position is required to maintain sympathy with the lead character. To make Big Scar a hero (since he is an active criminal) it is necessary that the Law be presented as a brainless abstraction. It is also necessary that all representatives of the Law—police, guards, wardens—be corruptly vicious.

Opposed to these monsters are the professional criminals. Some have honor. Others do not. Big Scar adheres to the law of the underworld: don't squeal on a pal (although Dashiell Hammett had some quick crisp remarks about the unreality of that myth).

But the Big Scar series is hardly constrained by reality. It presents the Law of the Underworld as a positive thing, even as it presents society as a fat melon supporting both the vicious creatures of the Law and The Underworld.

"Liberty For Sale" (December 4, 1926) allows Big Scar to break into "Copper John"—the Blackstone Penitentiary. He carries a bribe to an inmate who is a genius at arranging escapes. Big Scar has no difficulty breaking in, locating his man, or concealing himself the whole day inside the walls. The prisoner is rescued but is accidentally electrocuted as they escape over the walls, by which Big Scar concludes that he was guilty, after all, and his death a judgment of Heaven.

"The Tomato-Can Vag" (August 13, 1927) tells how a pair of crooks, masquerading as hobos, enlist his aid in opening a safe. Since this belongs to an old woman, Big Scar recants the job. The two crooks are taken and Big Scar slips away easily.

At this point, he escapes out of *Flynn's Weekly* and becomes a regular character in *Detective Story Magazine,* where he appeared for the next several years. The stories remained the same, which is to say crusted with yegg talk over a core of sugar syrup.

The September 10, 1927, "Buzzards at Bay," tells how he is sprung from prison by a political boss. There is a price: he is to infiltrate a gang that has threatened to murder the boss's daughter. Using hobo lingo and a rifle, our hero saves the girl and learns, to his chagrin, that the gang's mastermind was de buzzard in de next cell back at de prison.

This basic situation repeats throughout the series: Big Scar is constantly being snatched from the grip of the law by semi-respectable people who wish him to perform dark acts. As in "The Gold Room" (October 1, 1927)—a wealthy collector pays his bail and offers him a large fee to break into the museum. He is to steal a Greek statuette the collector can no longer live without. Double-cross follows double-cross, but Big Scar has seen through that tricky collector from the start and has arranged a double-cross of his own. You can't trust an honest man.

"The Crooked Cross" (November 5, 1927) is another variation of the same situation. A square lawman, fighting fire with fire, hires Big Scar to blow up the banks of a small town. This simulated crime wave is intended to drive from office a crooked city government, which it does, proving that fiction is stranger than the truth.

"Seven Grains and Chinese Cribs" (November 19, 1927) is a romp through Chinatown. Big Scar is caught cracking a Chinese merchant's safe. At the point of a poisoned dagger, he is directed to exchange the merchant's empty safe for a full one belonging to a Chinese bank. Escaping by a fluke, he returns the very next morning and lays an iron bar back of that crafty merchant's ear. He then loots the safe and departs, his heart singing.

You may conclude from these adventures that Big Scar is as sentimental as a concrete wall. As the series continues, however, the softer emotions, like a faint mist, creep stealthily into the prose. "The Man Who Couldn't Squeal" (September 1, 1928) presents him with an ethical quandry: how can he deliver to the Law a criminal so low that he stole the funds of the Prison Benefit Union? Big Scar's Code forbids him to squeal on a fellow con. And yet, yet.... He tracks this stealer down, finds him running a gambling hell in bland indifference of the police searching for him. But punishment is near. Big Scar merely shows his face, familiar on a dozen wanted posters. The police swarm after him; he ducks into the gambling den. The police follow and arrest everyone in sight, the stealer included, while Big Scar slips away over the rooftops.

More sentiment creeps into the February 2, 1929, "Menacing Bill." Big Scar aids a girl whose father is accused of counterfeiting. After some trouble, she locates the hidden plates, and the wicked crook responsible pays for his crimes. The wicked Law, by the way, holds the father in custody to blackmail Guffman and the girl into finding and turning over the plates.

"Too Cheap" (June 22, 1929) picks up Big Scar as he returns from three years in the pen. The story reads as if it were any old crook story, with Big-scar (the name is now written this way) being added as an afterthought.

The girl wants him to go straight, and he promises. Instead he slips out and steals a pearl necklace, the sly cad. Since this is *Detective Story Magazine*, Big-scar has been provided with a pursuing detective, Detective Binney. He is vaguely characterized as being overweight, tough, not too clever and, we may assume, wears a derby hat and puffs a cigar butt. Guffman sees Binney and stashes the pearl necklace among the fake pearls at a 5 cent & 10 cent store. When Binney shakes Big-scar down, he finds nothing but a moth ball, which suggests something about the rewards of crime. Later, Big-scar bolts back to the dime store. Too late. The necklace is gone.

Who do you suppose got it?

"...a poor old woman, with two kids..."

All of which is charming in its own way. Although it scarcely conceals the fact that Big Scar has no real life as a character. He is big, hard, scarred. From that point on, invent your own personality to fit these characteristics.

Like the other criminals we have met, Big Scar inhabits a universe carefully biased in his favor. All values are reversed. White becomes black, Law becomes Crime, and Crooks are either soiled but good or soiled and rotten.

The small-time professional criminal in fiction is made acceptable to the reader by distortion of the ethical situation or by the use of humor. Thus reality may be wrenched about to the point where the central character's villainy can be tolerated. A method less frequently used is to plaster the character, his point of view, the story, the sky and the grass with romance—glowing irresistible romance, gay-feathered and singing its giddy crystal melody, until the reader loses all sense of the world in which he bought his magazine and sat down to read.

The romance of crime. Its sheer swagger as its happy highwaymen, its brighter buccaneers, cuff aside those social formulas, worn and stale, that keep men tame and fetter their souls. And, quite often, keep them out of jail.

But arrest, trial, prison, and disgrace have no real meaning to a blithe criminal sparkling among those phlegmatic clods, the respectable. No, no. Romance calls. Adventure beckons. The shallow artifices fall away. It is burglary time and the hours quicken with golden excitement as your flashing wits dazzle and dart and prank.

The romance of crime excused much and so etherized the reader's moral sense that he could gobble a library full of stuff that, couched in other terms, would get him heaved out of Sunday School. Such long-lasting fellows as The Saint, Lester Leith, and the Spider (that is, Mr. Richard Wentworth), endured for years in a swaddling of romance. Not many small-time crooks in brief series managed this feat. Of the few that succeeded, two have particular points of interest. In the case of Maxwell Sanderson, The Noiseless Cracksman, the romantic criminal viewpoint which buoys up the hero is constantly melting away, mist in the wind. In the series featuring Sheik and Simpson, a merry duo, the romantic mists are barely dense enough to conceal the brazen rapacity of the characters. Both series provide fascinating glimpses of romance as a literary technique to cloud readers' minds.

4-

The Maxwell Sanderson series begins with the January 17, 1925, novelette, "All But His Hands," *Detective Story Magazine.* The character of Sanderson is Raffles—an Americanized Raffles, with strong insertions of material tested through ten years of pulp magazine criminal fiction. The author was John Jay Chichester.

Born in Kankakee, Illinois, Chichester became a copy boy on a Chicago newspaper in his late teens. Soon after becoming a reporter, he was held up by two gunmen as he was returning to his boarding house. They swiftly discovered that he was broke. ("Take a tip from me," he said, "and never waste time holding up a newspaper man.")[14] Whereupon the hold-up-men took him to an all-night lunch room and bought him a meal.

prisons and gained the confidence of the prisoners who talked to him and gave him an insight into their lives. Because of this first-hand information and his interest in the character of the people whom he met, he was able to incorporate in his stories a true representation and authenticity of his heroes and villains.[15]

According to Chichester, that pair of gunmen started him thinking about writing crook stories and over the years, his name appeared constantly in the Street & Smith magazines. His most popular series character, Sanderson, was created early, running from 1925 to about 1932, with reprints appearing until 1937.

The initial situation of "All But His Hands" contains some familiar material, particularly to those of memory long enough to recall the opening chapter in *The Amateur Cracksman.* As Raffles and Bunny Manders met, so did Sanderson and Barton Clark.

In through the window of the luxurious apartment, by night, slips Mr. Clark, desperate to steal $5,000. The apartment belongs to that idle young rich man about town and general wastrel, Maxwell Sanderson. Who catches Clark in the act.

How amazed Clark is when Sanderson reveals himself to be not just a wealthy young fool, but a rising young safecracker, whose expensive tastes have long outstripped his inheritance.

Sanderson became a thief purely by accident. Engulfed by debt, at the end of his financial rope, he was seated at a performance of *La Boheme,* immediately behind a quarter-of-a-million dollar necklace. Then the lights were lowered. When they rose again, the necklace was in his pocket and a new career beckoned.

He sold the necklace in Paris. He began to study safe mechanisms in the manner of other series characters before him and he developed a technique of drilling into a safe and using a bit of wire to work the tumblers through the hole. Soon the police hunted "The Driller," master mind (they suspected) of a vast organization.

All the stolen profits are hardly able to pay off Sanderson's larger debts and keep him from week to week. "I've never had a grain of common sense," he says, "when it came to the handling of money. It dribbles through my fingers like sand through the hands of a child."

Then he met Clark. They pool skills, rob the safe of Julius Rittenhouse. The adventure turns messy. Either Sanderson or Clark or both kill the butler. Clark barely escapes. Sanderson is barely able to alibi for him. Three months later, most of the $50,000 has slipped through Sanderson's fingers.

As told in "All But His Hands," he now develops an elaborate scheme for robbing an actress of her jewels while she is a guest on Adam Decker's yacht. Decker made a huge fortune on the shady side of the law, got out just in time, now amuses himself with ostentatious spending. He is a tough, grim, unrelenting man.

The jewels are stolen by a heavily disguised Sanderson. He escapes successfully, but Decker has recognized his hands and declares war. He hires a detective, Peter "Bulldog" Blodgett, and sets him on a full-time effort to get Sanderson.

Undismayed by the hound on his track, Sanderson proceeds along his merry way. In "Sinking Safety" (July 10, 1926) he impersonates an English butler to steal the lady's pearls. In "Helpless Hands" (three-part serial, January 8 through 22, 1927), Blodgett captures him on a train and handcuffs him. Sanderson is able to escape but finds himself penniless, both hands chained together, 1,000 miles from the nearest friend. At every step he is involved in more trouble. He accidentally discovers a suicide in an old house, ends up chased by half the law in the country. At the same time, Clark, also beset by difficulties, struggles across the continent from New York City to reach Sanderson in time. Yes, he does, But it is tight.

Soon after, Sanderson finds himself in a deadly struggle with that

King of Crime, Magnus, a completely paralyzed genius who schemes away as he lies slowly dying. Magnus has kidnapped the rich broker's daughter, Carolyn Wheeler. Naught can save her pretty throat from the knife—unless her daddy, an influential fellow—manipulates the stock market as directed. Is all hope lost? Certainly not. For Sanderson, who was resting from a bout of jail break, hears the news and comes foaming back to New York. Ah, he had so admired Carolyn, back when he was a social favorite, not an outcast. And so the intricate combat between the super cracksman and the super criminal begins.

After spoiling Magnus' every hope, Sanderson continues his optimistic career, as cheerful as ever. Decker is offering a $50,000 reward for Sanderson, now. The identity of "The Noiseless Cracksman" is known and warrants for his arrest are everywhere. Wanted or not, he insists on attending a Broadway show, triggering the events of "Sanderson's Rejected 'Moll' " (June 1, 1929). The Moll is Diamond Mary, raging because Sanderson had foxed her for the Shrewsbury necklace, tentatively hopeful that he will sweep her into his arms. But Sanderson does not understand these feminine flutters. That a woman hates because she loves, a chronic emotional condition of popular fiction, escapes him completely. And so she strikes. With a tough friend, she kidnaps Clark, forces Sanderson to open a safe packed with diamonds, locks him in a closet to be captured. After a series of escapes, struggles, and confrontations, he steals the diamonds from Mary's bag in the baggage car of a train and leaps bravely into the night, successful still again.

While waiting to sell these jewels, he takes it into his head to rob Decker's safe. And finds himself, as shown on the cover of the July 6, 1929, *Detective Story Magazine,* in a sorry pickle. The safe is a mantrap. As Sanderson reaches for the valuables, he finds his right arm caught. "Sanderson Handcuffed" is the story. Decker, beside himself with delight, sees our hero marched off by Blodgett, and the series would have ended right there if Clark, by nerve and good luck, had not been able to intercept the police car and free his friend.

Sanderson promptly returns to Decker's home. At pistol point, he forces Decker to insert *his* arm into the safe and so leaves his old enemy livid as Sanderson exits with the valuables.

A thoroughly engaging criminal, Mr. Sanderson.

To excuse his choice of profession, he has all the usual pluses of character:

It was typical of Maxwell Sanderson that he stuck as close to the technical truth as circumstances permitted, for while he possessed no apparent scruples...there was a peculiar quality in his make-up which shrank from lying, and more than once he had actually taken amazing risks of his life to keep inviolate his "word of honor"....[16]

This conventional characteristic is shared with figures as diverse as Buffalo Bill and Dr. Fu Manchu. Forgery, kidnapping, theft, assault bother Sanderson only lightly. But his word of honor, that fabulous thing, is to be preserved and maintained polished and blazing.

Like other popular characters on both sides of the law, Sanderson is particularly aggravating in being close-mouthed. He barely confides to Clark. Unlike most second bananas, Clark resents this bitterly. He is no Bunny Manders. Sanderson charms him without disengaging his

Flynn's (January 3, 1925). A short-lived fad for convict and jail fiction included Big Scar Guffman's adventures and culminated in the magazine *Prison Stories*.

Detective Story Magazine (July 6, 1929). The playful Sanderson, a Raffles variant, is trapped by his arch-enemy, Decker. But not for long.

judgment. Beneath his role as Faithful Friend lies a grim pessimism: The good days will end; the luck will pinch out. After that, the night.

He watches Sanderson spiraling upward on exuberant waves of optimism, risking thirty years' of imprisonment for a few seconds laughter. Enchanted, partly, Clark follows. Unlike Sanderson, he is aware of what failure actually means.

Chichester assures us that Sanderson is a masterly technician and strategic genius. But the man is also of that deadly temperament which glosses immaturity with personal charm.

Full of high humor, Sanderson glows. He tweaks Blodgett's nose. If the worst happens and he is caught, he has that boys' book remedy— a pill of cyanide concealed in the cap of his fountain pen. Only a harsh critic would observe that twice he is fairly caught and never reaches for this.

No. no. no. The pill is a bit of romance, an artifact of boys' play. If the pill is fearsome as a possibility, we may expect that Sanderson considers it a variety of sugar. His mind does not feel the reality that we know. To him, it is play. The meaning of what he does slides across his supple mind; it is not crime but romance, bright romance, where values twist at unfamiliar angles, and those imperatives of civilized life, responsibility and accountability, are blurred with egotistic intoxication.

Does he kill a man? Then he wills himself to forget it. Lo, it is forgotten. Is the butler dead? No, only forgotten. Except, perhaps, to the butler and his family. A murder. A robbery. What does Sanderson know of these things? He is a boy at play in a play world. At the end of the game, all dead butlers rise up. There are no consequences.

Sanderson is not really Raffles, that icy egoist, who knew, so well, reality's spiny surface. Not at all. Sanderson is Tom Sawyer, grown to adulthood and capering still among the fancies of an eleven-year old.

5-

This is the life we have permitted Sanderson, we who read the old magazines. It is our responsibility equally with Mr. Chichester and the magazine editor. Villain, hero, swordsman, jungleman, detective—all are equally stunted. When they tire us, when we wish to hear them speak as adults, they are necessarily silent. Our tacit acceptance of their imperfect adulthood has frozen them at immature levels. Black Star plays the menace. Barton Edgeworth plays the bad robber. Sanderson plays the gentleman cracksman. Their games are boys' games. They play, and we read, by our acceptance permitting their play, approving their lack of growth and pretenses to maturity. When their story closes, the simplicities stop. Around us then, like walls suddenly visible, stand the dire complications of the world we know.

We readers purchase these simple fictions. We cannot complain because they are offered for sale. They will be for sale as long as we buy. We dip our minds into simplified narrative where action replaces all else, where characters endlessly grapple. Obviously our lives are not like this.

Is this what we wish? To live as simply as the people on the other side of the print? Who measures the quality of our hearts when all are equally simple? In the labyrinth, where do the games end?

6-

From 1927 to 1930, *Detective Story Magazine* featured a series about a pair of bright young burglars. The scene was the Jazz Age in its final hours of glory. Readers apparently devoured the stories as, in more noble times, they would devour popcorn shrimp. Legions of these stories spilled through the months, each about 2,000 words long. They seem to have continued as inexorably as a pulsing heart.

The author was Roland Krebs. In common with so many other magazine writers, he was a reporter. Before the First World War, he worked on the St. Louis *Globe Democrat*. He enlisted in the Navy when war came. After mustering out, he worked on a newspaper in Cleveland. When he began to sell regularly to the magazines, he quit his job and moved to the Ozark Hills of Missouri. While there, he designed and wrote a real-estate booklet and found himself, quite unexpectedly, moving into advertising.[17] Two years later he entered the ad business in St. Louis full-time. His fiction gradually dwindled away.[18]

Kreb's fiction is short, brassy, comic, slangy, and about small-time crooks. Most have a strong family resemblance. Krebs had been writing about these people for almost a year, when he varied the formula slightly and brought forth Sheik Shannahan and Andy Simpson.

Sheik, the lead, is a young, high-stepping, fancy dresser, his hair greased back, gauded up in high-fashion clothing. His friend and series narrator, "Simp" Simpson, is more prosaic, slower, less social, and very intent on the dollar.

This pair of thieves carry the Raffles convention to its ultimate attenuation. Their adventures are fragile wisps, decorated by determinedly amusing dialogue and 1920s slang. Sheik, heading for a ball in a devil costume, causes a drunken rich boy to reform ("The Devil To Pay," June 2, 1928). Sheik absently locks his expensive gloves in a pillaged safe, which he must then re-rob ("Handle With Gloves," August 25, 1928). Sheik, dressed in a stolen bathing suit, hides in a flooded basement until the police leave ("Dressed To Rob," November 3, 1928).

Each story focuses on a single incident. After that incident, they escape with the loot, or receive an unexpected check, or are not caught. Their life is not quite a game, being dangerous, but it is hardly serious. At a sober assessment, it is infantile, mendacious, and self-serving, and is glossed over by justifications even more shallow than usual.

As Simpson explains it, everybody is a crook. We only steal from those who deserve to lose (he says). We clip the clipper. We bite the rich guy for the coin he sweats from the helpless.

Sheik attempts to steal the Stradivarius violin belonging to a prominent musician. By error, he gets the practice violin belonging to the musician's son. ("Fiddle Fooled," August 11, 1928).

May we suppose that the violin is returned?

You expect too much. Sheik trades the instrument for a box of water colors.

Sheik: "While society is pleased to term gentlemen of our ilk 'burglars,' the truth is we are far-seeing men of vision who recognize the inequality of the present distribution of wealth and plenty, and we are engaged in rectifying the error."[19]

"Here's How" (June 1, 1929) tells how the boys break into an expensive house and steal many bottles of old wine. Just as they are about to drink, they hear over the radio that the wine was bootleg vintage, manufactured from denatured alcohol and decked out in fancy labels. Shaken, they pour the wine into the radiator of their car on a freezing night. It eats out the hose connections.

"Sheik's Mice" (June 22, 1929): When Sheik drops mice at the tough housekeeper's feet, she forgets she has the drop on them. "Reward—500 Smackers" (June 28, 1930): Sheik fixes up a wallet with directions to a gold mine and offers a reward of $500 for the wallet's return. He then drops the wallet in the path of the town rich man. Just as the sucker bites and the sting is being applied, up drives a police car. Out step a policeman and an irate citizen to whom the rich man owes five hundred dollars. Immediately, the rich dastard takes Sheik's $500 reward money, pays off his debt, and exits, leaving the would-be con men greatly demoralized.

The Raffles series maintained an eerie sort of tension between the thieves and the society upon which they preyed. Their crimes were committed to maintain their positions in that society. They accepted its standards and mores in all but their source of income. As Raffles often remarked, other respectable men were equally great criminals, although their methods were less direct than burglarious entry. The justification is given easily, but Raffles' profession stiffened his life with moral tension. His activities outlawed him from the only society he found desirable. His crimes maintained his social position, at the same time that they made that position untenable.

No trace of these biting ambiguities trouble the Sheik and Simpson series. The stories bear a sassy surface flash; for all that, they are sickly thin formula stuff, morally bankrupt.

7-

Sanderson and Sheik, those naughty fellows, are two variations on the eternally popular figure of the romantic rebel. Their exploits are made tolerable to the reader by specious justifications, inversion of usual ethical positions, traces of humor, and heavy gilding on the woodwork. Behind them rears the dim figure of Robin Hood, whose benign example extends across the centuries to excuse the petty thefts of the 1920s.

Given the nature of the popular fiction medium, it is exceedingly rare for a series character to be an unsympathetic wretch; even Big-Scar, a hardcase if ever one lived, was provided with a heart of gold. If some daring writer elects to move counter to the flow of mainstream fiction, we may anticipate that his unsympathetic series character will be either a figure of fun or a wretch so incompetent that his failures, rather than his successes, make the story.

This is the case of Dr. Karl B. Krook, featured player in a short series containing no trace of the romance of crime. Dr. Krook was introduced by Arthur Mallory in the April 21, 1928, "Dr. Krook—Crook." He was another of *Detective Story Magazine's* patent criminals. As a doctor, he did harm.

Krook begins as a massive failure in the medical profession: no patients, shabby offices, debts. His slovenly life is matched by his slovenly thinking. Insurance swindles offer quick wealth; and so that patient, insured for $100,000 in Krook's favor, dies of anthrax.

It is murder for nothing.

Enter that shabby, diffident investigator, Bill Wright. (For every hare is tracked by a hound.) Wright's husky voice is soft, uncertain, and dandruff flecks his shoulders. But he swiftly picks out traces of the concealed crime—the stained floor, the tell-tale newspaper unburned. And now Krook must flee from Blanksburg, New Jersey.

He grabs a freight train out, running in fear, penniless.

We meet him again in Chicago, where he is employed as a ward orderly ("When Krook Meets Crook," June 2, 1928).

He is a hulking big man, heavy muscles under the fat; powerful white hands, dark hair thick on the backs of his fingers. Fear sours his guts. He waits to be caught. But he is not caught. One night he switches identities for an embezzling teller brought drunk to the hospital. Another man is buried under the teller's name. For planning this deception, Krook squeezes $5600 from the teller. Too late he learns that the man had absconded with $250,000. Rage consumes him. But by then, Bill Wright whispers his diffident investigation at the hospital. Krook must flee.

And he will flee again. For this is a morality play, the figures diminishing through the issues. The moral is ever before us—crime pays only tiny amounts.

Unlike most series, the saga of Dr. Krook decisively terminates. The final story is "The End of Doctor Krook" (October 6, 1928). Attempting to squeeze some insurance money from the wife of his last murder victim, Krook visits a slick shyster lawyer. Immediately the lawyer blackmails him. Worse, the doctor is also being blackmailed by Slash Jack Padrone, a killer Krook had hired to murder detective Wright.

Through compounding treacheries, Krook betrays and kills all who have dealings with him. Slash Jack goes down under police guns. The latest of the doctor's murder victims spills $200,000 insurance money into his hands. But hammering at the door is detective Wright, not dead at all. Krook flees into the alleys where he meets Slash Jack, not killed after all.

Slash Jack methodically shoots our hero eight times. As he sprawls there dying, up pants Wright. Krook attempts to stab him, misses:

"Not even that," groaned Karl B. Krook weakly. He began to weep slow, ineffectual tears, and, sobbing, died.

His story is a lesson to us all.

According to the article, "Popular Detective Story Writers," published in the June 2, 1928 *Detective Story Magazine,* Arthur Mallory was born in Chicago, 1889. He was a singularly powerful man, feats of strength and heroism studding his career.[20] He became a newspaperman and was fascinated by the shadows at the edge of crime. That fascination worked slowly into his fiction and informed his crime melodramas with the unromantic elements of shabbiness, confusion, greed, and failure. How far this is from Sanderson prancing among safes, and Sheik oiling his hair before leaving for an evening of robbery and dancing.

The joys of criminal life may not always be what the parson predicts or the doctor orders, but, for purposes of series fiction, they are substantial. In the world beyond your window exist such things as Swiss bank accounts and champagne days. As a matter of course, every coin having two sides, there are also unsympathetic police, cells smelling of inadequately washed men sitting close together, and television cameras recording you being led manacled from your eighteenth appeal.

It is not for popular fiction to dwell overlong on these disadvantages. The fine art of the crook story makes acceptable, or even delightful, behavior which, if encountered off the page, would provoke howls of anguish. The most direct way of lulling the reader to acceptance is to make the criminal character so interesting that his wickedness is hardly noticed. The personalities of Thubway Tham and Jeff Peters excuse much. Sanderson's nimble wits and Sheik's joy of life sugar coat their depressing social behavior. While such as Brannigan and Elegant Edward are poor souls and regarded with kindly contempt, the activities of others, equally reprehensible, may be excused (at least in print) by an occasional outburst of integrity or because of their unfortunate love life.

The writer's sleight-of-hand also glosses over magazine crimes. These are neatly scoured and scented to remove all taint of the absorbing self interest which reeks from everyday crime. So purified, they may then be presented as romantic adventures, an individual playing for high stakes while the world scowls. Or humor—as in the Big Nose Charlie series— may glaze the surface of the story with colors crisp and vivid. An equally effective writer's technique is that of ethical reversal: Either the criminal's activities are represented as a force for good, or, as in Big Scar's adventures, society, itself, is shown to be corrupt and the victims more disagreeable than those robbing them.

This latter method has been used for generations to justify the activities in a crook story. No literary con man ever stung a sweet old lady, not do the Barton Edgeworths of the magazines ever lower themselves to rob the innocent and good. The charm of fiction is that it can ignore so many of life's realities. And so the reader on the safe side of his window finds much to admire in criminals who prey entirely upon other criminals and battle evil with at least as much enthusiasm as Sherlock Holmes and his followers. The magazine criminal may disdain Law and jeer at police but he stands immovable on the side of justice.

The criminal who serves justice was thoroughly exploited by Edgar Wallace, an early master as unappreciated today as he was puffed during the 1920s. His Three Just Men, striking where the Law could not, were the first of that durable popular fiction type, the Justice Figure.[21] In the strict view of the Law, they were criminals, surely; in any larger sense, they were archangels of justice, acting as silent balance wheels to stabilize 1900s English society against the thrusts of untouchable crime.

In later series, Wallace turned repeatedly to the theme of the criminal who punished other criminals. These paragons include a number of series characters, among them, a feminine thief, two adventurers, and a public-spirited murderer. Like the Just Men before them, these characters visited rude justice on the dishonest and, for the most part, also earned themselves a respectable living. They are admirable. Even the murderer develops a puckish sort of charm, as Wallace transforms him from a public menace to a public benefactor.

But then Wallace, a master of the mystery-adventure story, regularly transformed stones into cakes.

IV—FOUR FROM EDGAR WALLACE

1-

In each country and each civilization, the ultimate sin differs. In one area of the world, a sly satiric grin at the name of Lenin will buy you three decades of scratching Siberian moss. In other places, careless use of pork in preparing dinner, or committing bagatelles with the opposite sex, or speaking disrespectfully of horses, are crimes serious enough to blight your opportunities and cause the world to consider you socially dispensable.

If theft of property is not the ultimate sin in the United States, it is at least one of the few that matters. The importance of property shines all through the popular magazines. Steal your neighbor's wife and he will lament for days. Steal his onyx ring with the diamond skull, and his howls ascend Heavenward.

The people of the dark side share this dire sin in common: they relish others' property. How diligently they con away funds, steal away jewels, fetch iced terror to the hearts of those who have. The rest of us, with ambivalent emotions and trifling stocks of cash and gems, read hungrily of these exploits. With exquisite tact, the authors of these stories avoid offending us directly; their larcenous heroes ignore the shabby reader, concentrate instead upon the vulgar rich whose pockets bulge so weightily and their counterparts, the wealthy crooks who prey upon the public and, in turn, are preyed upon by cool, skillful men and women.

The works of Edgar Wallace brim with bright young people who walk a little to the left of honesty. Some do so for adventure, some for the love of a full purse, while others, despairing of justice in this imperfect world, seek to punish and avenge. Their motives are mixed but their adventures, glittering froth, provide unalloyed joy.

One of the earliest of Wallace's series criminals was a young lady known as Four Square Jane. She was not the first woman to practice crime in the public print at the head of her own series—Henriette Van

98

Raffles, Mrs. A.J. Van Raffles, had appeared in her own book, *Mrs. Raffles,* in 1905.[1] Nor does Jane seem to have exerted the influence which was rightfully hers, for the publication history of her adventures is curiously involved. Still her series contained a central justification which would be used to rags during the 1920s and she is a most distinguished representative of one of Edgar Wallace's most popular character types.

Jane's adventures originally appeared in a newspaper, *The Weekly News.* The series, titled "Four-Square Jane," ran for nine consecutive issues, from December 13, 1919, through February 7, 1920, being signed John Anstruther.[2] The stories were collected and published in February 1929, as a red-purple, pocket-sized book titled *Four Square Jane,* the author revealed as Edgar Wallace. One story from this collection, "The Stolen Romney," was reprinted by Ellery Queen, with slight editorial deletion, in his anthologies, *101 Years' Entertainment* and *The Female of the Species.*

That Jane has been so little reprinted is perhaps because only the first four stories stand alone. By the fifth story, the series converts to a serial with a murder mystery at its core. All nine stories comprise a brief novel which begins with the accomplishments of a clever girl thief, gradually throws out plot threads, invents character relationships, develops a central situation (during the third, fourth, fifth, and seventh episodes) and the murder mystery (beginning with chapter five). In the ninth and final chapter, these loose parts are sewn together. It is an impressive demonstration of improvisational story telling, resembling a hawk floating in ever tighter circles until, at last, it drops direct upon its mouse.

As mentioned, the first stories are less interested in plot than in the exploits of this new-fangled thief. The first installment (titled "The Theft of the Lewinstein Jewels" in *The Weekly News* and simply "I" in the book) introduces Mr. Joe Lewinstein, a newly rich fellow who has invited guests for a gala weekend at his mansion. To protect their jewelry from the attentions of that wicked thief, Four Square Jane, he has hired a private detective, a woman who can mingle with the guests and listen and watch.

The detective gives him little confidence, for she is small, slender, dark-haired, and barely twenty-three. However she knows all about Jane—and the square sticker she leaves at the scene of her crimes: Four small squares arranged two on two with a capital "J" in the center. (This label, we later learn, is to identify Jane's work, so that the servants will not be blamed.)

No sooner is the detective in the house than she takes sick and must be put to bed. Her illness is diagnosed by a doctor (who happens to stop at Lewinstein's to borrow some gasoline) as scarlet fever. During the night, the girl recovers both from the scarlet fever and her identity as a detective, and becomes Four Square Jane, gliding through the silent house, opening doors with one of those semi-magical devices, beloved by fictional characters, a special skeleton key. (By adjusting the mechanism of this key, it can be made to fit almost any lock and Jane uses it constantly. We may assume that it was made for her by the same clever Swiss who manufactured a similar key for The Phantom Detective in 1933.)[3]

The jewels of Lewinstein's guests fly away, but before this is discovered, the doctor arranges that an ambulance carry off the stricken detective. Both the doctor and the ambulance driver are aides of Jane. And so the first episode ends, a story slender to transparency but very sprightly. Jane is only a clever thief and no hint of complexities to come sullies the dancing prose.

In the second story, "Jane In Custody," we meet the disagreeable Lord Claythorpe. Among the Lewinstein loot was Lord Claythorpe's gift to his wife, an armlet of a Doge of Venice. Jane sends this treasure to a hospital in financial shoals. Lord Claythorpe offered a 10,000 pound reward for the armlet's return, until the hospital returns it. Then he quibbles and scowls. This unsportsmanlike attitude marks him as Jane's prey. But how is she to crack the barred, guarded room with seven wall safes, only three of which hold the Claythorpe jewelry collection? Worse, two policeman apprehend Jane lurking about outside and bring her into the Claythorpe mansion to be held until the paddy wagon arrives. For safe-keeping, she is tucked into the vault room, the most secure room of the establishment, in the company of a scowling detective. From that room she is presently gone with all the jewels, leaving her sticker on the door. The arrest and the detectives were hoaxes all, but the theft is real enough.

With the third story, "The Stolen Romney," we are introduced to that dedicated young policeman assigned by fate to dog the slippery heroine. He is named Chief Superintendent Peter Dawes, a fine young fellow who remarks: "...I am pretty certain that (this Four Square Jane business) is not going to bring kudos or promotion to me."

To flesh out Jane's professional background, Dawes now summarizes her history for those of us eager to learn. Her crimes began about a year ago. She is "constantly robbing, not the ordinary people who are subjected to this kind of victimization, but people with bloated bank balances...accumulated as a direct consequence of shady exploitation companies."[4] (This justification is later discarded, as the basic series situation clarifies in Mr. Wallace's mind.)

All valuables that she steals except cash seem to be donated to medical charities. The cash stays right with Jane. "...she is," remarks Dawes, "the cleverest criminal that has come my way since I have been associated with Scotland Yard. This is the one thing that one has dreaded, and yet one hoped to meet—a criminal with a brain."[5]

After such a recommendation, it is only proper that Jane is able to steal a very large painting by Romney from a guarded, barred room. She did it by strategy, misdirection, and some slight help from Edgar Wallace. And she returned it the same way.

With the fourth episode, "The Sister of Mercy," plot enters the series and matters begin growing complex. Meet the charming young Joyce Wilberforce. Her uncle left her a fortune, and a stupid will stipulating that she marry the choice of Lord Claythorpe, trustee of the estate. Claythorpe has elected his driveling son, Francis, as Joyce's husband. Joyce, herself, prefers Jamieson Steele, a penniless engineer and possible forger.

It seems that the check Steele cashed bore a strangely written version of Claythorpe's signature. Steele maintained that Claythorpe gave it to him; Claythorpe maintains that is a lie. The bank and police, however, agree with Steele, although he does not know this. He has bolted—but not so far that Scotland Yard doesn't know where he is. So, by altering his signature, Claythorpe has eliminated a suitor for Joyce's hand. And tomorrow she is to be married to that numbskull, Francis.

She does not, however. Sometime in the night, Four Square Jane strikes, stealing both the wedding ring and the marriage license. Evidence suggests that Jane is likely Jane Briglow, a maid discharged for incompetence by Joyce's mother. There is certainly some connection for, as Mrs. Wilberforce notes, "All the people she is robbing are personal friends of ours, or of dear Lord Claythorpe."

Dear Lord Claythorpe is violently annoyed. He has been counting on the wedding, now postponed a year, to refresh his "almost bankrupt estate." And now death enters the story.

"The Murder in St. James' Street" concerns the death of Donald Remington, Claythorpe's confidential clerk. Remington intends to retire, as soon as Claythorpe pays him ten thousand pounds for services rendered. But payment is never made. Remington is found shot to death before Claythorpe's open safe. In the dead man's hand is the visiting card of Mr. Jameison Steele and on the safe door is the seal of Four Square Jane. It is at this point that the series gives a little shake and converts itself to a serial.

In the sixth episode, "Robbing the Royal Mail," it is immediately evident that Steele is being framed, for Scotland Yard knows he was in Falmouth at the time, with his wife. The mystery is not particularly deep, since Claythorpe has in his possession an American debenture certificate for 500,000 dollars—all that remains of Joyce Wilberforce's legacy. He seals this into an envelope, preparing to mail it out of the country for safety. But the envelope is seen by Joyce and, that night, Four Square Jane and a male assistant rob the mail and carry off a sack of letters.

These are returned to the post office in episode VII, "The Actress's Emerald Necklace." Since Joyce is now without a fortune, she receives Claythorpe's permission to marry whom she wishes. After inveigling 20,000 pounds from the Lord as a wedding present, she reveals that she has already married Steele and that some mysterious person had left the $500,000 certificate in her mail box.

At this point, Superintendent Dawes arrives, filled with suspicions as to the identity of Jane and the identity of the murderer. He visits Lewinstein, who points out that Jane, in most cases, has stolen nothing but presents given by Claythorpe. This is not particularly true, but Mr. Wallace is working hard to tie up the larger fragments of his plot and it would be discourteous to deny him that privilege.

Now follows the incident of the theft of an emerald collar during Lord Claythorpe's dinner party. It is a collar the Lord had given to an interesting actress. And then there is a scream, the lights go out...

VIII: "The Secret of a Box of Cigars": While members of the dinner party mill frantically about, Dawes recalls that one of the waiters had a stunted little finger. And so does Jamieson Steele. Immediately Dawes goes to Steele's apartment, finds that clever gentleman just returned from Scotland Yard. A search of the apartment reveals nothing.

No sooner does Dawes leave, than Steele removes the emerald collar from the bottom of a box of cigars and prepares to flit away. But he has been observed by a concealed Scotland Yard man and is arrested in the hotel lobby. At that very moment, Joyce arrives, flings herself wailing upon him, neatly slipping the collar from his pocket.

No, neither representative of Scotland Yard notices anything. It is a new low in detection.

After Joyce goes her way, *appassionata*, it occurs to the detectives to search their prisoner. But they find nothing in his pockets, nothing at all.

The rapturous improbability of these proceedings affects the modern nervous system like some irritant gas. Mr. Wallace, entirely unabashed, glides luminously along, impervious to the outrage of future generations.

One thing the police do accomplish: They discover a fingerprint on that visiting card held in Remington's dead hand. The print belongs to Lord Claythorpe and he is briskly arrested. He remains jailed only long enough to eat a poison button and so exits, grimacing horribly, from the story. These exciting events begin the final episode of the series, "The Great Escape."

It is Peter Dawes' sad responsibility to arrest Four Square Joyce and spouse. He goes to their apartment reluctantly, for all her crimes (except for robbing the mail) have been to recover portions of her legacy stolen by Claythorpe. Or so it is claimed, although the reader may notice that it took Mr. Wallace some time to arrive at this justification. The Steeles offer Dawes a cigarette and blithesomely confess the Four Square Jane crimes. Too late Dawes discovers that the cigarette was doped. While he slumbers, the Steeles exit over the rooftops, recover the $500,000 debenture from Claythorpe's desk, and leave for South America.

So ends the adventures of Four Square Jane, glittering froth, as previously mentioned but pleasantly appealing.

2-

Four Square Jane is an early work and a casual one. Its internal inconsistencies and incessant self-correction suggest that it was improvised in weekly installments, bursts of *Jane* being emitted like beams from a pulstar between intervals of more serious work.

For all its structural fragility, *Jane* incorporates at least one narrative element that sustained many another piece of 1920s crook fiction. This was the situation in which a bright young person must steal back his stolen inheritance. Although the literary origins of this theme have not been traced, it is suspected that Wallace adapted it from the ideas circulating at that time. During the 1920s, that theme, variously cut and polished, recurred in pulp magazine novels and such representative series as The Thunderbolt and The Avenging Twins *(Detective Story Magazine)* and Pat the Piper *(Flynn's Weekly)*. Wallace's influence in these series may be suspected, although the direct influence of *Four Square Jane* does not seem probable, since the stories were buried in the files of a weekly English newspaper for more than a decade and do not seem to have been reprinted until the book was issued in 1929.

Edgar Wallace exerted enormous literary influence during the 1920s. He was the great original, the glaring success, the master of the thriller. In both the adventure and the mystery-action story, he was supreme, playing melodramatic plots against fairly realistic backgrounds. He did not often venture into the closely related field of the mystery problem novel, then being tilled by Christie, Freeman, Wells, and a multitude of shining others.

A variety of American magazines published Wallace's short stories, serials, and articles. During 1918-1919, both *The Popular Magazine* and *Everybody's* featured his short stories. *Argosy All-Story* published "The

Policy Sleuth" series during 1920-1921, and *Short Stories* printed various novelettes during the 1920s. Other material appeared in the *Saturday Evening Post* (1922-1925) and *Collier's* (1926-1928). *Detective Story Magazine* began extensive publication of Wallace serials in the mid-1920s, adding series about The Ringer, the Just Men, O. Rater, and Sergeant Sir Peter during 1928. *Flynn's* published a series about Mr. Reeder in 1924, which was partially reprinted by the 1931 *Dime Mystery Book* and several novelettes were reprinted in the 1929 *Best Detective Stories*. Later Wallace appearances included reprint of some Sanders stories in the mid-1930's *Golden Book* and the late 1930s *Jungle Stories*. He also had published crime articles during 1930 in *Clues* and *Detective Fiction Weekly*. (A partial listing of Wallace serialized novels is provided in the Checklist.)

In his book, *The Durable Desperadoes*, William Vivian Butler remarks that Wallace was so popular during the 1920s "because he supplied heroes with whom anybody, in any walk of life, could comfortably identify."

That Wallace was a master of the action narrative had something to do with it, too. But it is true that his heroes, and his scoundrels, had an easy charm. As do most of the people passing through his pages.

They make up a reeling cast of characters: Aristocrats, gamblers, civil servants, policemen, money-lenders, bankers, newspapermen, and foreign fiends. These are well mixed with Americans, sea-faring men, Canadians, Australians, and ex-Colonels with bright red faces. All are tangled together, small criminals and great, members of the working class, members of the Establishment, their fates interwoven as tightly as a Chinese rug by mutually-shared secrets and plans.

Wallace did not deal in complex characters as much as complicated situations. Manfred of the Just Men is about as far as Wallace goes in presenting a complex personality. He is willing to suggest complexities, even to show a progression from bad to less bad. But the story is the prime object. Wallace's instinct was for action and the people of the story are stirred by constant gusts of emergency, dark gray menace, the vivid white line of violence. The characters sail to the demands of the plot, revealing themselves or not as it all works out.

Through the fiction move a great number of Lords and Ladies, Marquis This and Earl That and miscellaneous other bearers of noble blood. Some are impoverished. Others have not counted their millions. There are many fools, more of wit and ability. The affairs of the nobility customarily polarize the story. Around them, actively fermenting, boil all the other groups—criminals seeking wealth, business men with strange secrets, police who have to stop all those killings somehow.

Wealth generates problems that are particularly suitable for an action novel. Who wishes to bamboozle the poor and rob the pauper? That only happens in real ife. It is much more interesting to begin with a plot against Lady So-So, who has so much more to lose than Milly the Shoe Clerk.

Wallace views his Lords and Ladies with an ambivalent eye. If he were personally drawn by the advantages they enjoyed, his view was nonetheless dispassionate. Being born high was not sufficient. These Lords had to do something: stand for a principle, possess measurable skills. Otherwise you hear his pen grate bone.

For all his upper-class characters, Wallace managed a consistent, middle-class point of view. This is shared by all his main characters, noble or otherwise. They share a remarkable similarity in their thought patterns, ethical choices, and fields of interest.

The Wallace hero (and heroine) believes in the work ethic and social stability. He respects the value of information. He possesses sufficient physical strength and technical skills to prevent him from being either pushed around or easily fooled. He glories in technical expertise, respecting those accomplished in applied technology, whether they are whiskered tramps or paragons of perfect dress.

His sense of humor is quick, his integrity unshakable. Once his word is given all the powers of Hell cannot force a retraction. And all the heroes, from first to last, radiate such confidence that a glow of security fills you when they appear on the page. You can imagine how they affected the beleaguered heroine.

If a Wallace hero is ever ready to use his long-barreled Browning, he doesn't use it that often. The usual characteristic is not blood-thirstiness but omniscience. The Wallace heroes are incredibly well informed.

They have excellent memories and more than excellent information sources. Without hesitation, they can reel out the background and prison record of every old lag they meet. They know the secrets of Lord Deveny and Lady Helen. They can recount, down to the final seedy enterprise, how Major Carr sought enrichment. They know. Mr. J.G. Reeder knows. As does The Sooper, Sanders, the Just Men, and Four Square Jane.

Women share major roles with the men. Frequently three hundred pages of violence condense about the heroine. But she does not stand there passively, smelling of violets, while the villain weaves his web. Instead she plunges into the general melee.

Whether she is brunette or blond (almost always with grey eyes and a wide humorous mouth), whether she is short, tall, slender, or well formed, she is always intelligent. And unmarried. Most novels end with her engagement to the hero—and the audience sighing with satisfaction.

That's the way it should be, for these are fine girls. A few of them are crooks and a few more of them love crooks. A very few are damn fools who cause untold misery before they get their heads turned around. Whatever their characters, they participate actively in the adventure. They accompany the hero down sweating limestone steps into black peril beneath the mansion. Or they go there alone.

They handle a pistol almost as well as Nick Carter's Ida Jones. Under stress, they do not faint and they do not lose their poise. Most of them realize that something is very wrong when the sallow family lawyer urges them to sign a document and don't bother to read it.

Most heroines end up in positions of high peril, but they don't arrive there by being vapid. The villain must sweat blood to ensnare them.

The villain is another, less laudable, matter. In Wallace, we have no great difficulty determining who is the primary bad apple of the novel. Frequently he is a scientist or a doctor of something. His competence glitters; his intelligence is towering, if warped. His plans are vast, his assistants ready with knife and cosh, his facilities rich with automobiles, airplanes, and elaborate installations containing rooms filled with snakes and secret doors and concealed elevators or chambers that can be flooded and spectacularly wired houses.

A certain percentage of the villains are noblemen whose schemes have soured. Like Lord Claythorpe, they feast at the lip of bankruptcy, their reputations eroded and their prospects ash. Recoup their position, they must. They have drained the estate, the bank, the company, but more is needed to sustain the illusion of their integrity and worth. And so from crime to crime, their hopes flaking away as the chapters fly, and the girl's hand and the girl's fortune inexorably recede beyond their straining hands.

The lead criminal so completely concentrates self interest that he glows like a neon tube. His preoccupation with himself results in a lopsided character, rounded only by wickedness. His immediate aides are usually more complex. The secondary male criminal lead—often supported by a secondary feminine character—are usually developed in more detail than any other character of the novel.

In a customary subplot, the secondary criminal becomes revulsed by his actions and slowly grows to oppose the plans of the primary villain. Often he breaks free of the master mind, stealing quantities of the gang's funds and bolting from England.

These secondary characters, male and female, are firmly drawn. The men have a worn gentility that frays to desperation during the course of the story. The women tend to be sharp tongued and a little faded. These people, you feel, engaged Wallace's attention more than the predictable leads. You don't begrudge their escape at the end of the book, even though they gave the heroine a terrible time during early chapters.

Wallace's police are sympathetic and professional, although it is still years before Marric's Commander Gideon. With the exception of such early works as *Four Square Jane,* Wallace's police and Scotland Yard detectives are not fools. They have no illusions about crime, and unlike more modern characters, that knowledge has not soured them. They perform their jobs with discipline, usually without weapons, and with a gruff fondness for the petty criminals they arrest.

Among Wallace's law enforcement characters, two major types frequently appear. The first of these is older, given to cryptic statements and largely eccentric; they are inclined to investigate on their own and hold scandalous opinions of their superiors. In their ranks may be found Sgt. Elk, Superintendent Minter (The Sooper), and the admirable J. G. Reeder of the Public Prosecutor's Office.

A second recurring character is the wealthy young police official who looks and acts like a dude. (You will find him splendidly alive in *Angel Esquire.)* Glossy frivolity masks his acute mind. His clothing is faultless, his upbringing superb, his chatter volatile, but concealed within that impeccable sleeve is an arm of steel.

Since Lawrence Treat and *Dragnet* led us to sophistication, this character seems improbable. He works too much on his own, glitters with too hard a polish, reports to higher authority than any young man should chum with. And he has, even for fiction, a particularly flexible working schedule. Still, how efficient he is. How nicely he fits into the novels. What a fine fellow lies beneath that decorative facade.

Over the years, the major characters of the novels take on a predictable sameness. We wait for the entrance of the bright Scotland Yard genius. Or the cracked professor with a secret process and things to hide. Or the heroine, grey-eyed and lovely; somehow the fortune she knows nothing about is all tangled in the schemes of a crooked lawyer/banker/business man. She ought to love the hero but she is perverse, not acknowledging what her heart tells her.

Endless variations are played with these characters. It is never safe to assume that they will behave as they did in the last novel. Some plots wrench bitterly at the people. Others mechanically invert all characters on the final page—the good ones being revealed as evil wretches and the reverse. You are never sure. But the gray-eyed girl is almost always good.

3-

Several of these character types are foreshadowed in the pages of *Four Square Jane*. Here are the efficient young girl, the culpable nobleman, the high-ranking Scotland Yard youth. They are not yet quite in focus. Their outlines shimmer uncertainly, although, in them, you see the shape of characters to come.

In the two crime series that Wallace wrote immediately after *Jane*, the blithe young man steps to the center of the stage and establishes himself solidly as a character type with a very long shadow. In one series, he is named Anthony Smith; in the other, he is Anthony Newton. They are so closely similar that you have a persistent feeling of double vision.

The adventures of the Anthonys are given in two collections: *The Brigand* (January 1927) and *The Mixer* (August 1927). Each book offers the selected adventures of a splendid young man who supports himself handsomely by preying on crooked wealth. In each case he is an ex-military man who begins jobless, friendless (save for an Army crony or two), without prospects and without funds. He adapts his wits to the adventurer's life, ultimately finding success and, at last, the perfect girl.

Both Anthonys wear clothing to perfection and radiate a high-spirited innocence. Behind their guileless smiles lie minds shining with wit and imagination. They have a will to fleece the world's fleecers, to con the con men, and to extract from the shady rich, a tribute of gold.

Anthony Smith: "I am out to make money. I am the Invincible and Incomparable money-maker... And I have discovered that the easiest way to make money is to take it from men of your kidney."[6]

Both Anthonys are blood relations to a character type which Wallace got down on paper in the 1908 *Angel Esquire*, and which George Bronson-Howard had been featuring in a series since 1905. (His character, Norry, the Diplomatic Agent, appeared in *The Popular Magazine* from 1905 to 1923 and will be discussed later in a later volume.) This character type is that of the highly competent adventurer whose abilities are concealed by the perfection of his clothing; he seems a society dude, wealthy and brainless. The Dude had been a figure of fun on music-hall stages and in dime novels for at least fifty years before his assimilation into more formal mystery-adventure fiction.[7]

The first of Edgar Wallace's Anthonys enjoyed a publication history even more tangled than that of Four Square Jane. Anthony Newton, The Brigand, began his fictional career under the name Captain Hex. Together with his close, good friend, Belshazzar Smith, Hex glided through a short story series in the weekly newspaper, *The Sunday Post*, beginning February 9, 1919. The series was titled "The Adventures of

Captain Hex" and was signed E. Graham Smith, possibly a house name and certainly a pseudonym for Edgar Wallace.

About two years later, the series was slightly rewritten and republished in *The Novel Magazine,* 1922-1923. At this time, Hex seems to have been re-christened Anthony Newton and Belshazzar Smith became Big Bill Farrel. Four years passed before the stories were once again revised and collected in the book, *The Brigand* (1927). Five years later further reprints of the magazine stories began appearing, causing unutterable bibliographic complexities which need not ruffle the serene surface of this account.[8] Of all these appearances, only the lively book *The Brigand,* remains reasonably available to readers with a voracious appetite for out-of-print book lists.

For all the eccentric publication history of Newton's adventures, his book is a major link between the rather thin-blooded heroes of the 'Teens and those polished gentlemen rogues of the 1930s, The Saint, The Toff, The Baron, and Lester Leith. The Brigand is a happy combination of urban pirate, justice figure, and man about town, who contrives to live luxuriously by punishing the felonious, plucking away their stolen gold as deftly as would the reader, had he a little more time.

Newton does not begin his career in such brilliant circumstances. The series opens at the end of the First World War. London's streets are packed with ex-military men, unemployed and clawing for jobs that do not exist. Iron need clenches them. Among these men stands Anthony Newton, an ex-lieutenant of the Machine Gun Corps, a "soldier at sixteen; at twenty-six...a beggar of favors, a patient waiter in outer offices, a more or less meek respondent to questionnaires...."[9]

He is put out of his rooms for non-payment of rent. With no more than a coin or two in his pockets, he cons a lunch at a splendid hotel. Immediately he is marked for plucking by a confidence man who draws the wrong conclusion from Newton's glossy manner and impeccable clothing. The con man is rather crudely swindled out of a thousand dollars and Newton darts away to the delight of Sgt. Maud of Scotland Yard, who has watched it all.

The central theme has been struck: Newton will earn his living by exploiting the dishonest and Scotland Yard, slightly grinning, will tolerate his activities. For above all else, as Wallace puts it, "Anthony Newton was an honest adventurer."

Polite brigandage has its novel aspects and its moments of fascination. Vulgar men, crudely furnished in the matter of ideas, may find profit in violence, but the more subtle and the more delicate nuances of the act of gentle robbery had an especial attraction for one who...could count the game before the prize.[10]

In the second story, "On Getting An Introduction," he is still seeking honest employment. He attempts to get an introduction to millionaire Gerald Mansar by faking an automobile accident with Mansar's daughter, Vera. Mansar, however, recognizes Newton as an adventurer and, to teach him a lesson, sends him off to Brussels on a confidential mission, carrying a letter to Mansar's manager there. The letter merely instructs the manager to pay Newton's way back to London. The joke backfires. Newton returns to London, but does so via Berlin, Vienna, Constantinople, and Rome, expenses paid by Mansar's office.

The following story, "Buried Treasure," introduces Big Bill Farrel, Anthony's reliable, slow friend, also a hungry ex-military man. Together they swindle a millionaire butter king who is led by greed, and a forged document, to seek a box of diamonds buried under a little house in the country. They sell him the house. The document gets into the butter king's hands by incredible coincidence and equally incredible luck. But these are not stories to be read with a critical eye.

The fifth story, "The Lady In Gray," introduces a larger cast of characters, a group of out-of-work young ex-officers willing to assist Newton with some of his larger schemes. He enlists their aid with the same type of justification that excuses the activities of justice figures the world over. And most of the criminal figures so far viewed in this book.

Newton (to an eager audience of unemployed officers:)"...the surplus wealth is in the hands of two classes—the honorable and the dishonorable—the honest and the thief. And as there are quite a large surplus of thieves to operate upon, you needn't worry about...busting a band. The thing is to find a man with ill-gotten gains.... We, being soldiers of considerable merit and valor, find ourselves still at war with the enemies of honest finance and lawful behavior."[11]

It is virtually their duty, these guardians of finance and honest behavior, to strike the dishonest hip and thigh and pocketbook. And so they do. They swoop down upon two gambling clubs run by an unsavory and clean them out, somehow leaving the impression that they are police without ever saying so. During these raids, Newton manages to restore to a charming young lady—the lady in grey—the IOUs she had given to the head gambler. (The brute was forcing her to serve as hostess in one of his infamous houses; why, a man like that deserves to be...)

The group of officers reappear in the eighth story, "The Guest of the Minnows," assisting Newton in selling a defunct gambling club to a South American nogood. "The Bursted Election" recounts how Newton wins an election by tricking his opponent into temporary residence in a insane asylum; The Brigand becomes a Member of the House of

Commons for one week, before magnificently resigning. And in "Kato," Anthony and Big Bill assist an unfortunate Japanese gentleman seeking revenge and are nearly involved in a murder.

"The Graft," the final story, reintroduces Vera Mansar and her wealthy father. Perhaps you never expected to see them again, but every series must end in crinkles of happiness and it's best to crinkle with an engagement and two loving hearts entwined.

At any rate, Anthony Newton has become wealthy and successful. While doing a favor for a convict, he learns something about the activities of a Mr. Sadbury, a successful bigamist, and while he is musing upon the wickedness of men, meets Vera again. His heart pulses but she is not to be his. She is marrying her cousin, the rotter, Philip Lassinger. Her father, the bull-headed Gerald Mansar, insists. Does she love him? Certainly not. But then she is not sure whether she loves Anthony, either. Since the ending of a story this brief must be foreshadowed in the beginning, it will hardly disturb you to learn that Lassinger is really Sadbury, eager for additional bigamy. Anthony exposes him at the door to the church—and two months later is engaged to the trembling Vera.

The story of The Brigand concludes with an engagement and a smile, ingredients as essential now to the spun-sugar of television, as to the spun-sugar fiction of that remote time.

These fragile stories float like gossamer above the harsh times that birthed them. They give the impression of well-planed surfaces and sound angles, a geometric solidity bathed in light. It is illusion. They are as insubstantial as painted cobweb. Most of the characters are faceless, existing as an adjective, a trick of speech, a habit of action. Coincidence dominates the proceedings. Wallace's hand deftly arranges the scene and plants his devices as smoothly as a three-card Monte artist. The stories are half plot, half charm, all fluff, beautifully devised bubbles of entertainment.

The adventures of Anthony Newton, The Brigand, and Anthony Smith, The Mixer, are as intimately interwoven in time as cords in a macrame hanging. Smith's blithe activities began about a year after those of Captain Hex and in the same weekly newspaper, *The Sunday Post*. The series was titled "The Scallywags," written by Wallace under the name, John Anstruther. Ten episodes were published from April 25 through June 27, 1920. About a year later, the newspaper published a second series of eight short stories under the title, "The Return of the Scallywags," May 1 through June 19, 1921.

Six years later, both series were collected, revised, and published as *The Mixer* (1927), two additional stories being added for a total of twenty. The author was now given as Edgar Wallace. Two years later, during 1929-1930, the *Topical Times* magazine republished both

Scallywag series in their original form, crediting them to Edgar Wallace, rather than John Anstruther.[12]

These much reprinted adventures are bright romances, light hearted and filled with ingenious situations. The main action is carried by The Mixer, a cheerful twenty-four year old named Anthony. Whether his last name is Smith, which he once signs in a hotel register, or something less obvious, is not made clear, and the text dances along evading all efforts to provide Anthony with a family name.

The book begins with "The Outwitting of Pony Nelson," confidence man and card sharp, who is about to take an extended vacation. But before he leaves, he elects to earn another hundred pounds for expenses. He selects, for this purpose, a pair of drunken young men in evening dress:

They were not only well, but foppishly attired. Their gold-headed canes were thrust under their arms, and from the pocket of the handsome and noisy youth dangled a watch, the face of which was set about with brilliants. His companion was slightly older, less handsome, less boisterous, but obviously not less inebriated.[13]

Pony invites them for a nice game of cards. They accept and, after an hour's pleasure with a stacked deck, identify themselves as The Mixer and his friend, Paul. Mr. Nelson is then belted on the head with a Browning, and, as he sleeps, is relieved of 40,000 pounds, the proceeds of his activities to that time. It is not a particularly graceful robbery. It has the simple directness of Big Nose Charley's operations, a limitation likely imposed by the newspaper's restricted space.

In the following adventure, "The Great Geneva Sweepstake," a con man with a fraudulent sweepstakes scheme is tricked out of half his profits. The trickster is a very bright and talkative ex-Army officer named Smith, who was intended to become the patsy when the scheme finally collapsed.

"The Bank That Did Not Fail" tells of the downfall of Mr. Digle, a money lender who has also been collecting forged claims from the estates of dead officers. Learning from a client (Anthony) that his bank is about to fail, Mr. Digle draws out his funds. Then appears a fake Scotland Yard detective, a doped cigarette, and Mr. Digle awakes under a bush, handcuffed and thoroughly robbed.

Three young men are involved in these crimes against criminals. Anthony Smith, who wears clothes so well, is a combat officer who was "kicked out of the army most ignominiously for punching in the eye a young person who wore the badge of provost marshalship, but was not entitled to any other decorations because he had not been to France."[14] (It is the old quarrel between the combat and the garrison soldier.) He

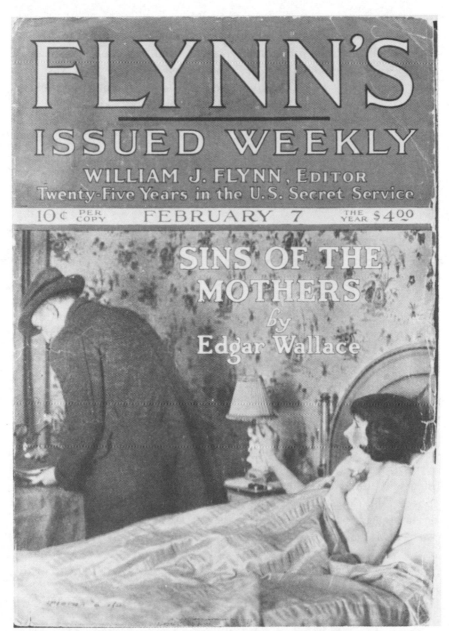

Flynn's (February 7, 1925). The serialized novels of Edgar Wallace, the most popular mystery writer of his day, swarmed through the 1920s magazines.

is a splendid actor and can compose his face into a mask of such cheerful blankness that swindlers feel their hearts rise at the sight of him.

His friend, Paul ("my secretary, companion, and general assistant"), is also an ex-combat officer who overstayed his leave and was court marshaled out of the service, regardless of his League of Honor award. Like most seconds to a brilliant lead, Paul is slightly slower than Anthony, slightly less prone to take risks. Anthony remarks that Paul is "an extremely moral man (who)...would have taken to rascal-skinning on his own account, being very unwilling to return to hum-drum pen-driving, and very tired of looking for it, when I met him."[15]

Moral rascal-skinning is a dubious profession that works only because:

...the Mixer is one of the mildest, most unobjectionable heroes imaginable.... Edgar Wallace had given a still semi-puritanical public a crook hero whom they couldn't fail to warm to, because he was *as morally judicious as they were.*[16]

The third member of the team is Sandy, Anthony's batman during the war, now become a combination valet, chauffeur, and talented handyman. He performs all those essential tasks required to make the plot work, the silent engineer oiling the machinery.

The three of them make a pleasant team, but matters do not invariably go their way. In "A Speculation in Shares," Anthony passes some worthless shares to a swindler, only to discover that they were of value, after all. And in "A Close Call—And Its Sequel," that sly woman, Milwaukee Meg, supplies Anthony with counterfeit bank notes and he narrowly escapes arrest. He returns the favor by sending her a purse lined with the same notes and she is arrested. She reappears in "Mr. Sparkes, the Detective," determined to get The Mixer before she leaves England. Anthony strikes first, however. Disguised as a seedy private detective, he drugs Meg and friend and departs with all their worldly goods. And, incidentally, saves the innocent young Agnes Stillington from the evil intentions of one of Meg's lieutenants. (By the end of the series, Miss Agnes will become Anthony's intended. Since Mr. Wallace failed to provide her with any personal characteristics, other than an inability to type, she will not be described in these pages.)

Meg is penniless but her mind flares with schemes. "The Submarine-Chaser Coup" tells how she cleans out Anthony's safe-deposit box and leaves England, hauling along the gullible Agnes. Anthony intercepts their ship with a war surplus submarine chaser he has purchased. He swings aboard in a naval officer's uniform and, in a matter of pages, has secured the stolen funds and swept Agnes away to Spain.

"A Strange Film Adventure" is the final story of the first series. Agnes has been sent back to England, preserving her moral perfection for another time, and The Mixer and Meg have a last encounter—to his profit and her rage.

Now a year passes in the life of the series. As it is explained in "The Girl from Gibraltar," first story of the second group:

After a long holiday, The Mixer had ventured to test the forgetfulness of those whose vigilance had made it advisable for him to leave this part of the world some time ago.[17]

During this story, he swindles a gambler and saves the virtue of a foolish young lady who trusts the wrong man. Back in England, he finds a way to embarrass a rich pain-in-the-neck ("A Gambling Raid," Chapter XII of *The Mixer,* and one of the episodes added for book publication). Then, in quick order, he fleeces another swindler ("The Silk Stockings"), a designing woman ("The Case of Dolly De Mulle"), and a con man out to defraud an Indian prince ("The Seventy-Fourth Diamond").

"The Billiter Bank Smash, Chapter XVII of *The Mixer* (and the second story added to that collection), tells how Anthony locates an absconding bank director. Following that exploit, he punishes the practitioner of The Spanish Prisoner confidence game, and resteals some stolen German crown jewels.

As his last act in the series, he clears up a will fraud which would have left Agnes Stillington a pauper. And with this, the adventures come to an end, gloriously. Just in time.

The Miser: "...I think I have gone just about as far as I can, and I am not at all anxious to take a term of penal servitude, particularly as I find my bank balance in a condition most conducive to virtue. I have arranged to leave this country in a month, and I am taking with me a wife."[18]

Which may have been news to Agnes; on this glowing note, however, *The Mixer* closes.

Neither *The Brigand* nor *The Mixer* seems to have been published in the United States, although a significant number of copies leaked in from England and Canada. They do not appear to have leaked in sufficient number to influence directly the development of American series criminals—if people as mild and good-hearted as the Anthonys could be classified as criminals.

Their influence was exerted indirectly (which would have pleased these polished tricksters) through the far more spectacular activities of

Simon Templar, The Saint. The scale is quite different. The Saint's incandescent white glare obliterates the Anthonys' modest candlelight. Templar is a figure towering more than life size, richly developed, the quintessence of the romantic outlaw at large in the modern world. He is his own man. Cascades of books from 1928 through the 1970s, at least forty-six by Leslie Charteris and others, have traced his life and developed his personality to complexities undreamed of by the Anthonys.

Yet traces of The Brigand and The Mixer linger in the earlier Saint adventures. Like the Anthonys, he dresses at the crest of fashion and taste. He earns a splendid living by his wits, preying on distinctly unpleasant criminals, avenging their victims, and administering a rough justice which is as often witty as violent.

Through the Saint, the impeccable young adventurer, facetious, lethal, and admirable, entered the bloodstream of 1930s fiction. Which is another, later story. He is a giant. But more than the legend of Robin Hood energizes his bright buccaneering.

4-

Crime against property was a popular story theme in the 1920s (popularity being a convenient measure of readers' suppressed impulses of sin). Crime against the person was also a popular theme, but less often was it the forte of a major fictional character. We may count Fantomas, The Just Men, Hopalong Cassidy, and Mr. Chang among the few characters who habitually killed, yet survived in series.

Henry Arthur Milton, The Ringer, is one of these elect.

From the beginning, there is no question about Milton's predilection for blood. He is an escaped convict with a knife and a clear, methodical intelligence. He is out for revenge, "...a cold-blooded, logical man, without the slightest respect for human life—or personal property."[19]

His wife, Cora Ann, has even more positive emotions:

"God, how that man frightens me—frightens me sick! He's got one idea—kill...kill...kill!"

What makes Milton particularly dangerous is that he is a genius of disguise. Only Colonel Clay and Fantomas are his equals.

His name reflects his gift. "The Ringer" stands for "Ringer of Changes." He is, first of all, a character actor of towering gifts. He flows into a part and his ability to create convincing personalities with a minimum of make up is fearsome.

Police records describe him as being 33 years old, 66-inches tall, fair complexion, with light brown hair and gray eyes. He speaks fluent French, German, Italian, Arabic, and American. He is independently wealthy. At first, his deadly work is done with knives, although he later adopts other weapons.

During the First World War he was a Captain in the Flying Corps. Even then, he had an aversion to being photographed, never appearing in the squadron's commemorative pictures. Nor was he interested enough in the small change of heroism to accept the medals offered him.

How this coldly self-effacing man married the vivid Cora Ann is hard to understand. How the marriage endured is stranger.

Cora was originally a member of a United States blackmail ring. Slipping from the States ahead of the police, she met Milton on board ship, married him. Thereafter, she spent a lot of time wondering where he was—and who he looked like.

She was a dainty little exquisite, beautifully dressed, lavishly perfumed, golden haired, with a strong American accent.

Her features were regular and small, the chin too full for perfection, her eyes a limpid blue. She owed something to art for the clarity of her complexion and the redness of her full lips.

The Miltons are genuinely in love—the blackmail shill and the murderer adore each other. But it is a difficult marriage. The police use Cora as a stalking horse to locate Milton, for there are warrants against him in eighteen countries. It becomes dangerous to come near her. He is reduced to standing disguised in places where she walks, so that he can look at her. Only once does she recognize him. It is a somewhat tenuous relationship.

The Ringer first appeared in Edgar Wallace's novel, *The Gaunt Stranger* (1925), US title, *The Ringer* (1926). In 1926, the novel was extensively ploughed up and turned into a play, "The Ringer." The play, in turn, gave birth to a motion picture (1928) and a renovelization of the play. This later book, for clarity also titled *The Ringer* (1929), is largely different from *The Gaunt Stranger*.

During 1928, Wallace had continued the character in a series of seventeen short stories, some of these appearing in *Detective Story Magazine*. The stories were later collected into the book, *Again the Ringer* (1929) (US title: *The Ringer Returns*, 1931).

These facts do not quite tell the story. For the first part of his career, Milton is that standard figure of the thriller—a murderous escaped convict seeking vengeance. During the later part, he metamorphoses to a justice figure, a direct literary descendent of the Just Men.

All this makes a curious history.

The Gaunt Stranger is a richly atmospheric novel of suspense. It

follows the crooked lawyer, Meister, through the final days of his life—
a network of plots, intrigues, manipulations, all well basted in a simmer
of terror. He had betrayed Milton; now he waits to die.

The disguised Ringer—seen only in brief sentences—edges slowly
toward his victim, patient, inexorable. If he is invisible, the menace he
represents is as real as the smell of ammonia. His presence swells ever
more horridly behind the complex tanglings of the sub-plots.

As the story progresses, Meister slowly disintegrates with fear. He
is one of Wallace's unpleasant men, a liar and seducer, a calculating
cheat. By the end of the book, he has earned every inch of the blade
that slays him.

The Ringer strikes. Two swift murders. And then the police trap
snaps shut on Milton. With characteristic foresight, he has provided
against even this. As the police lead him past the car in which Cora
sits:

There was a thundering report, the 'flick' of a white flame, and Henry Arthur Milton
dropped into the detective's hands, dead.[20]

Which should end The Ringer's story. However, as you recall, the book
became a play.

The play became a large popular success. (Leon Gonzales, one of
the Just Men, attended it and was struck by the blackout scene in which
Meister is murdered.) The play, however successful, severely reworked
the book material. The brooding tension was diluted by more obvious
thrills: Sinister faces peer through windows, broad red herrings are hauled
flopping across the stage, and a new character, Inspector Bliss, is
introduced. All this in addition to a massive reconcentration of the main
sub-plots, during which the melodrama of the book is heightened and
simplified.

When Wallace later prepared a renovelization of the play, he dedicated
the revised book to Sir Gerald DuMaurier, who had staged "The Ringer."

This book is "The Gaunt Stranger" practically in the form that you and I shaped it
for the stage. Herein you will find all the improvements you suggested for "The Ringer"—
which means a better story than "The Gaunt Stranger."[21]

Mr. Wallace is by no means the first author to misjudge the value
of a work. The 1929 version, *The Ringer,* is a much lighter book than
The Gaunt Stranger. It is filled with described stage effects, which may
have worked for a play, where visual effects are essential; the same effects,
translated to fiction, contribute little.[22]

The play did have one unexpected side effect: It resulted in The

Ringer's survival as a series by returning him to life.

Cora still shoots him. But this time, the cartridge is a blank.

Wembury...wrenched the revolver from her hand. As he did so, The Ringer rose swiftly from the place where he had been lying limp and apparently lifeless, and walked out of the door...[23]

(It is narrated stage direction, you may notice.)

From the play, Wallace also drew a new major figure, Inspector Bliss, who will appear throughout the short stories. In the 1929 novelization, Bliss is a short little sourball who wears a clipped black beard and is cordially hated by his associates. That portrait was drastically altered in the later fiction.

As the 1928 story series opens, The Ringer is still a fugitive, still disguising himself with genius. But Wallace has moderated Milton's homicidal streak to a mere scarlet line. In every way, The Ringer is less the active criminal of *The Gaunt Stranger*, more the disengaged observer standing outside of society who intrudes when pernicious wrongs need be corrected. It is the classic position of the justice figure.

As a wealthy man, unfettered by economic need, The Ringer slips invisibly about England and Europe, interested in everything, molesting no one. Although he will strike with no gentle hand if an incautious criminal uses the name of The Ringer in vain (as in "The Murderer of Many Names") or pontificates about him in the newspapers ("The Man With the Beard"). His response is not always murderous, for The Ringer is much tamed. Perhaps the killing of Meister has calmed him. Now his mode of action is similar to that of the Just Men, although The Ringer kills with rather less restraint, when he kills.

But first, in the manner of the Just Men, he sends warnings. These are typed on a portable machine whose out-of-alignment 's' and faint-tailed 'p' are only too familiar at Scotland Yard.

The warnings are terse:

Find another occupation. I shall not warn you again.

Others arrive as business-like death notices:

On this date, you did thus-and-so. The consequence was that... (Like other Wallace characters, The Ringer's information is detailed and correct.) As you are a man of considerable property and may wish to have time to make arrangements as to its disposal, I will give you a little grace. At the end of a reasonable time I shall come to London and kill you. ("The Man with the Red Beard")

Those subjects of his terminal art are painted in shades of black, unrelieved by human warmth. In "The End of Mr. Bash—the Brutal," The Ringer deftly fools a slugging safecracker into smashing a globe of poison gas, believing that it is his wife's head; and in "The Blackmail Boomerang," a blackmailer is dispatched for draining a particularly nice woman.

Such people are casually stamped out with the readers' tacit approval. But to a large extent, that quality of kill, kill, kill which so horrified Cora Ann has faded from these stories. It has been replaced by "a broad streak of altruism...perhaps, as big a streak of impishness."

In one instance, he saves an innocent man from execution by impersonating a particularly pig-headed politician ("Case of the Home Secretary," which appeared in the June 2, 1928, *Detective Story Magazine*, as "The Ringer To the Rescue.") In other episodes, he runs down a scientific murderer of the aged in "The Sinister Dr. Lutteur"; he forges a will to frustrate a thief who is stealing an estate ("The Fortune of Forgery"). And he finds a way to blackmail a sexy professional blackmailer ("The Complete Vampire," also titled "The Ringer and the Vamp" in the June 23, 1928, *Detective Story Magazine.)*

These neatly plotted little stories, bright as candy drops, are warmed by humorous understatement:

'If I drop dead this minute,' said Cully virtuously, 'I burnt them letters.'
He did not drop dead that minute, proving beyond any doubt that Providence gives a miss to the most tempting invitations. ("The Blackmail Boomerang")[24]

Or this:

It was a tiny house with a tiny garden; and if the brothers had searched diligently in the untidy forecourt they would have discovered a board announcing that this "desirable residence" was to let. ("The Obliging Cobbler")[25]

Or this,

Colonel: "Is (the Home Secretary) likely to be influenced by you, Inspector?"
Insp. Bliss: "If I agree with him, yes; if I don't, no."[26]

The Inspector Bliss of the short stories is a more popular man than in the novel. Still close-mouthed, he has grown uncommonly efficient. He is the Yard's Ringer specialist and, for him, The Ringer has a warm admiration. Twice he saves Bliss' life ("The Escape of Mr. Bliss") and in all episodes, keeps him well supplied with typewritten notes of advice and guidance.

Throughout the short stories, Bliss is saddled with Chief Inspector Mander, a gentleman who had "a wonderful knack of appearing clever to the right people." Mander is, unfortunately, a popinjay of insignificant intelligence, whose role in the story is to be deflated by The Ringer. He provides a humorous figure against which the darker elements of the story may be played off, and he gives the reader someone to feel superior to.

Mander's first appearance is in "The Trimming of Paul Lumiere," where The Ringer makes a fool of him—with the considerable help of Edgar Wallace. Thereafter he appears in seven other stories, full of the conceit that never learns. "A Yard Man Kidnapped" describes his meeting with Cora Ann. Mander doesn't know her. She feeds him a doped cigarette and he ends in an intensely embarrassing situation from which the sardonic Bliss must retrieve him.

Even the longest series winds at last to the sea, its adventures expended and its readers gone in the crush of years. So, in the dreadful slipping of time, the brief Ringer series should have snuffed out, an artifact of the past, treasured only by those living artifacts who rake the cinders of old books. But it did not happen that way. The Ringer is remembered, in England, at least, and his books remain alive through the generations. He has joined that happy few, The Just Men and J. G. Reeder among them, who survived along the road from the 1920s. What they lack in realistic tension and sexual situation, they more than make up for by their charm and joyous rightness. They are simple as a pearl necklace and glow as warmly. They offer no complex emotional states, no questing after those ethical ambiguities that prick our modern minds. They do depict violence and glimpses of angry men, yet they also offer views of a world where violence and anger are not the only available currency. They are possessed by optimism. They glitter with it, like waves in the sunlight. The water beneath may be dangerously deep and haunted by terrible teeth, but concealed danger by no means invalidates the sunlight or its bright reflections.

5-

The Wallace vision brightened two generation of pulp magazine fiction, for he was highly influential. His personal success beckoned others to follow after him, eager for such portions of the Golden Calf as their wit might earn. It is said that the house name, Robert Wallace, appended to the 1933-1953 Phantom Detective novels, was coined to skim some of the magic associated with Wallace's name. But few could imitate his bright style, witty and contemporary, that provided an object lesson in the techniques of spreading melodramatic action on realistic bread.

They tried. In a thousand derivative stories appeared his plot twists and devices, his point of view, his costumed villains, his competent heroes racing through the night, his firm-minded heroines. Through The Saint,

Wallace's glossy young adventurers, quick-minded and brash, became a literary type, recognizable at a glance. His altruistic justice figures, social prophets with heavy-caliber Brownings, condoned violence for the public good and so set the stage for the generation of 1930s mystery figures and crime avengers.

To the formal language of early 1900 fiction, Wallace brought the sting of contemporary dialogue. He gave faces and voices to a novel slice of the social scene—the petty professional criminal. Only in O. Henry do you find a similar swarm of the modern, urban lost— the burglars, failed salesmen, and seedy touts, the street crooks and the night floaters-that move through Wallace's fiction. They are minor figures all, but presented sympathetically; he understood the unsuccessful. They live warmly on his pages. He intensified the literary tradition in which he worked. Those contributions he made to the craft of the mystery-adventure have since been obscured by the vivid technical abilities of those who followed him, their excellencies enabled by his. But he led the way, and his charm binds you to him.

V—IN NAME ONLY

1-

People are too perverse to remain labelled for long. Call a man wise or a woman an angel, if it pleases you. But be prepared, before the day is out, to change your opinion. Call a man a criminal—a more vivid opinion than either "wise" or "angel"—and you may be shocked to find yourself wrong again. For on the eighth appeal, his conviction may be overturned, freeing him, righteous and unstained, to continue improving society in his own, unique way.

If it is hard to identify a criminal in life, it is nearly impossible in fiction. Each of those we have met so far is a special case: This master criminal is really a naughty boy who loves to tease; that stick-up artist is only an urban adventurer expressing his annoyance at a limping social system.

And this splendid group of men and women gathered here, well-washed, soft-spoken, intelligence and competence illuminating their faces. Criminals? You may call them so. But they are criminals in name only. In reality, they are frightfully misjudged.

No urge for easy money tarnishes their minds. They may be trusted to invest the widow's mite and scorn the politician's deal. They abridge no man's right, pay women equal wages, drive at the posted speed limit, pay every splinter of their income tax. They are model citizens. Yet every one is smirched black as Rafferty and Big Scar with crime.

It is limited, specialized, restricted crime, having that peculiar literary knack of breaking the letter of the law to preserve its spirit. Part of this group includes some splendid thieves and daring adventurers who have gone wrong for likely very good reasons. They balance raffishly between banditry and social protest. Their faces are unknown, for they would stoop to nothing so vulgar as a police record. And in their hearts grow the seeds of reform, forever promising leaves and weighty fruits. If their past is not blameless, their future is richly promising. They repent youthful folly; they acknowledge error in their old ways; they attempt to peel away crime's old skin, although circumstance and unrelenting authors persistently work against them.

123

A second group of criminals is even more blameless. Of these, some merely pose as criminals to avenge wrongs. Others seek to punish a small coterie of the unrighteous, who sit serenely armored by wealth and social or political influence. Those proceeding outside the law to avenge or punish are, technically, criminals. Still, we know they are not. Like Four-Square Jane, they turn to crime for only a brief period of time, for only a limited purpose. Once their mission is complete (leaving the wicked twitching like grubs amid the shards of their schemes), these criminals are criminals no longer.

It is all highly satisfactory, in a literary sort of way.

2-

In the doorway crouches a terrible figure.

Nondescript black clothing covers his husky body. From one black-clad fist juts a heavy automatic. The figure has no face—only a smooth, black, horribly sleek head.

It is an illusion. The head and throat are concealed beneath an elastic black hood. Thin slits have been cut for eyes and mouth. On the shining black forehead is painted a yellow lightning bolt.

"Don't move," grates a low, tense voice, "or you will never again cheat another orphan or widow."

The Thunderbolt has come for your ill-gotten gains.

Which assumes that you are one of the Big Six—those crooked financiers.

Young John Flatchley, back from the first World War, finds himself heir to his uncle's $200,000 estate. So immense is this inheritance that Flatchley investigates its origins. He discovers that it is fat with the profits his uncle realized from a shady deal, nothing less than legal robbery. And six other financiers participated in the swindle and in the spoils.

To these six men—the Big Six—goes young Flatchley, his jaw grimly set.

Flatchley (pointing accusingly): "You are thieves who robbed widows and orphans. If your deal was legal, it was morally a swindle. To cleanse the name Flatchley, I am returning the money my uncle left me. I want you to return your shares."
The Big Six: "We scorn your unrealistic proposal."
Flatchley: "You will pay, willingly or not."

Scotland Yard (August 1931). The costumed criminal and his hordes further spiced the melodramatic violence of 1930s pulps.

With this premise, the story of The Thunderbolt opens. It was a six-novelette series that ran in the *Detective Story Magazine* during 1920 and 1921. It is a pleasing example of the limited-objective criminal hero theme, a justice figure stalking outside the Law to punish the wicked, secure behind their lawyers and their police. It is also one of the earlier examples of the costumed hero.

At the time The Thunderbolt appeared, the costumed series hero was still a novel magazine device but it was not a new device. Before McCulley's characters, the Baroness Emmuska Orczy's popular hero, The Scarlet Pimpernel, had appeared on stage and in novel, in 1905. Before The Pimpernel, the dime novels and story papers sparkled with heroes— cowboys, detectives, and general avengers—who donned costumes to champion the right. In those remote times, however, costumes were primarily reserved for the more dramatically inclined criminals, whose gaudy schemes of loot and murder were enhanced by equally gaudy outfits. Through the dime novels had pranced a long series of criminal fiends outfitted as devils, buccaneers, Restoration gallants, clowns, little known monsters, and fearsome specters. They stalked about weirdly, glaring and orating, a joy to the discriminating taste. Their costumes were limited only by the writers' ingenuity and the readers' willingness to believe anything.

The dime novels had drawn their wonders from many sources, among them hooded figures from Gothic novels and the more contemporary Ku Klux Klan, and mystery figures from the deeps of the literary tradition formed during the early 1700s.

The mystery figure, which developed as a separate costumed line, lurked and spied and glided weirdly through the night, often laughing in a terrible voice. It was dramatically enveloped in a great black cloak and slouch hat, revealing only a pair of burning eyes and deathly white hands and face. Its role was that of half-seen menace and it could be either saint or devil, which added a desirable pinch of dread to even the most leaden Gothic fiction. In later years, it was employed by such diverse talents as Charles Dickens and Louisa May Alcott. The mystery figure appeared in the dime novels about as frequently as exclamation points. As we have previously seen, it also popped up in French popular fiction as Fantomas, that monster of evil, and, during the 1930s, as The Shadow, lethal figure for justice.

While a distinct convention in its own right, the mystery figure is a branch of the costumed tradition. That tradition reached a crescendo of sorts in the magazines, books, films, and radio drama of the 'Thirties. For almost a decade, the volcano of popular fiction hurled out a dazzle of Argus-glass helmets, bat-winged capes, colored hoods, devil suits and octopus suits, Lama robes, and masks, masks, masks.

The fad exhausted itself in the early 1940s. It collapsed into that permissive sanctuary, the comic book, where it remained, like beer fermenting in the basement, until the coming of television.

So the convention of a costumed figure capering through mystery-adventure fiction did not spring up unexpectedly, like a pay raise in Congress. The costumed figures of the 1930s were an extension of roots evolved across the generations and exploited in the pulp magazines of the mid-'Teens and 'Twenties. Particularly these figures had been exploited in *Detective Story Magazine,* where the foremost practitioner was Johnston McCulley, that great popularizer of costumed adventure.

McCulley's first costumed series character was Black Star (1916), that robed, masked genius of crime met in Chapter II. A few years later in *All-Story Weekly* (1919), McCulley introduced Zorro, a caped, masked justice figure of Old California. Both characters demonstrated once more the viability of fiction featuring a costumed lead character. Then in 1920, McCulley created the first of his urban, costumed justice figures. This was The Thunderbolt. Following him, in 1921, came The Man In Purple, and, in 1926, The Crimson Clown—a bent hero who preyed upon wealthy untouchables.

The costumed strain that flared so brightly in the 1930s pulp magazines owes a great deal to McCulley. The convention was long established when he adapted it to his fragile fictions, bright and shallow as a trout stream, with energy and good humor replacing realistic settings and character depth. But if he did not originate the form, he certainly confirmed it as an acceptable part of the popular fiction scene.

The Thunderbolt, then, was the first of the modern costumed heroes. He prowled the city, pistol in hand, fantastically dressed, every man against him. But what is that to an essentially innocent heart; it is a matter of record that he shed not one drop of blood. The qualifications of John Flatchley, The Thunderbolt, are those of every outstanding Street & Smith hero. A combat pilot in World War I, he "loved excitement and adventure. He had hunted big game, been a member of a North Pole expedition, and made a record for bravery in the war."

He is thirty years old, a wealthy clubman of prominent old family, a bachelor. He is a talented student of architecture. He likes fast cars and boats. He flies airplanes. He is tall, broad-shouldered, an athlete. Rarely does he come near the girls. For in his heart blazes the image of Miss Agnes Larimer. Yet he cannot speak to her of love. Not yet. Not until The Thunderbolt has finished striking.

This is the situation as the first novelette begins, "Master and Man" (May 4, 1920).

The first of the Big Six selected for punishment is Conner Bradford, his mansion safe crammed with crooked gains. Through the darkness, The Thunderbolt glides unseen.

But hark!

He hears a panting, fumbling approach.

He closes with the newcomer, there in the darkness:

"Silence! Don't make a move. You're a dead man if you do."

The Thunderbolt has captured Saggs, a petty crook. Worse—an incompetent, bungling crook. So inadequate is Saggs that no other crook will have anything to do with him.

Five feet four was Saggs. He had heavy, stooped shoulders, short and thick arms, and gigantic hands. His head was poorly formed. Any scientist would have declared that the ears stuck out too straight from it, that the eyes were too small and glittering and much too close together, the lips rather thick and the lower jaw too heavy.[1]

Saggs has failed at everything—at valeting, at the crook business. Broke, friendless, disdained, he has slunk into this mansion hoping to find something he can pawn.

To continue. . . .

The Thunderbolt recognizes Saggs as being a fear-crumpled petty crook. This being a Johnston McCulley story, his natural response is, "Come along. If I take a fancy to you, your future is assured."

Together they slip into Bradford's bedroom. There The Thunderbolt shows Bradford the hollow end of an automatic (he carries the weapon unloaded but who's to know). Like all McCulley millionaires, Bradford promptly disintegrates with terror. Slobbering, sweating, shaking, he begins to dial open his safe.

Meanwhile. . .

Detective Martin Radner, of the police force, has spotted Saggs slinking across the mansion lawn. Hoping to capture him and impress Bradford (who might do something nice for Radner's career), the detective sprints away for a squad of police. When they arrive, wearing cardboard noses and sugar-loaf hats, Saggs glimpses their arrival. The Thunderbolt eases him away, leaving behind the Bradford pearls. Radner and police give chase but are successfully dodged at Flatchley's club. Thereafter, Flatchley takes Saggs to a fourth-floor apartment in a towering building. It is "furnished lavishly, yet in excellent taste."

Then and there, Flatchley explains all about The Thunderbolt.

"I am determined to rob those crooked financiers, and then send the proceeds anonymously to their victims. I am going to force them to pay back every penny with interest. And

I have just six men upon whom I am to work."[2]

To the cynical modern reader, whose heart is as a shriveled radish, it would seem the height of brainlessness to confide your secret and illegal business to an obvious crook with a poorly formed head. But self preservation is not a virtue practiced by 1920s heroes. They don't know what fear is. Or discretion, either.

Tonight, Flatchley says, tonight he intends to strike. And off they go once more, via a dumb waiter to the basement of the apartment house, from the basement back across town to the Bradford mansion. There Radner lingers, discoursing—no less—on Black Star. In from the gloom darts The Thunderbolt. He shows them his pistol and ties both up. Then he opens the safe, accidentally setting off a secret alarm. Swarms of police promptly swoop down once again. But The Thunderbolt has foresightedly planned an alternate escape route. He and Saggs go slipping down the electric cables between house and alley and so vanish again into the night.

The second story occurs two weeks later (series time) or on June 29, 1920, *Detective Story Magazine* time. In this, "The Kidnapped Midas," The Thunderbolt's identity is guessed by all participants, from the millionaires to Radner to Miss Agnes Larimer.

> *Agnes:* "I think that you are taking things from those men who were associated with your uncle."
> *Flatchley:* "...I'll not have your name mixed up in it at all.... We can have no (engagement) announcement as long as there is danger of me being apprehended."[3]

That reasoning accounts for the very large number of unmarried heroes in the 1930s pulps. As you may recall, Richard Wentworth, The Spider, kept his fiancee, Nita Van Sloan, waiting for 118 issues, for the identical reason. Agnes' wait will not be so extended.

And now, as omnious purple clouds lower balefully in the sullen sky, and the Heavens mutter with thunder's hollow guttural, in the apartment of John Flatchley, grave doings eventuate. Flatchley beckons his new valet, Saggs, to approach. The plotting of crime impends.

These conferences most usually begin with a moment of droll foolery:

> *Flatchley:* "Do you happen to notice any sort of change taking place in me, Saggs?"
> *Saggs:* "No, sir."
> *Flatchley:* "Nevertheless, Saggs, I am changing. Watch closely, Ah-I am no longer John Flatchley—now I am The Thunderbolt."[4]

By an identical magic, Saggs ceases to be a valet and transforms to The Thunderbolt's assistant. The transformation is accompanied by a sudden deterioration in the precision of his English.

Then to the immediate problem. Out there, in popular fiction land, a shuddering millionaire trembles behind a screen of police. By his elbow glowers Martin Radner, shedding cigar butts like a Cuban Christmas tree.

How can The Thunderbolt strike through Radner's defenses?

Flatchley has a plan. Good gracious, he always has a plan. He is a most audacious young man. The plan in "The Kidnapped Midas" is to abduct Cyrus Grantburg from his bedroom. He will then be lugged across town and forced to open his office safe, although the office suite is guarded by layers of detectives.

Back at Grantland's apartment, Radner smokes peacefully, lulled by the sound of Grantburg's snores—for, as a snorer, the millionaire is equal to 12.3 on the Richter scale. Too late, Radner discovers that he has spent the evening listening to a phonograph record of snoring.

By then Grantburg has been thoroughly robbed, the criminals long escaped to their fourth-floor nest, the black costume long concealed somewhere in the kitchenette.

Humiliated, Radner calls down the flaming hosts:

"I have arranged to have Flatchley watched every minute day and night. He is to be shadowed by our best men. His apartment house is to be watched all the time. We have placed a reliable operative in his club to watch him there. He will be trailed by good men wherever he goes."[5]

Little good does this vast expenditure of talent and money. At a society dance, The Thunderbolt steals the fabulous Flaming Star—a ruby cluster—from the wife of one of those reprehensible millionaires. (The story is "The Big Six," September 7, 1920.) Instantly Flatchley is grabbed and searched. The guests are searched. Flatchley, the house and the grounds are searched.

Nothing.

No wonder. The Flaming Star has been slipped into Radner's pocket. He does not discover this until The Thunderbolt swoops down on him in the park, ties him up tight, and departs with the cluster.

Nor does anyone see John Flatchley enter or leave his apartment house, Of course not. In these stories, any policeman can be lured from his post at any time. They are good-humored fellows and enjoy giving Johnston McCulley a lift over the rough edges of his story.

Flatchley needs little help to enter or leave. During "The Thunderbolt Collects" (December 11, 1920), he arranges to have himself locked into a small vault. It is part of a fancy society magic show. Manacles bedeck him, and Radner's own handcuffs secure his wrists. Yet The Thunderbolt (conspicuously unfettered) strikes the financiers still again. And when the vault is opened, there lies Flatchley, still gripped in Radner's handcuffs. Only once does Radner come close to sending The Thunderbolt down. This occurs during "The Thunderbolt's Engagement" (July 30, 1921). Flatchley has reached the end of his mission: He is robbing the last safe of the last of the Big Six. And at this delicate moment, enter Radner, eyes hot, pistol steady.

The worst has happened. The series is about to end in arrest, disgrace, misery.

Then Radner's attention wavers for a microsecond. Flatchley instantly whips out his automatic, shoots out the lights. He flees. Behind him races a sprawling pack of police, shooting, shouting through the dark streets. In all the confusion, they fail to check that innocent trash can.

Within lurks Flatchley, concealed until the police depart and Saggs arrives with the car to drive him away.

It is the moment of The Thunderbolt's departure.

Saggs drives to a woods near the river. Flatchley leaves the car and

"....went into the woods for a short distance.... There he stripped off the thin black coat and trousers, put them into a pile, and added his gloves and the hood of The Thunderbolt. He emptied the bottle of kerosene over the pile...

"This was to be the death of The Thunderbolt. His work was at an end...

"He stooped and touched a match to the pile, watched the flame start, then darted quickly through the woods."[6]

And so these revels end.

Punished, humiliated, sour, the six financiers glower over rich cigars. Radner, for his arrogance, is razzed by the newspapers. Widows and orphans finger piles of restored money, their pallid faces bright, their eyes straying to advertisements for Florida Real Estate.

Agnes and John will marry within the month.

And Saggs studies grammar.

Within the river's woods, a small charred patch, melting in the rain, marks the passing of a wonderful figure. Johnston McCulley has contributed another step in the development of the costumed hero. And, as a matter of course, some six years later in 1927, Chelsea House (the book branch of Street & Smith) gathered the Thunderbolt stories into two books: *Alias The Thunderbolt* and *The Thunderbolt's Jest*.

Books? It seems an extravagant gesture to place The Thunderbolt's adventures between hardcovers. These are such fragile entertainments, delicate wisps so insubstantial that they dissolve in direct light. The characters of the series, the action of the stories, seem to occur in some far, strange place, a distant Frost Kingdom, unveiled by reality or human passion.

In the Frost Kingdom, only ice lives. There glide glittering figures, most exquisitely shaped—human forms whose skins are delicate glazes, whose eyes are crystal, whose hearts glitter richly blue-green.

One touch of your coarse hot human flesh, one pressure of your breath, and these shapes burst sparkling to crystal and eddy and fall away, an iced mist, leaving a few drops glinting frozen on the frozen floor.

The Thunderbolt is frost and dream and all his adventures are a special fooling in a world untouched by human breath. McCulley has written down, all neatly spelled and punctuated, fantasies from early boyhood, the dreams of wonder and accomplishment, in which every action is successful and the hapless opposition gapes agog.

His fiction is written in dream and frost, soon gone. But what delightful patterns while they endure.

About two years later, McCulley brought forth another variation on the theme of the limited-objective criminal hero. Again the magazine was *Detective Story*. The central situation, thriftily brushed up for reuse, had already yielded two similar series—The Thunderbolt and The Man In Purple (who will be discussed in the following chapter). But McCulley could wring a gallon of juice from the rind of an exhausted idea. Thus a new series rose from the old, the chief difference being that no costumes were used this time, and the hero was a pair of identical twins. The Avenging Twins.

Their names are Peter and Paul Selbon, "tall, broad-shouldered, good-looking pictures of health." The balance of their physical description is left for the reader to fill in as best he might.

The history of the twins has a familiar ring, as if somewhere a voice sweetly sings that old refrain.

Their parents died and the boys were reared by kindly old Uncle Ellis Selbon, who shared his fortune with the unfortunate orphans. After graduating from a university, loaded with honors, they toured the world for a few years and ended in South America. There, on the pampas, in the jungle, they earned a small fortune, some $500,000. During these activities, Peter became the amateur heavyweight champion of Argentina, and Paul, less discriminating, earned a reputation as the toughest "rough and tumble fighter in all South America."

It was splendid training for the leads of a magazine series. And necessary. For while the twins were smashing around down there, back in New York City, kindly old Uncle Ellis was being ruined by six wealthy men, "leaders in the world of finance and politics."

Within a few paragraphs, Uncle Ellis is dead of poverty and disgrace, and the twins come roaring back to the States, their eyes hot and iron in their hearts:

Peter: "We are out to square accounts with the men who ruined our dear old uncle. All the crooked financiers in the city, the crooked politicians, and their crooked friends cannot stop us."[7]

The boys take a bachelor apartment at the National Apartment House—a building they soon buy to secure more freedom of movement. Then they secure the services of Attorney Fornaser, a noble old lawyer who has known the boys since childhood. In the coming series, he will prove a valuable ally, providing endless alibis and spouting white-hot legalese at those annoyed by the Twins' activities. All the while keeping himself neatly dissociated from their activities.

These commence at once.

Each of the six wicked rich men receive a brief note:

For that which you have done, you are to receive punishment. One by one, the six of you shall receive attention. You cannot escape! Through that which you value most shall we strike you!

THE AVENGING TWINS

And off we go through a series of six stories, published at intervals during 1923 and 1924. These were later reprinted in two Chelsea House books, *The Avenging Twins* and *The Avenging Twins Collect*, both 1927.

Although the six millionaires are not nearly as cowardly as those quaking through the pages of The Thunderbolt, other things are the same. The detective assigned to the case is Milton Griff, "the best man attached to the force." He has been assigned full time to protect the Six against the Twins. In due time, he will head an army of private investigators, police guards, watchmen, and such vigilant people. These saturate the stories, fumblers all, each one armed with two or three pistols which are repeatedly emptied during the story. The trail of the Avenging Twins is marked by gunfire. No one is ever wounded, but all that shooting adds excitement.

In pursuit of their revenge, the twins have agreed upon certain basic operating rules. They will alternate their attacks on the Six, beginning with Paul. One of them must be highly visible, establishing an alibi, when the other is off on a job. Their purpose is to cause severe loss to each rich man, depending upon what is closest to his heart.

During the initial story, "The Avenging Twins" (May 12, 1923), the first victim is forced to burn $200,000 in cash and bonds. It almost kills him. Paul then makes a clean escape, leaving behind stacks of detectives he has rendered unconscious by a trick learned in jungle fighting—the victim is gripped from behind and an arm clenched across his throat. Suddenly he blacks out for whatever period of time is required by the plot.

Use of a pressure point to incapacitate a foe is a technical device used to distraction by later writers. The technique was silent, efficient, harmless, required no tying up, and gave the hero a decisive edge over the glowering hordes thirsting for his blood. Use of this device seems loosely correlated with an enthusiasm for *ju-jitsu*—variously spelled—which cropped up as magazine advertisements during the early 1920s. These advertisements promised the physically insignificant a sure-fire means of resisting bullies and other muscular oppressors. In a later Street & Smith publication, the *Doc Savage Magazine* (1933-1949), the Man of Bronze customarily gripped his enemies from behind, clamping thumbs against sensitive neck nerves. The end result was temporary paralysis and unconsciousness. From Doc Savage, the method spread through 1930s pulps like ink through water. Any hero could jab, squeeze, strike an opponent's neck and down he would go. Only a rare villain mastered this art. (It was far more artistic than slugging heads with a .45 automatic.)

As "The Avenging Twins" draws to its satisfying conclusion, the telephone rings. At the other end sounds an exquisite dainty little feminine voice. Somehow she knows all about the twins and their vendetta. Her name is Aletha and, like the Toscin of the Jimmie Dale series, her information is immediate and exact.[8] Unlike the Toscin, Aletha has no motive other than to wish the twins good hunting. She promises to supply them with useful information, then rings off, leaving a bewildered Peter. How did she know of them? Who is she? Why, why, why?

All will be answered in good time, although Peter fears for the worst: "We do not want one of these mysterious dames to wreck our plans."

No such thing. After each raid, the boys receive a complimentary telephone call:

"This is Aletha. I do not know just what you have done, Avenging Twins, but I do know this much—you have certainly fussed up several people."

Indeed they have. Immediately after the incident of the burnt fortune, Detective Griff and the outraged victim rush to the Selbon's apartment. There they run into a legal technicality that would have pleased Erle Stanley Gardner. One of the twins has a perfect alibi, having talked with the apartment house manager and Attorney Fornaser for hours. The other twin? Who knows where he was. For all that, who knows which twin he was. Since the boys look exactly alike, how is Griff to arrest the guilty one? If he makes an error, it's a lawsuit.

And he cannot arrest one twin as the principal, the other as an accessory, because he does not know which one is the principal:

Fornaser: "Let me call your attention to the point of law that says that an accessory implies a principal and cannot be convicted until after the principal has been convicted. Choose one of these men as the principal, and you will fail to convict him, as I have pointed out. So you'll fail to convict the other, also, if you try and turn around and make the accessory the principal—"⁹

It's rather academic, at that. The terrible robber who presided at the money burning was masked and otherwise anonymous.

Thus aided by Aletha, the law as interpreted by Fornaser, and assorted ropes, glass cutters, suction cups, pistols, flashlights, and black masks, the twins proceed to raise Merry Ned with the six millionaires.

"The Avenging Twins Try It Again" (three-part serial, June 16 through 30, 1923) tells how they steal away a priceless painting that one of the millionaires has concealed in his bedroom. The painting was stolen from an Italian museum and it is returned to a museum, after a loud, violent chase which leaves Griff, again, with empty hands.

Then follows the kidnapping of millionaire Byard, just when he has rigged the market for a stock raid ("The Avenging Twins' Third Trick," three-part serial, August 25 through September 8, 1923). The raid fails, with the agreeable consequence that the financiers lose millions. Byard wakes up in a park, some days later, having laid in a drugged sleep within a secret compartment behind radio equipment. Yes, it was in the twins' apartment. But who's to know.

Griff redoubles his efforts. A dictograph is slipped into the twins' apartment. A false Aletha calls on the telephone. The apartment house personnel are bribed. But no stratagem works.

"Pearls of Great Price" (November 10, 1923) tells how the boys steal away both a pearl necklace and its paste replica. Griff is thrown off the scent by the presence of a real jewel thief. Before he discovers his error, the twins are gone, having flipped both necklaces casually into the river.

"The Avenging Twins" Fifth Victim" (February 23, 1924) is caused to lose $100,000. Aletha, herself, all done up in a mask, helps the twins to escape. She slips away before they can question her.

Only to return once more in the final story, warning of an electrical trap set for them ("The Avenging Twins' Last Blow," two-part serial, April 5 and 12, 1924). Crafty millionaire Calwood has placed $50,000 in marked bills in a wired desk that has been further protected by an electrified floor plate. The next room swarms with detectives who spill out into the hallway and cluster around the mansion outside like unsettled bees.

To get into that protected room requires smoke bombs, wall scaling, and liberal squeezing of pressure points. Once inside, Paul is trapped behind a screen, an unconscious detective trussed at his feet, the room full of men. Disaster impends, not seriously. You can depend upon Johnston McCulley.

Enter Betty Calwood, niece of Calwood the wicked financier. She looks behind the screen, smiles at the masked man with gun and reports that no one is there. None of the detectives think to help her look, since they are McCulley detectives and good only at falling down.

We have, at last, met Aletha. She has helped wonderfully and the series ends not in arrest but in a glow of good feelings, millionaires excepted. Even Detective Griff is rewarded. Although he didn't capture the twins, he will be made police chief anyhow, a little gift from a grateful political boss.

My, what an odd world.

The Avenging Twins is written at the same level of seriousness as the sayings on a party napkin. The stories are studded with bits of repetitive foolishness inserted to make glad readers' hearts.

Peter: "Perhaps you'd better elucidate."
Paul: "Gosh, that's a dandy word."

The catch word is "dandy" and the joke is worked to exhaustion and beyond. As are the mock solemnities of the two-man committee meeting:

Peter: "Time for the meeting to come to order. Let's have the report of the investigation committee, please."
Paul: "Of which I am the chairman. Beg leave to report..." (He discourses briefly)
Peter: "Now I'd like to hear from the committee on suggestions."
Paul: "Of which I have the honor to be chairman." And so forth.

The joke is worked until the jolly reader is forced to lie down. You wonder what level audience it is all directed toward, these flashes of boys' book humor intermixed with bits of legal lore, hard-action cops and robbers chases, and characters as simplified as the illustrations in a kindergarten coloring book.

It is pleasant, shallow fun. Even the dullest reader could understand the appalling cynicism of the message—the only justice you receive is what you make for yourself. Established social mechanisms are in the hands of the privileged and police, courts, political power are eager tools of the wealthy, who ruin and defame with impunity.

Like other McCulley heroes, the Avenging Twins strike at these problems without ever changing them. They bruise the enemy. In no way can they correct the situation or remove the enemy from position of power and abuse.

Beneath the Selbon's amiable chatter lies pessimism. They can punish; they cannot correct. The ills persist, no matter how many avengers, costumed or otherwise, strike from the darkness, and laugh, and slip triumphantly away.

3-

Not all criminal heroes pursuing limited objectives were created by Johnston McCulley and not all radiated such jaunty good humor as they tugged the Establishment's tail. You have no doubt that The Thunderbolt or the Avenging Twins are upstanding young men of integrity most bright. You are sure that, once they have confounded the wicked, their illegal activities cease. Their task is over; now to other matters.

You are hardly so confident about other criminal heroes. They are so criminal. Their associates say so; the heroes, themselves, say so; even the police say so, if that makes any difference. Only the reader may have doubts. The reader knows that it is a habit of writers to favor stories with surprise endings, when the whole fabric of the narrative is abruptly reversed, revealing an unsuspected pattern in which black has become white and guilt, gleaming innocence.

That ultimate narrative twist is sorely provoking, although its use seems established beyond correction. No cry of rage, no chiding tear has an effect. Blinded by his folly, the writer grinds out, still yet again, another story of a criminal hero who is, in the final pages, shown to be good wholesome decent and admirable. He is unorthodox only in his method of correcting wrongs and performing services.

For example, the Scarlet Fox.

The Scarlet Fox series appeared in the 1923 *Black Mask,* back when that magazine, later honored for terse sentences and unflinching characters, was still in the larva stage. The 1923 *Black Mask,* was then no more than the uneasy child of the *Smart Set,* unsure of itself or its direction. The stories read as if their authors were giggling behind their hands.

The *Black Mask* of that time was a watered-down version of *Detective Story Magazine,* containing all that magazine's faults of preciousness and sentimentality and none of its virtues. The fiction *Black Mask* was published was pretentious, shallow, and self-consciously cheap, apparently written to the editorial policy of "Give the Boobs Junk."

Junk they got.

Including the Scarlet Fox series. Six connected episodes under the general title, "The Trail of the Scarlet Fox," ran in the magazine in early 1923. (These episodes were dated January, the 1st and 15th of February and March, and the 1st of April.) An additional short story, "The Footprints of Doom," was published January 1, 1924.[10] In 1927, the six connected parts were published as the novel *The Scarlet Fox*.

Thus early began *Black Mask's* habit of publishing a series of independent, if closely linked, stories which would be later issued as an episodic novel. Most early magazines used some variation of that technique, although *Black Mask* continued to do so throughout its great days, extruding by inches such classic hardboiled novels as *The Glass Key, The Dain Curse, Green Ice,* and *Fast One.*

The Scarlet Fox is as far from a hardboiled classic as *David Harum* is from *A Farewell To Arms.* No hardboiled school existed in 1923, although Carroll John Daly and Dashiell Hammett (writing under the name Peter Collinson) had published a few stories in the 1922 *Black Mask;* and in the *Adventure* magazine, one or two very tough people, Gordon Young's Don Everhard chief among them, conducted their affairs with a spleenish indifference to genteel ways.

No such lapses occur in the Scarlet Fox stories. The hero is aristocratic to his least capillary, handsome, well-bred, debonair, and red-headed. His eyes are the usual steel-gray, a characteristic designating the hero in all popular fiction. He is, in fact, nearly perfect. The other characters adore him:

Nurse: "He's the Prince of Robin Hoods! He gets away with the biggest deals in the country—picks only on rich crooks who stole their millions from the widows and orphans and helps every poor crook he knows, sending them straight. The only time he was ever arrested was when he let them nab him, to save poor Louisville Liz from the penitentiary.... And the only time they got him—he was absolutely *innocent!* Clever cops!"[11]

Detective (After Knocking the Fox unconscious): "Poor lad! He looks like a regular aristocrat laying there now. Too bad that with all their education and good blood some of 'em goes wrong. I'll do my best when he gets jugged to have it made easy for him."[12]

Criminal Mastermind: "He's the most remarkable young man I ever met..."

Gangster "De greatest one of 'em all!"

Crook's Wife: ".....what a man. He doesn't seem to be one of those sporty society swells who can't stay straight because they gamble or drink or hit the dope.... And I never heard of him after the girls or saw his picture in a newspaper scandal.... I wonder what made a crook out of *him?* Well, God have pity on him if he ever gets into trouble, for he's helped enough other poor devils this last few months, when every man's hand was against them."[13]

And why is this paragon a crook. Well, he isn't.It's all a delightful trick by Mr. Eustace Hale Ball, author of the series. Following closely the convention of the period, Ball has manufactured this scintillating young hero as the model of the *wunderkinder,* who can never err, who is widely admired at and gloried over and looked up to, who shines at the top of his profession like the star at the tip of the Christmas tree. A crook? He is no crook at all. If you believe that he is, you have been reading too much Eustace Hale Ball.

Now it is true that the Fox is a convicted felon. He went to Sing Sing on a purse snatching charge. He took the rap, as previously mentioned, for poor old sick Louisville Liz. Another stretch would have killed her. And so the Fox assumed the blame.

Why then his formidable reputation as a master among thieves?

For that simplest of reasons: the plot of *The Scarlet Fox* demands it. And what is easier, in this world of casual fiction, than to ascribe to a man a reputation that he could never have earned, under any circumstances, in the world of real mean streets.

There is point to all these convoluted writhings. But it is not yet time to reveal that point, which glitters like a zircon at the bottom of the swill bucket. First it is necessary to review The Scarlet Fox's personal background, his associates, and his adventures. Then the zircon may be removed and made much over; although, admittedly, it is a very small stone, hardly large enough to embellish a friendship ring.

The Fox enjoys a personal history that was, even for 1923, entirely conventional for a magazine hero. He had served in the French Foreign Legion. Later he joined the A.E.F. serving as one of Pershing's most brilliant espionage officers. He became a Captain and fought in the Argonne Forest—a combat in which half the magazine criminals and all of the magazine heroes participated. After the war, he returned to the United States, only to discover that his father had died, leaving all his property entailed and all his assets thieved away by business associates.

At this point, you may anticipate that the Fox will meet a petty crook he had known in the Army and help the poor wretch out. You will be correct. The Fox had saved Jem O'Brien's life in the Argonne Forest and now meets him again in New York City. Jem, a walking cliche, looks like a worried jockey, is a former burglar, thinks the Fox the greatest of men. Greater, even, than Woodrow Wilson.

The two join forces. Jem does not know the Fox's real name—which turns out to be John Smith—nor does he know anything other than the Fox's reputation according to Mr. Ball. With all this background nicely laid out, omitting only the zircon, we may now consider the story.

It concerns the recovery of the fourteen sacred emeralds making up the amulet of the Nadir of Sadkara. Should the superstitious hordes of India learn that the amulet is gone, they will rise in race war, shouting slogans and hurling curry at each other. Something must be done promptly and Scotland Yard does it: It offers a 200,000-pound reward for the return of the amulet intact.

This may prove difficult, since Singh, a Hindu of royal blood, took the amulet apart and sold most of the stones to entertain his fiancee, a dancer of the *Folies Bergere*. Only four stones remained when he came to New York City and was promptly set upon by thieves, who burst into his hotel room, and beat him until he died. At the last moment, they were driven off by a red-haired young man with a pair of guns who then snatched the four emeralds and vanished.

This romantic tale provides the thread, and some of the characters, upon which the Scarlet Fox episodes are strung. The Fox is out to collect the emeralds and does so at the rate of two per episode. Fortunately for him, all the stones have gravitated to New York City, where they are scattered far and near—in a pawn shop, in a fat woman's purse, in an Hindu's turban. You or I would be baffled to locate even one. Not so the Scarlet Fox, who prances briskly about, simply shoveling them in.

He meets obstacles, most of them human. Around the Fox swirl people whose motives are mysterious, whose identities are confusing. They double cross and triple cross and lie and deceive and strain themselves to make the action as confusing as possible. Included are Dr. Alexis Benguique, jewel expert and schemer, out to snatch emeralds by means foul. Here smiles that fragile jewel, Phiphi Villette, a dancer and society pet, who can hardly be trusted near a green stone. There glide hot-eyed clusters of Hindus, slinking, whispering, hurling baskets of cobras in through the window. And here, deadly Chinese leer, as cliche piles upon cliche, and grubby gangsters speak an amusing form of English.

Behind them all hovers an invisible menace, a master plotter without name or substance, manipulating so silently that his existence is never expected until the final chapters.

Nor are these people the only complications. Indeed, not. From Chapter One, the Fox is tracked by that tall, burly, Irish fellow, Detective Lieutenant Peter Brady, splendid in a derby and carrying an automatic pistol on each hip. It is Brady's desire to capture the Fox and so earn the reward of a trip across the ocean to County Galway with his faithful wife, Mary.

Ah, sure, and never did a stout-hearted Irish policeman so admire one of the Devil's own as Brady admires the Fox, that blithe rascal. Blessed by shamrocks that lad must be. Let him humiliate Brady, foil him, baffle him, tie him-up tight. That only increases Brady's admiration for the spankin' young lad, indeed so.

And doesn't Mary, too, have a sneaking fondness for the Fox, who called her up on Christmas Eve to tell her that Peter was safe, only tied up a bit in a little room, and now wasn't he sure Peter would escape soon, such a fine figure of a man he is. And doesn't that bit of gallantry win Mary's heart, so that she admires the Fox as heartily as Brady himself. You betcha.

So here we go, light heartedly collecting emeralds among most awful perils. There is the theft at the pawnshop of the emerald (strangely priced at $17.17.) The episode of the fat woman's purse (snatched by a pitiful little ragged girl who looks much like Phiphi Villette; the Fox deftly saves her from arrest, for he is very slick).

And there is the exciting experience of the basket of cobras flung into Phiphi's skyscraper apartment. The penetration of Dr. Benguique's secret lair...

The action accelerates, and the violence, those strong wines. For the reader demands something for his effort. If he is denied characters more complex than a sneeze, a situation that is not a string of cliches attached to a search, incidents that in some way resemble human experience, and a writing style that does not irresistibly suggest stewed bread, then he will settle for violent action. When all else fails, let the guns talk.

And so they do, aboard the yacht of a rich fool who has sailed across the Atlantic to New York, emeralds in his pocket and, although he doesn't realize it, opium and cocaine and bootleg whiskey hidden in his ship. Hijackers strike. Dr. Benguique and Phiphi are in danger as the guns roar and the rich fool dies. Then the Fox rips off his clever disguise. The guns go some more and the reader, properly thrilled, feels at last, the story is beginning to move.

But it doesn't. Fox gets emeralds and escapes as the police come swarming onto the yacht.

Now the final scenes rise about us. Time for another adventure or so, breathtaking suspense, revelations and breath-catching climax. To provide this, Mr. Ball sets blood-thirsty killers after Phiphi. The Fox protects her. She points a gun at him. By a ruse, he disarms her. Enter Brady, who points a gun at them. By a ruse, they disarm him. Brady wiggles free and, by a ruse, subdues the Fox. All others escape.

Is all lost? Certainly not. The Fox escapes, flexing his lithe muscles, and strikes a deal with Brady: Work with the Fox, and after they have jointly captured Mr. Big, Mr. 17-17, himself, the Fox will surrender.

Before Brady can quite grasp the joy and wonder of this promise, Mr. 17-17 has been doped with the Fox's tricked cigarettes—and Brady has been forced to shoot down that killer fiend, Chem Jow—and Phiphi's identity as the Singh's one-time fiancee is revealed—and the Fox has flitted away.

As he leaves, like Santa Claus rising into the night, he shouts a few words of instruction to Brady. The Fox is less succinct than Santa Claus and requires eighty-six words, a considerable number to shout from the darkness when someone is glaring after you, waving a gun. Brady does not open fire, nonetheless, and the Fox is gone. He is still promising to meet Brady at the Inspector's—perhaps he means the Commissioner's—in an hour and to be in handcuffs.

The Fox goes, and this is the last we see of him in this story. The rest of the chapter is devoted to a long explanation by Phiphi concerning the Fox and his strange secret.

It is strange to Brady. To those of us saturated in popular fiction, it is the usual ultimate twist that makes white black and naughty boys good. In brief:

Back in the days when the Fox had returned to New York City and was feeling blue and lowdown, he was commissioned by a family friend, the wealthy Montague Shirley, to hunt those stolen emeralds. To do so, the Fox became a Secret Service operative, working under the authority of the Department of Justice. This must have tickled the rest of the Secret Service operatives who were working under the Treasury Department.

Regardless of which fragment of government turf he occupied, the Scarlet Fox was set for action. He had a solid official job, a badge, and Shirley's fortune to pay all expenses. Now the Fox was able to obstruct the police, break and enter, conspire against justice, steal boats, administer unlawful drugs, hit people on the head, shoot holes in them, and drive very fast. All the things a hero must do if we are to take him seriously. None count as crimes in the 1923 *Black Mask*, providing that you are a member of the Secret Service.

And what about his responsibilities in the Secret Service? His criminal reputation? His months in Sing-Sing?

It is annoying that you bring all that up when the story is finished. If you don't mention it again, no one else will, either.

So Brady captures Mr. 17-17 and can take Mary to Ireland. The British government gets peace in India. John Smith, the Scarlet Fox, gets $1,000,000, a spotless reputation, and, very likely, the hand of Miss

Villette. These terminal matters having been settled, all hands adjourn for a big corned beef and cabbage dinner at the Brady's. The reader will get the indigestion.

Even age's patina can confer no distinction on the Scarlet Fox series. Its chief merit is accidental: It concentrates in one place most of those fictional conventions defining the limited-objective criminal hero, as of 1923. We observe that this version of the hero is a free-lance adventurer and operates as such; that he is foresighted to the same abnormal degree as Nick Carter and other dime novel heroes; that he is hunted by crooks and police; that he is assisted by a shabby little crook; that he is partially opposed by a beautiful woman of ambiguous circumstances, as well as by criminal types conforming to the most depressing cliches of the period; and that he is widely admired because of his personal charm and private charities. We should also note that the vivid spectrum of his transgressions is excused and justified on the grounds that he is, somehow, associated with the Secret Service.

This last point was a universal excuse in those innocent days. If associated, however vaguely, with law enforcement, the hero could do pretty much as he wished. The reader would admire in the fictional detective what he would despise in the real policeman. Official status justified every scrap of the hero's illegal behavior. It is a point of view to be much discussed some thirty-five years later at the Nuremberg war criminal trials. Not that the horrible moral deeps probed at Nuremberg were visible in these sunny 1923 shallows.

Throughout the Twenties, the convention displayed so fully in the Scarlet Fox energized hundreds of other short stories. (Not that the Fox exerted any influence; it merely mirrored the existing convention.) Few of these stories comprised a series. Fewer still presented limited-objective criminal heroes. Only infrequently did a character appear in a story series that established a goal, reached it, and concluded.

The *Flynn's Weekly* series about Pat the Piper was one of these.

The story group was written by Joseph Harrington—or signed with that name, at any rate. Pat is a charming girl crook, a pale, beautiful young lady with melting eyes and well-modulated voice. A dainty little darling, dressed in rich good taste, she is a sparkling, original, and accomplished liar. Hence her name. On the spur of the moment, she can "pipe up" a story so believable that it slips her from trouble.

She is a jewel thief. At the beginning of a series, in "An Up-To-Date Cavalier" (Flynn's, March 5, 1927), she is caught in the bachelor apartment of Jimmy Van Beuren, young idiot about town. Jimmy is properly amazed. In about seventy-three seconds, she persuades him that the two detectives chasing her are jewel thieves. He holds them at gun point. Meanwhile, she opens his safe and cleans out his jewels. Then she relents and writes an improbably long letter telling him that he was so sweet to allow her to escape, she has left the jewels under his pillow.

Comments of the detectives are not recorded. For the story, they neglect to identify themselves as detectives. Thus the series begins with a disagreeable cheat.

A month later, Jimmy meets her again at a party given by his sister. ("The Piper Pays," March 12, 1927.) Pat has already filched three jewels, smuggling them from the party in his coat pocket. (He is not searched as he leaves because, obviously, no young man would rob his own sister.) Pat leaves another note—she writes as copiously as Black Star—telling him where to find the jewels. She can't steal them, you see, because they belonged, after all, to Jimmy's sister.

You do see, don't you?

Still later, her identity is revealed to Jimmy. She is Patricia Clifford, rich society girl ("The Piper's Name," March 19). Since Jimmy has the intelligence of a sea squirt, he is inveigled into working with her.

He is intrigued. About her hovers a mysterious secret which cannot be revealed yet, most likely because the author hasn't thought it up.

Soon, in "The Piper's Partner" (March 26), Jimmy finds himself disguised as Humpy the Hunchback and lounging in a noxious dive— the kind Nick Carter used to enter when disguised as a prize-fighter.

The Piper, all golden hair and smiles, moves gracefully through this awful place. The boys greet her with warm respect. Nobody attempts to deflower her. Two crooks, off in the corner, are planning to rob an old woman. Pat tips Jimmy off. (We gather that she had been reading about Jimmie Dale and the Toscin). At the robbery scene, Jimmy leaps in through a window, grabs the swag, escapes. He turns it all over to Pat who keeps the jewels (for reasons undisclosed) and returns the money.

What is her amazing secret?

Why is Jimmy Van Beuren such a boob?

"The End of the Piper" (April 16) reveals all.

She is attempting to clear her father's reputation. Seven years earlier, he was framed to prison by the town's leading wholesale jeweler, a sinister plotter named Danforth.

So, while Mr. Clifford sits in prison, Mrs. Clifford, quite naturally, dies of heartbreak. But Pat plunges into the underworld to track down the criminals responsible. She takes safe-cracking lessons. She steals and robs. She learns to smoke cigarettes.

Everything that she steals and robs, she hides away. What she sells to the fences are her own jewels, large quantities of which remain from her father's collection. In due time, all stolen items will be returned.

But she must seem to sell stolen jewelry so that, eventually, she can reach—The Chief.

The Chief, that figure of mystery. Whispered about. Never seen. Pat sees him. She has some rose diamonds that he wants. In a secret luxurious office, he hunches over a desk, his face concealed by a black silk mask.

An appointment is set up for Pat to bring the stones to The Chief's concealed headquarters.

To this place, Pat and Jimmy come creeping, an hour before the appointment. Time enough to locate the hidden safe and extract the receipts that prove the innocence of Pat's father. You gather that the receipts have been preserved for this very occasion, although any super-criminal in his right mind would have destroyed them years before.

It is Pat's hour of triumph. And her hour of defeat.

Suddenly burst in The Chief and a henchman, bristling with guns. Gotcha.

No, not exactly. By a subtle trick, Pat gets The Chief's gun. During the following confusion, the henchman accidentally shoots The Chief dead, an error solving all manner of tedious problems, as would confront these people in a flesh and blood world.

The henchman bolts away. Pat and Jimmy confirm that The Chief is really wholesale jeweler Danforth. Then they, too, slip away, leaving behind for the police the evidence that will clear her father.

That terminates the activities of The Piper, closing the series, and, incidentally, leaving Pat stuck with Jimmy. It is a fate she did not deserve.

If this series were conceived as other than a group of feeble vignettes, Mr. Harrington conceals it well. The characters are shallow and inconsistent, the action preposterous, the prose clamorous with echoes of others' work. You are left with the impression that Harrington drifted into the series, beginning with nothing more substantial than a glib girl thief; only later did he insert a few bones to hold the pieces together. But as we have already remarked, Harrington was not the first writer to begin a series with no clear idea of its direction. Edgar Wallace did it with Four-Square Jane, and many E. Phillips Oppenheim series reflect similar improvisations.

4-

Some hearty souls pretend to be criminals. They swagger through ill-smelling dives, blacken their own reputations, wear remarkable costumes. They go creeping through the night. They cultivate an air of wickedness, although their hearts shine white. They are, in short, good men playing bad men for the reader's pleasure.

So many odd things please readers. Back long ago, at the opening of the Roaring Twenties (which looked exactly like today in period costume), readers not only enjoyed stories about imitation criminals, but stories about criminals who wished to reform.

They wished to; they wanted to; they were never allowed to.

If a criminal reforms, he takes up life as most of us know it. No longer does he whisk great bags of gold from great fat bankers. He ceases to dumbfound the police with crimes of dazzling execution. He turns from the silken palaces where he used to banter with hot-eyed adventuresses, sketchily dressed. He gives up excitement and danger and crackling wits and schemes, wonderfully profitable. All this he surrenders for the more modest joys of the sweet little wife, the junior clerkship, and a lunch sack containing a sandwich and an apple.

Such is the perversity of readers that they will not willingly read fiction about lives like their own. They know too much about lunch sacks and not nearly enough about hot-eyed adventuresses. They will tolerate a criminal hero. They will even admire his resolution to reform. But when he does reform, they drop him instantly.

With the result that no criminal hero ever manages that final step. Like Jimmie Dale before him, he longs to give up the life of crime but does not. He wishes himself away from those evil companions but is not. He earnestly yearns to be married and at peace but cannot be.

Not if the writer and his editor have anything to say about it.

5-

The White Rook was a thief with a sense of humor. Besides being a master artist in his profession, he was a joker who took a malicious pleasure in tantalizing the police by signing each masterpiece he left behind for their inspection, much as the painter scrawls his name on his canvas and the author signs his finished manuscript.[14]

Trade-marking your handiwork was all the rage in the magazines of the 'Teens. Witness the illegal activities of such characters as Jimmie Dale (the Gray Seal), Zorro, and Black Star, who left behind them an irritating trail of small gray stickers, "Z's" slashed into foreheads, and tiny black stars glued to everything in sight. It was a habit continued into the 1930s by the Spider, who stamped the foreheads of his victims with a crimson spider, and the Black Bat, who left bat seals to attest he had been there.

The Spider and the Black Bat were relatively more deadly than the "thieves with a sense of humor" who caper so preciously through earlier mystery-adventure fiction. These get the colly-wobbles if they think of blood. All of them are descendents of Raffles—at least to the extent that they hold safe robbing to be a merry prank.

It is Jimmie Dale, the Gray Seal, who first elected to go robbing
and pranking and jesting through the American pulps. It would appear
that the White Rook had read some of Mr. Dale's early adventures, for
he shaped himself into the very mould of the Gray Seal. Perhaps this
was because Mr. Hugh Kahler, author of the White Rook series, had
willed it so. Or perhaps it was so because Street & Smith published
both *People's Magazine,* in which Jimmie Dale appeared, and *Detective
Story Magazine,* which featured the White Rook. It is possible that some
concealed editorial guidance is at work here.

Whatever the cause, the Gray Seal and the White Rook have things
in common. Instead of sticky, gray diamond-shaped seals, the Rook used
handcarved ivory chess rooks. At each crime, one of these was left behind
to bother the police. And so it went through 1918 and into 1919—another
cunning master criminal, so very smart, so very clever, you wonder why
the police didn't pay him to retire.

The series begins with "White Rook's Pawn" (*Detective Story
Magazine,* October 1, 1918), a story which achieves the distinction of
introducing a series without presenting the main figure. Not only that,
the Rook is not among the characters, not even in disguise. The Rook
exists only as an off-stage name, not mentioned until Chapter V.

The story concerns a sissy rich fellow named Warren Charlock, who
sees a murder in the house next door. Snatching up an Army Colt .45
single-action pistol, which he neglects to cock (and incidentally
demonstrating that heroes of 1918 stories are not good for much in the
way of action), he lunges loudly into the night.

Whereupon he is hit violently upon the head. He is dazed. The
dark garden rustles with mysterious figures but he finds nothing. The
next day, the police are suspicious and suddenly there appears a beautiful
girl to warn him.

More sinister doings follow: Secret rides with the beautiful girl, who
is being blackmailed into service of the shadowy Rook; secret rooms
in which strange people sit mysteriously. It is all incomprehensible.

Charlock meets at least one authentically tough guy, who will stand
for none of this pansy dilettante stuff. Only after many chapters is the
whole wild activity explained away as a police attempt to ensnare the
White Rook. This fails. At the end, Warren Charlock is in rather a hopeless
mess, neck-deep in suspicious circumstances. However, he pulls his social
position and the police apologize for thinking ill of him. Thereafter,
he marries the beautiful girl and the Rook sends them a nice piece of
silver. It is the only thing in the story that the Rook does.

After this holocaust of trivia, Mr. Kahler buckles down to a series
featuring the White Rook in person.

Astonishing as it may seem, the Rook is a manufacturer of safes. (How these Jimmie Dale resemblances do creep in.) He is about thirty-five years old, beginning to put on weight, his hair just touched with gray. He has money and social position. Why then safe-cracking?

For the fun of it, for a diversion. Why else? "...theft for the thrill of danger and the zest of outwitting rival makers of safes."

Why then the elaborate buildup in the first story, during which the Rook seemed to be blackmailing people to squeeze from them the plans of the mansion and the location of the safe.

Sorry. That can't be explained.

The Rook is no professional criminal. He is merely a jolly amateur who steals but never sells his loot. He collects it—paintings and jewels, a gold nugget stolen from the Mint, an empty safe-deposit box extracted from a Trust Company vault. Even a collection of papers stolen from a safe in the office of a rival safe manufacturing company.

All these trophies the Rook stashes in a concealed safe inside his own mansion. Certainly he should get rid of it all. It's nothing but massed white elephants. He doesn't need it, doesn't want it; yet he can't part with it.

His name is Enfield Bray.

Since it is the tradition that every master criminal must be chased by a master detective, Bray is hunted by Raybold, Headquarter's resident genius. When Raybold was still an obscure cop in Breck Village, the Rook visited there and got himself mixed up in a murder. He was so impressed by Raybold's performance that he pulled strings to have the man transferred to the New York City detective bureau. It's more fun, you see, to be chased by a clever man.

Now, Raybold is a deliberate, cool operator, a clear reasoner who wastes neither time nor motion. He gets along well with Bray and together they look into a few White Rook cases. Then comes serious trouble.

The Rook's identity is learned by a hard-nose named Wake Deckerman. He gets a signed confession from Bray, then forces him to obey and commit bad crimes.

After much excitement, Bray steals back the confession. Only to lose it to Deckerman's valet, "a mysterious, silent figure of a man, known as Ramsgate." He is a violent man, too, for he kills Deckerman and vanishes for three years, leaving Bray with his heart in his mouth. And for three years, the Rook remains inactive believed dead.

As in the case of Mr. Jimmie Dale, all the fun has gone out of crime.

These adventures are recorded in the stories "The Rook's Defense" (November 5, 1918) and "The White Rook's Secret" (November 26, 1918).

Now begins "The White Rook's Mate" (December 31, 1918), during which many of dangling threads are resolved.

Bray has employed as his secretary, the reformed thief Leila Craig, the most intelligent individual in the series. At this time, Raybolt has reasoned out that the Rook must be a wealthy amateur who stores his loot in one of those impregnable safes—just like Bray builds. He offers Bray police immunity to break into various mansions and check the safes there for the Rook's loot.

Bray agrees to do so and provides himself with sweet Leila's assistance. Unable to resist the opportunity, he leaves some White Rooks in a plundered safe. A mistake, Up rears Ramsgate, the long lost valet, threatening Bray with exposure unless he obeys commands.

In the face of all this, a sensible man would skip the country. Bray, however, being a Street & Smith hero, continues to break and enter for the police department. During his next foray, he discovers that the safe he is to open is all tricked up to catch him. He gives up the mission and returns home—where he finds Leila in the act of ramsacking his possessions. She knows that he is the Rook and is trying to get all that valuable junk out of his safe before the police arrive.

There is nothing to do but help her loot his own mansion and see her gone. And, at this point, he discovers that he has been out-generaled. The police are not coming after all. Leila had fingered him for the last job—he had missed capture only by a fluke—and she has decamped with every last thing in his home.

One flicker of sunlight remains. Since Leila felt a trifle sheepish at her ice-cold deception, she had considerately stolen his confession from Ramsgate. All in all, the Rook has come out ahead.

But to think that a mere slip of a girl. . . .

You might assume that the series would end on this minor chord. Series, however, have their own lives. And so, in the February 4, 1919, issue of *Detective Story* appears the coda to the White Rook adventures. Titled "Thirty-three," it is a whopping 46-page novelette, packed with incident. It is a solid piece of structure, tightly suspenseful and tangled with plot.

The Committee of Thirty-Three has offered $25,000 for the capture of the Rook. This is a vigilance committee that is cracking down on crooks the police can't seem to catch. Bray is offered a position on the committee, only to discover that the Thirty-Three is actually a crime syndicate controlling an army of criminals through blackmail.

Complexities tug at Bray. Raybolt is having active suspicions as to the true identity of the Rook. Leila Craig reappears, her hands overflowing with illicit money; she is, perhaps, an agent for the Thirty-Three.

At this point, a stranger is arrested and sent to prison for being the Rook and Bray is blackmailed into getting the man out. He does so with little difficulty. Since the reader swallows this without strangling, he also gets down the next event—which is that Bray marries Leila.

As others have discovered, marriage creates new problems. No sooner has he claimed fair Leila's hand, than he is forced at gun-point to rob a safe for the Thirty-Three—or rather for its sinister head, Mr. Kew.

Mr. Kew has simple tastes and uncomplicated wishes:

"I'll rule the world, Bray—rule it with an absolute, unchallenged supremacy with all the petty little powers..."

He's thinking in terms of a glorified Mafia, with himself as the Don of Dons.

Unfortunately he has babbled out his confession before the hidden Raybolt and is promptly hauled away, foaming and screaming. Peace now descends. Raybolt is finally convinced that the Rook was Leila's brother (imaginary) and that he is dead. No longer is Bray under suspicion. The Rook is gone forever. The series is over.

Mr. Hugh Kahler, author of the series, went marching on. He had been born in Philadelphia in 1883, wrote fiction for the early pulps—particularly the Street & Smith magazines—appearing not only in *Detective Story Magazine*, but *Popular, Western Story*, and *Best Detective*. He successfully made that difficult transition to the slick magazines. He became the Fiction Editor for the *Ladies Home Journal* (1943-1960) and contributed to the *Saturday Evening Post, Collier's* and the *American* magazine. He died in 1969.

6-

More than six months before the White Rook made his first appearance, a particularly striking young lady had entered *Detective Story Magazine*.

Her hair was a wavy chestnut...; there was the flush of a healthy tan on her face and consequent faint border lines on her throat and forearm...; her eyes were gray, and they could be very soft or very hard in a shifting flash; her body was strong and lithe, every move gave hint of steely muscles, of perfect synchronism; each movement was timed and there was no lost motion.

One thing was stamped on her. She was bred to the great outdoors.... (She) was about the swellest bit of feminine loveliness that (the guard) had seen in a long time....

...a sudden soft movement had come to him out of the corner of his eye...Detective Gillane was looking straight into the business end of an automatic gat.... Her whole being had undergone a swift and almost unbelievable change. Warmth and sunshine were at once transformed into blued steel. When next she spoke, her words were snapped off in short, crude phrasings:

"Stick'em up!"[15]

The adorable young lady who turns to metal is Miss Blue Jean Billy Race—a curious name that has nothing to do with the style pants she wore. "Blue" for the ocean and "Jean" for the gracious gift of God. The rest was her father's name, old William J. Race, old Quality Bill.

By profession, Billy is that unique thing—a pirate, a "Highway Woman of the Sea" as the author archly remarks. At the beginning of the series in *Detective Story Magazine,* her attention is more often on shore. But within a few issues, the action veers out toward the brine and salty to her prime targets—the yachts of rich men, bloated, arrogant rich men, puffing $2.00 cigars as they brag fatly of how they skinned widows and crippled children.

It is night.

Over the yacht railing glides a slender figure dressed in black, Blue Jean Billy in full war attire. She pads to the main cabin. There revel the hordes of sin—the exclusive party well washed by bootleg fluids; the card game rigged to trim the sucker. Here jewels glitter about wealthy necks and wallets swell fat with goldbacks, perhaps honestly earned but probably not.

The door clicks open. Into the room jets the muzzle of a heavy automatic, circling ominously. Behind it, the girl stands tense, surveying her catch, her brown eyes iced, contemptuous, chilling as the moving muzzle.

Protests shiver up. What giant of industry wishes to bend submissively to a slender bit of a girl. It's indecent. Unmanly, even.

She is a buxom little thing, at that, hardly weighing one hundred pounds. She is soaking wet, dressed only in a simple swimming suit, her 1918 ankles immodestly revealed.

Let some red-faced captain of industry protest and gun sound hacks across his words. Bullet impact splits the table top. Usually that violence quells rebellion. The red faces shine wetly. It is terrifying—a crazy woman. No lady shoots in the presence of gentlemen.

No lady talks to gentlemen as she does, either.

Billy begins the proceedings with a long speech. It looks good on paper, but, since it runs almost a column, we may suppose that Mr. Charles W. Tyler, author of the series, has expanded her comments. These are concerned with the disagreeably low morals of those facing her gun. She points out how unworthy they are; what liars and cheats they are.

The purpose of this lecture is to lend a high literary tone to a hold-up. To judge from her comments, Bill is serving humanity by robbing these cultured scum. After several stories, Billy gives up this sermonizing, and just as well. It reminds you of the pious remarks made by Jesse James before cleaning out a bank. You know how he ended up.

Mr. Tyler rather sweats to justify Billy's reputation in terms of an avenging administrator of justice. He can't do it. True, she preys on crooks and near crooks. But her trade is piracy and grand larceny and all the world's glowing rhetoric fails to conceal that.

Now back to the robbery. Once pockets are emptied and necks stripped bare, the swag is wrapped in a rubber bag. Blue Jean slips silently back into the night. As she scurries along the deck, she stuffs the pistol into a waterproof pouch worn low at her waist.

Thus disarmed, she is immediately vulnerable. A dozen men, flushed with belated courage, drive at her. Too late. Already she is over the railing. They hear her splash into the black water. Then silence.

Occasionally the narrative action is varied by adding a chase—search lights jabbing about, motorized launches butting among the waves. Once, twice, there are gunfights out on the face of the ocean—orange flashes at the wave bases, the boats pitching, the heaving black surface concealing the adroit swimmer. Silent as light, she slips along wave troughs to a distant fishing boat.

The pound of a two-cycle engine recedes in the night.

Charles W. Tyler wrote the series—one of the several that he provided for *Detective Story Magazine*. Born in North Hinsdale, New Hampshire, he was, in turn, a railroad fireman, draftsman, and steamfitter. Information on his career is extremely scanty, but it is known that he began publishing fiction in the general pulp magazines during the late Teens. He appeared in *Railroad Man's Magazine, People's Magazine, Ace-High Magazine,* as well as *Detective Story.* Later work has been noted in the 1943-1944 *Argosy.* According to a particularly uninformative profile in *Detective Story* (July 20, 1929), the Blue Jean Billy stories suggested themselves to him while he was cruising the coast of Massachusetts in an old power boat.[16]

The Blue Jean Billy stories appeared during the first half of Tyler's extended professional career. The series began at the height of *Detective Story's* infatuation with criminal heroes, when readers could indulge their anti-social urges by liberal applications of Black Star, Big-Nose Charlie, White Rook, Thubway Tham, the Spider, Boston Betty, and such amiable folk, a glut of lawlessness for the law-abiding. Unlike most of these characters, Blue Jean Billy was featured in a sequence of loosely-linked novelettes. These ran chronologically with vast time breaks between, each threatening to be the last. From 1918 to 1931 approximately a dozen stories were published. The first half of these was collected in two Chelsea House hardbacks, *Quality Bill's Girl* (1925) and *Blue Jean Billy* (1926). Each book contains three novelettes, whose beginnings and endings were editorially mangled to provide a trifling amount of continuity and to give the illusion that each book was a novel.

Billy's career begins with some spectacular crimes. The initial story, "Raggedy Ann" (March 26, 1918)—the name refers to an island out in the Atlantic off the Massachusetts coast—tells how she held up the fancy engagement party. Not only does she carry off all the expensive presents, but she kidnaps the groom, who rejoices in the name Algernon Whosis Pinagree Smythe.

Because of this crime, the celebrated detective, Robert Wood, sets out on Billy's trail. In "Raiders from Raggedy Ann" (July 16, 1918), she saves Wood's life and foils a pack of crooks with political connections. After this exploit, Billy invests part of her stolen proceeds in the "Nix's Mate" (March 11, 1919), a shabby boat with a souped-up engine. The rest of the loot she spends on a few fancy dresses and the purchase of a society gambling house.

Once this place is packed with jeweled women and florid men, Billy and her father's old friend, the Shanghai Kid, hold up the whole crowd and rob them clean. Away the pair dart through a secret tunnel, barely evading the police. After a violent encounter with a gang of wharf thugs, they escape to sea.

But the crooks come snuffling her out. In "The Haunt of Raggedy Ann" (October 7, 1919), one harsh event follows another, including a full-scale gun fight. The *Nix's Mate* sinks and Shanghai is killed, his death occasioning a thousand tears. Billy and Wood, tightly trussed, are imprisoned aboard a beached wreck captained by a crazy man. At this very moment, a furious storm breaks, as storms are apt to do in this series. The crooks die in the waves. Billy reforms and marries Wood, who retires from the detective trade to become a lobsterman.

How a sweet young buxom girl got into all this hurrah makes a surprising story. It seems that her father, William J. Race, old Quality Bill, was arrested by error and crippled during a police third degree. Raging he turned to a life of crime, hating society and all its shams. His daughter, Billy, was brought up in his path—although he came to doubt that he had done the wise thing.

He died, leaving Billy an old brick house at 19 Green Street (city not specified) and a shanty, where Billy had been born, located out on Fiddler's Elbow, a sand spit angled very far out into the Atlantic. He also left her with an abiding contempt for liars, cheats, double dealers, and those who use wealth and social position to sock it to their neighbors.

Three family friends were entrusted to keep an eye on Billy as she grew up. It was a deadly assignment. Shaver Michael died standing off wharf rats in "Raggedy Ann." The Shanghai Kid died in a hail of gun fire in "The Haunt of Raggedy Ann." So far as is known, the third friend, the tough old, one-handed Kil Van Kull, lasted the course, although the law was hot after him for months.

All this history of crippled hopes is provided to justify Billy's violently anti-social activities. To emphasize that she does right by doing wrong, strong social distortions are written into the narrative. The wealthy folk Billy robs are uniformly corrupt and venial, using their high positions to scoff at the law. Obviously such people exist to be robbed; it is only right. By which reasoning, Billy, the Highway Woman of the Sea, joins that distinguished group of characters who worked outside the law to punish those deserving it.

The ruthless distortions used to characterize Billy's victims are also applied to her opponents. These come in three classes: First, lawmen of transcendent goodness who perceive her excellence and forgive her actions; these are contrasted with a second class—lawmen of corrupt cruelty, simple as a rubber stamp; and, third, there is a faceless mass of thugs, wharf rats, cut-throats, sneaks, and assorted waterfront scum whose one-dimensional qualities add menace without fatiguing the reader.

The June 25, 1921, "Blue Jean Billy At Fiddler's Reach" picks up after a three-year gap in narrative time. Immediately, Bob Wood falls victim to the curse hovering over the spouses of series characters—he gets drowned in Chapter One. While Billy struggles to revive him, she is recognized by the ferocious detective, Jerome Birwell, one of those baaad lawmen. He was "a veritable human bloodhound. He was possessed of an almost uncanny ability to ferret out clues..."

Birwell just misses capturing Billy and his brutality hurls her back to lawlessness. It wasn't her fault. She wished to reform. But Birwell wouldn't let her.

Away we go once more. During "Blue Jean Billy At Fiddler' Reach" and "Highway Woman of the Sea" (August 19, 1922), she holds up boats, gets chased by Birwell and his horde of dock scum. She makes them look foolish. At one point during the activities of "Highway Woman of the Sea," she gets hit on the head and captured. But not to worry. She promptly escapes and rescues the very nice police captain and his wife. The story ends in a scene requiring two hankies or a small thick towel.

Now comes a two-and-a-half year gap in the printed record of Billy's adventures. *Detective Story Magazine* rolls onward, while readers wonder what could have happened to their favorite pirate. When at length the series picks up again in the April 4, 1925 issue, with "Blue Jean Billy, Sky Pirate," she has modernized her techniques. She uses a seaplane to rob a private boat. On this vessel, a naughty fellow is tricking the foolish with crooked cards. Billy arrives and shows her gun and carries off all the money and the deck of cards, complete with the signatures of the crooks. They are desperate to recover the evidence and hire a detective to hunt Billy down.

He does so by aerial reconnaissance. Before you know it, Fiddler's Reach is again invaded by a snarling gang of cut-throats. The friendly detective gets somewhat shot, but Billy saves the day without his assistance.

In "Blue Jean Billy and the Lone Survivor" (August 22, 1925), still another gang of thugs kill old Lobster Joe. They lay the blame on Billy, causing her to settle their hash in short order. The November 6, 1926, "Blue Jean Billy, Waif of the Sea," features the ultimate final invasion of Fiddler's Reach. This time, Billy is falsely accused of bank robbery and murder. After clearing herself, if barely, she determines to cut all ties with the past. She fires the Fiddler's Reach establishment and leaves forever, amid cascades of pathetic adjectives. Renaming herself Arlin Shores, she becomes the resident guest of the Peasleys—Captain Lige and Aunt Sophy.

For a year, all is quiet and peace. Happiness days, warm and sunny, described in prose concocted from sugar paste, slush that affects even locale names. These appear to have been lifted from a copy of Raggedy Ann and Andy in Candyland.

The monotonous lapping of waves on the pebbly shore of Blue Gingham Bay. Distant surf breaking on Shabby Rocks....The Lazy clang of the bell off Pumpkin Knob....

On the slope behind the bay, a single light glimmered. It was in the window of a big rambling white house in Calico Lane.[17]

No mistake. It is Candy Land.

Both "Blue Jean Billy Plays Fair" (January 18, 1930) and "Sea Law and Blue Jean Billy" (November 14, 1931) play variations on the same idea. As Arlin Shores, Billy saves incautious teen-agers from rum-running gangsters. In the process, her true identity is disclosed but nobody cares; all think she's wonderful.

At this late date, the menace of the story is no longer a tough detective or a batch of wharf rats. In their place are sure enough Al Capone gangsters, complete with sneers and pin-striped machine guns. "Plays Fair" concludes with a gun fight in which Billy kills her first and last thug. During "Sea Law" she rescues the fool girl, hijacks the bootlegger's boat, and lures a boatload of killers to destruction on the shoals. The ending is a high-tension chase terminated by a perfectly enormous storm which arrives in the nick of time.

After this peak of tough excitement, it all oozes away in syrup:

> Guns and crooks seemed very, very far away from the big rambling house, with its apple trees, its lilacs, its old-fashioned garden, the wall-bordered lane with Blue Gingham Bay at its foot. A dream world, Calico Lane, through which one journeyed in eternal peace and security.[18]

If you can overlook this drivel, you can find a number of hardboiled moments in the series. Billy is one of the earliest figures of the tough crime story. The initial novelettes combine wisps of dime novel action with hints of *Black Mask* ice to come. In action scenes, the prose grows tightly impelling and takes on a vaguely hardboiled tone. Only when the setting is static does the language change to candy. You can reproduce the general effect by reading *Black Mask* while a string quartet plays sentimental favorites.

A series written by Charles Tyler, that renowned chronicler of Big-nose Charlie, should shine with light playfulness. Or so you might expect. But no real laughter lightens Billy's adventures. The prose stomps soberly along intent on the menace, the chase, the bellowing sea storm, the sentimental tear that blurs the eye.

In spite of the narrative style, many stories generate strong dramatic tension. They climax if slowly, to endings that shake with suspense, full of guns and blood. The series holds your interest, if precariously— and in spite of all that high-calorie sweetness out Calico Lane way.

7-

Good gracious, it is hard to reform. The will to turn your back on crime is not enough, as the agonies of Blue Jean Billy demonstrate. Once you crack a safe, once you leave a mocking token of your presence at the scene of the crime, and forever afterward, your liberty is forfeit to your concealed identity. Once your identity is known, you are helpless. Time and again you are pulled wiggling, repentant, sorrowful back to crime's abyss.

It happened to White Rook and to Blue Jean Billy, and it happened to The Joker.

"The Joker...was the most whimsical, impudently clever rascal in criminal history." Robs when and where he wishes, naming the place beforehand, always succeeding. At the scene of his jokes—crimes, you might call them—the wicked scamp leaves a tiny playing card. It is hardly necessary to specify which card.

The police are helpless, They growl and lurch, their great feet thudding. Even that famous private detective, Martin Quay, is rarely successful. The Joker detests Quay, who has spoiled some rare thefts. Often Quay is able to return the stolen property.

But more often, The Joker makes Quay look a fool. Several times, he has left Quay tied and unconscious at the scene of the crime—a merry jest. Again, again, again, The Joker has escaped. Always he returns, forever sending such notes to the newspapers, sending malicious notes to Quay.

That man Quay is an old-line police detective. Once head of the detective bureau, crooked politicians threw him out. He set up a private investigation agency, but this did not prosper. Not at first.

Then came The Joker.

The very first thing, The Joker robbed Quay, himself. Wrote a witty account of the robbery to the newspapers. Quay was much embarrassed. He should not have been. New business began pouring in, and the more The Joker mocked and cavorted, the better business became for Quay Investigations.

This desirable state of affairs couldn't continue forever. Eventually, The Joker's identity was discovered. Only by luck, and a delicate touch of blackmail, was the secret kept—that the jocular thief was Martin Quay and The Joker, an inverted advertising gimmick for the detective agency.

And what, may you ask, became of the stolen goods?

The Joker "was very careful never to profit by his thefts. If he couldn't safely restore the loot to its owners he saw to it that it was destroyed, if intrinsically valueless, or distributed among deserving charities....."[19]

Nothing could be more fair than that.

After the exposure of his alternate identity, Quay sensibly decided to retire The Joker. The agency was a success, and Quay was content to grow fatter placidly, smoking his black cigars, forgetting the joys of twirling the dial to someone else's safe. The Joker, he claimed, is dead.

Peter Kane did not agree with him. Kane was the fellow who assumed Quay's old job at the detective bureau. "The Joker's laying low," he bellowed. "Sooner or later—mistake—make slip—police will capture— long sentence—too often to the well!"

Quay agreed. And because of his discretion, the history of The Joker is (as can best be determined) given in only three or four stories from the Detective Story Magazine. These include "Left By The Joker" (July 18, 1919), "A Deal In Silence" (September 16, 1919), and "The Joker's Last Card" (October 14, 1919). All were written by Hugh Kahler, author of the White Rook series. That explains much, for parallels between the White Rook and The Joker are obvious.

The stories are solid, big novelettes, fifty pages or more, longer than many later pulp magazine novels and simply crammed with plot. During the final story, "The Joker's Last Card," Quay is called to the home of wealthy Myron Soule, who has just purchased that gigantic, maleficent diamond, The Rogue.

That same night, a swarm of crooks (all working more or less independently) descend upon Soule's mansion. All lust for The Rogue— none more hotly than Quay. He resurrects The Joker for the last time in a complex narrative involving crooked butlers, secret panels in the ceiling, phosphorus bombs, a beautiful girl suspected, and finally murder.

Inspector Peter Kane lumbers glowering about, suspecting all the wrong people. Quay is eventually able to steal the gem, then finds his identity known to a blackmailing voice on the telephone.

His secret, he learns, is in the hands of a madman whose mission in life is to murder precious stones that have evil histories. He kills them in an electric furnace.

"We kill men when they commit a murder, but I'm the only one who dares kill diamonds that have killed men."

Ha ha ha ha hahahahahahaha!

He drops dead from sheer joy and Quay's secret is safe once more. Apparently it stayed so. You are the first to learn it, after all these years. Please be discreet.

Evolution works its accidental magic on the stuff of literature as surely as on living protoplasm. Change is the only constant. Ten years is long for a story type. After ten years, literary pressures have modified yesterday's successes and new forms shine.

In that series of stories written by Herman Landon about the Gray Phantom, the change occurs from story to story. The series is a textbook example of character modification. It's rather like watching an orange become a hen.

Landon, a professional newspaper man, seems to have been highly sensitive to the winds that ripple public taste. Born in Stockholm, Sweden, 1882, he came to the United States when seventeen years old, began newspaper work when he was twenty. He became a special features writer on the *Chicago Record Herald* (1910-1914) and the managing editor of the *Washington Herald* (Washington, D.C.), 1915-1917. In 1914, he organized a syndicate to distribute to newspapers, motion picture plots written out as narratives. (The idea was later adapted to *Movie Action Stories* magazine during the 1930s.)

Landon began contributing material to *Detective Story Magazine* around 1917 and immediately created the first of his two major series characters for that publication: The Gray Phantom arriving in 1917, the Picaroon in 1921.

The Gray Phantom began as that most usual of *Detective Story* types, a brilliant, ruthless, criminal master mind, heading a world-wide organization. They headed world-wide organizations more gracefully then than now. The Phantom requires no computers, no bookkeeper, no clerks, or motor pools, or daringly tinted secretaries. He is the quietest master mind you ever met.

To the world he was known as a wealthy speculator, and few suspected that his exploits on Wall Street were but an avocation and a studiously calculated pastime that cloaked other and more mysterious activities. To society, the newspapers, the philanthropic organizations, the clubs, and the world of finance he was known as a successful, through somewhat eccentric, business man, one who preferred quiet and intellectual pursuits to the razzle-dazzle with which many others in his sphere of life whiled away their leisure time. But to a few—a very select few—he was known as the Gray Phantom.[20]

To someone—whether editor or author isn't known—he was also known as the Gray Ghost, a name which crops up repeatedly in the printed text. But don't be disturbed by an occasional small discrepancy; just wait till you meet the big ones.

The Gray Phantom's name, in the florid style of the 'Teens, is Cuthbert Vanardy. You would think Landon had better sense.

....there was a suggestion of gray elusiveness in the lean, clean-chiseled face and the strong, feverishly active eyes that upon rare occasions could be as dreamy as a young girl's. His figure was tall, lank, springy, and somehow it made one think of a cocked trigger. There was a mere suggestion of gray at the temples, and this color conception was vivified by the ash-gray eyes and the gray business suit he usually wore.[21]

These winding sentences, studded by subordinate clauses and improvisational diction, give little hint of the vigorous pulp writing style to come within ten years, vivifying the conception of action writing and brushing the ash-gray sluggishness from the temples of detective fiction.

However meandering this descriptive prose, the adventures of the Gray Phanton were tight, tense, and often peculiar.

The earliest story noted is "Seven Signs," *Detective Story Magazine,* December 18, 1917. A portion of the Russian crown jewels has been stolen by The Duke, that master criminal with a world-wide organization and "a representative in every large city in both hemispheres." The Duke is strong in Europe, but the Gray Phantom is the power in the United States.

The Phantom decides to hijack the jewels from The Duke. The treasures are being smuggled into the country in kegs of herring, then collected by The Duke's man in New York. This fellow is James P. Loring, commission merchant. The Phantom calls in his two lieutenants—fat Wade and hard-faced Liggett—and explains all this background information to them, while the reader listens in. The plan is to swoop upon Loring and carry off the treasure.

Since the Phantom is head of a world-wide criminal organization, he decides to do the job himself. That very night, he is to attend a dinner party at Loring's. Where he finds mystery.

Loring has been slugged unconscious in the street. Nothing was stolen but his little finger, which had been neatly amputated and the stump bandaged. Who knows why.

At the dinner party, a bullet flicks across Loring's forehead. Then an explosion rocks the mansion. As the guests stampede, Loring darts away to check his secret vault in a secret room. Vanardy slips after him, blackjacks Loring—accidentally killing him—and cleans out the Russian jewels.

The theft is interrupted by the entrance of a mysterious woman who arrives and departs without being clearly seen. It was probably intended that she kill Loring while he was unconscious. However, that thread is dropped in the general excitement and Vanardy carries the blame for it—a unique example of a sympathetic criminal hero who commits murder. It was just not done back then.

Vanardy is much touched by this dismaying event. He has never, never permitted murder during any crime. He is so distressed that, as he leaves, he drops his diamond-studded morocco pouch.

"It did not matter," he reflects later. It is a judgment that makes you wonder at the quality of 1917 master criminals. For the pouch is emblazoned with the initials CV and contains a notebook filled with encoded notes concerning the Phantom's operations.

The necessities of fiction dim even the sharpest wits. The Phantom is not disturbed by this loss because the morocco pouch is a plot device, essential to the resolution of the story.

The Phantom now leaves inconspicuously in a basket suspended beneath some sort of flying contraption. Returning to his mansion, he gloats over the jewels—particularly a huge diamond. Then he locks them away and is immediately knocked unconscious. When he wakes, his little finger has been amputated.

Even as Vanardy stares in horror at his bandaged stump, Detective Peter Trask is investigating back at Loring's mansion.

Trask has learned strange facts. He has learned that the Russian jewels are in the United States. That they include the celebrated Koh-i-tur diamond, which had once been the eye of an idol in Dabaredyh. That the diamond, enormously large, is worth two million, 1917 dollars. And that the diamond carries with it a seven-step doom: loss of a little finger, a narrow escape from death, mental agony, death of a friend, branding on the forehead, a second escape from death, then death by dagger.

Since Loring lost a little finger, Trask suspects secrets. But Loring has vanished. In searching the mansion, Trask discovers the concealed room, the vault, Loring's body. And that lost morocco pouch. From this he deduces that the murderer was Vanardy and that he can be located at The House on the Point, latitude and longitude given in the cryptic notes.

And so he can. Vanardy has moved the jewels to his house on The Point, a strip of beach extending into the Atlantic. He has buried the jewels at the tide line. Returning to the house, he discovers his faithful servant, Dulla, dead of a slit throat.

The meaning of his accumulating misfortunes he learns from a book in his library, conveniently enough. The book explains the Seven Signs of Doom associated with the Koh-i-tur, afflicting Vanardy with the superstitious fits. Even as he shakes and sweats, he is attacked by someone—or something—and a red swastika is stenciled on his forehead. Before he can get his mind organized, a woman appears—a beautiful Indian woman, introducing herself as The Voice and The Hand.

(Her face) was dusky of hue, and its exquisitely chiseled lines formed a picture of sorcerous beauty, despite the fixed look of relentless cruelty and unswerving purpose that flashed from the large pools of her eyes. Her mouth was formed into a hard but bewitching smile.[22]

She has come, with two assistants, to collect the diamond—or else. But the Phantom's equilibrium has been restored by the sight of a corporal antagonist.

Vanardy: "So you have taken all these elaborate measures to restore the missing eye of the idol of Dabaredyh? Why not try something original? Don't you know that trinkets stolen from idols were figured in nickel movies and cheap novels for years? If you want to be theatrical, why not exercise your imagination?"[23]

So much for *The Moonstone* and its two hundred imitators. Impressed by the Phantom's reasoning, The Voice and The Hand admits that she is indifferent to the needs of the idol. She is doing all this for her father, the Nizam of Dadaredyh, who has met financial reverses and cannot finance an expedition to aid the Allied cause in Europe. The idol's priests have promised two-and-a-half million to the person recovering the diamond. She is determined that her father will get the money, and the excellence of her cause will, of course, excuse her excesses in the reader's eyes.

Vanardy refuses to be forced to do anything. Is he not the Gray Phantom? He is lightly tortured to intensify the drama, then tricks his captors by leading them to dig up an abandoned grave. This sacrilege so shocks them that he easily knocks the whole bunch out.

Having reasserted his superiority (is he not the Gray Phantom?), he then gives the girl the diamond.

Vanardy: "I like to express my admiration for a worthy foe. And I can afford to be generous now."

As the Voice and The Hand glides away, sweetened by gratitude, from out of the darkness rushes Trask. Dropping the rest of the Russian jewels, the Gray Phantom melts away among the rocks. He has lost the jewels and murdered another criminal; on the other hand, he has indirectly aided the Allied cause. Surely that counts for something? You can forgive a master criminal almost anything, providing that none of the loot sticks to his fingers at the end of the story.

Having avoided Trask, the Phantom continued his adventurous life, plots by day and thrills by night, enjoying himself as only as master criminal can. That is to say, he acts as a free-lance adventurer. His mighty world organization exists only to help Mr. Landon over boggy patches in the plot.

Even master criminals grow weary at last. By 1919, unfailing success has so jaded Vanardy that he retires, disbands his organization, pensions off his lieutenants. As it is explained in "Grey Terror," *Detective Story Magazine,*

Nothing but sheer boredom had caused the Gray Phantom to suspended the spectacular criminal activities that had made his *nom de guerre* famous on several continents. Never having cared for money for its own sake, his only object in taking to crime had been to drain an extra thrill from existence, to find an outlet for his tremendous energies, and to obtain the excitement he craved. The novelty had quickly worn off, the excitements had degenerated into a tedium, and finally the Gray Phantom had grown weary of his criminal career.[24]

Retirement affects people in unpredictable ways. In Vanardy's case, it seems to have caused his little finger to grow back. It also resulted in the resurrection of Dulla, faithful even past death.

In spite of these miracles, in spite of his youth and wealth beyond calculation, Vanardy limps glumly about, bored, a pitiful sight. Dulla cannot cheer him up. Nor can Vanardy's close friend, the cheerful fat Pellington, managing director of the Pellington Detective Service.

To this point, the fiction is mixed blandly from those staples of wealth, boredom, uneasy retirement, and a detective antagonist. From this unpromising blend, something peculiar rises.

Vanardy resolves to come from retirement to create one final criminal masterpiece. He recalls his two lieutenants—fat Wade and clever young Liggett—ordering that they assemble two dozen of the best men from his disbanded gang. They are then to secure four monkeys, two sightseeing automobiles, and the collar size of forty prominent citizens from the town, Bostburg.

That catalog of improbable requirements is sufficient to inflame the most jaded curiosity. It is followed by an explanation that would sound almost reasonable were it not over the border into science-fiction. Vanardy knows a crazy inventor who has perfected a device for the execution of kings and emperors. This is a serrated rubber collar which, when latched about the neck, proceeds promptly to strangle the wearer. It contracts inexorably and, since it is filled with fulminate of mercury, cannot be cut loose without exploding. The collar separates only along one concealed line and for each collar, the line is different.

Vanardy's plan has the simplicity of dawn. The Gray Phantom gang rolls into Bostburg by night, closes in on the forty prominent men, and collars every last one of them. Just too late, a squealer in the gang tells Pellington that Vanardy is the Gray Phantom. Before the detective can act, the collars are in place. And a public demonstration with the four monkeys shows that the devices cannot be removed without terrible results.

From this point on, ingenuity yields to pure extortion. Either the town permits its six banks and two jewelry stores to be looted—or heads will fly. As Vanardy is explaining to Pellington and the city fathers the unfortunate consequences of resisting his will, they seize him and thrust him into a small vault. He promptly secures his freedom by snapping a collar around his neck. If he dies, all die. Only the Phantom knows how to remove the collars without adverse side effects.

After the forces for good are soundly quelled, the theft proceeds quite openly. Black Star would be pleased. No vulgar shooting or shouting. Only nice safe relaxed stealing.

After a leisurely escape, the gang is paid off. Vanardy comes drifting back to town, having removed all the collars, to advise Pellington that most of the stolen property has been buried in the local park. The city may have it back, minus $750,000 expenses, the price of relieving Vanardy's boredom.

And how does Vanardy now expect to escape?

He does not. In the stress of freeing the unhappy forty, he lost the combination to the collar that is still around his neck. Soon it will strangle him, unless he first sets off the explosive. "I'm a doomed man, Pellington. Nothing on earth can save me. Gray death for the Gray Phantom seems rather fitting. Anyhow, with this thing accomplished, I should soon lapse back into boredom again. I don't know but that death is preferable."

He rushes away into a small park. A knife glitters in his hand, An explosive crash rocks the area. The series ends at its beginning.

Nonsense. Nothing ends a character except reader indifference.

The story picks up several months later ("The Gray Phantom Goes It Alone," November 25, 1919.) There sits Vanardy, now nicely black-bearded and very very bored, in his luxurious home at Azurecrest by the Susquehanna River. He is unharmed, unknown, and unwanted by the police, who apparently believe that he was exploded to a cloud of atoms. In these stories, the police believe anything the author wishes.

The Gray Phantom's gang is entirely dispersed. Only Clifford Wade remains; he has grown immensely fat, adding a touch of comedy to these serious proceedings.

To Azurecrest comes determined Helen Hardwick, tiny pistol in her tiny hand. Her father's museum was recently looted and he is a broken man. Helen has reasoned that a collector of rare curios has done this thing. She has sought out whispers and rumors and hints, and, by a type of reasoning peculiar to women in pulp fiction, has decided that the recluse by the Susquehanna is the thief. He collects curios; he is solitary; and therefore, Q.E.D.

With Helen, thought and action are one, although thought is not essential. She appears suddenly within Azurecrest, showing her little pistol and demanding that Vanardy return the stolen treasures.

She is in error. Vanardy is too bored to consider robbing museums, small prey after the wholesale stealing of the past. He is, however, mildly revived by her spunk and promises to restore the museum's property within a week.

Off he travels to New York City. Advertises for curios. Is immediately given a drugged cigarette by a lovely woman, brains of the Duke's gang. By Chapter VI he is in the Duke's power.

The Duke, mentioned in "Seven Signs," has now dwindled to a rival gang leader aspiring to equal the achievements of the Gray Phantom. He hates Vanardy, loathes him, would destroy him, even kill him. First, before murder, he wishes to learn the location of Azurecrest, for he intends to take the whole of the Phantom's treasure.

Although the Duke is described as a fearful terror, he is most inefficient. Vanardy escapes. Two chapters later, he finds himself nailed up inside a coffin.

A minor problem. After all, he is the Gray Phantom.

"The Gray Phantom has always lived up to his name, hasn't he? Whenever he was thought to be cornered he always found a way out. Every time he was believed to be in a given place it developed that he was someplace else. Some people have gone so far as to credit the Phantom with occult powers. Perhaps they are right."[25]

Perhaps they should have credited him with a tiny kit of emergency tools. Using these, he digs free of the coffin, finds himself in a sub-basement packed with the loot from the museum.

Bored now? Certainly not.

Down in the deeps of that sub-basement, Vanardy and the Duke face each other. The gangster rages and snarls and calls down all his men, forty or fifty of them, to view the Phantom at bay.

The Phantom's situation is unpromising. But what would paralyze a lesser man does not ruffle his cool superiority. In a moment, he has shot out the lights and suddenly:

...a wisp of gray light...appeared at the other end of the room. It wavered and fluttered, like luminous mist in the surrounding darkness, shooting into slender tendrils that were gradually rising higher, forming a pyre of cloudy rays.[26]

It is apparent to the weakest intelligence that the Gray Phantom has become a column of mist. The forty-odd crooks promptly empty their pistols at this column, pumping about three-hundred shots into the narrow basement room. In spite of this lead cascade, not a single person is hurt. No ricochets. No flying bits of brick. It is a miracle. At least as great a miracle as getting all those people to believe that a cloud formed by an ignited phosphorous-compound was the Gray Phantom dematerializing.

During the uproar, the Phantom slips from the room and blocks shut its only door. He then calls the police and the action portion of the story is over.

In due time, he reports back to Miss Hardwick and wins from her a single kiss, "a thrill of such hallowing influence as I never dreamed existed."

Reformation by love is a convention of the criminal hero story. Love spoiled the promising careers of such illustrious masters as Jimmy Valentine, Cleek, and the Lone Wolf. All these loved and repented and sought salvation from the mire of their past by good deeds in the present. If love were not quite enough to redeem the character in the readers' eyes, the author was quick to revise past history and provide a mendacious justification.

(Vanardy) wondered why his restless spirit could not have found a different outlet. Perhaps the reason was to be found in the remote and dimly remembered past when, friendless and homeless, he had derived his philosophy of life from thieving urchins and night-prowling gangsters.[27]

Environment will do it every time. He got to playing in the gutter with Mike Lanyard and Tony Trent, and, before he realized it, he was a master criminal. Happens constantly.

Once corrupted, he moved "like a swaggering Robin Hood from one stupendous adventure to another."

...he gratified his thirst for thrills and excitement, always playing the game in strict accord with his code and invariably planning his exploits so that his victims were villains of a far darker dye than he. Always his left hand had tossed away what his right hand had plucked. Hospitals, orphan asylums and other philanthropic organizations became the recipients of donations that were never traced to their source. Princely and mysterious gifts poured into garrets and hovels in a way that caused simple-minded people to believe in a return of the day of miracles.[28]

It is necessary that the page be flooded with this bosh, for Vanardy's criminal record is being expunged in a flood of sugar water. The simple-minded reader, unable to remember the constricting collars of 1919, two years earlier, must surely have been convinced. With all his virtues stated right there in type, it was obvious that the Gray Phantom was not the sort to choke and explode forty businessmen, thereby gratifying his itch for thrills and excitement. No Robin Hood could be so wicked. Forget all that. Mr. Landon has. The Gray Phantom is only a poor orphan boy who grew up friendless. At that, he only robbed the evil and gave the proceeds to the homeless, ragged poor.

By George, he is one fine fellow.

Lieutenant Culligore thinks so.

Culligore of the Homicide Squad is the resident policeman of the series. He is a tall, lanky fellow with cinnamon-colored eyes "and a complexion that seemed to indicate that he drank too much coffee and smoked too many cigars."

During the course of the series, he will capture the Phantom at least two dozen times. He also releases the Phantom two dozen times. Even if Vanardy has found it necessary to smack the Lieutenant's head. Even if outstanding warrants exist for his arrest. Culligore is sympathetic. I'll bet a pair of pink socks (his favorite expression) that he is. You see, the Phantom never lied to him. And at the end of each story, the Phantom turns over to Culligore a carload of crooks, already caught and tied. You have to admire a sincere crook who plays by his code.

Culligore admires Helen Hardwick, too.

Everybody admires Helen. Even Mr. Landon, who dedicated most of the Gray Phantom books "TO THE OTHER HELEN WHOSE NAME IS SOMETHING ELSE" or, more delicately, "TO H. B., THE OTHER HELEN" or, archly, "TO A CERTAIN BRUNETTE."

(Mr. Landon had married Heather Benjamin in 1922.)

Helen is a woman of accomplishment. She has written a successful play and handles a pistol with skill. Her curiosity and intelligence lead her from one tar pit to the next. She is described as having a "fresh young charm and frank brown eyes." Also a firm, oval face. For those astrologically inclined, she was born under Uranus, meaning, perhaps, that she has a tendency to get kidnapped. That habit forces the Gray Phantom to perform all manner of feats he would not otherwise undertake, being a man of sense. Except where Helen is concerned.

One flaw blemishes this otherwise superb woman. She has cultivated a whimsical, arch manner of speaking to her "Phantom Man" that causes constriction of all your major blood vessels.

Helen: "I love clouds—dark, sullen, scowling ones. And I love lightning and storm, too. The sunlight is all the more beautiful after they are gone.

Translated to English, this means that she loves adventuring with Phantom Man, and they have just survived another series of experiences that would leave less lucky people in a sad state of repair.

Cute references to clouds hang, like wens, at the end of many Phantom stories. Since television has dulled your awareness, you may now find them blatant jolts of sentimentality. Back in the 'Twenties they left readers feeling warmly secure.

After the Gray Phantom's first adventure, he threw off the shadow of Black Star, met Helen, and cultivated reform. At that point, a giant mechanism in the sky began grinding out a novelette or serial about every six months. Publication was so spaced that the reader could overlook certain similarities of treatment.

One form of story is about as follows:

The Duke's men, seeking revenge, frame the Phantom. He must face dire peril rather than allow Helen to lose faith in him. At the last possible instant, when all is lost, he faces several hundred snarling criminals and turns the tables on them by a clever trick. (Thus, typically, "The Gray Phantom's Defense," *Detective Story Magazine*, six-part serial, June 1 through July 6, 1920.)

A second form lightly varies the first:

A secret genius of crime either kidnaps or frames Helen. This ensures that the Phantom will perform certain special services, rather than endanger one sweet hair of her head. When all is lost, the Phantom and Helen face two or three hundred leering criminals and turn the tables on them. (Thus, typically, "The Gray Phantom's Surrender," *Detective Story Magazine,* October 15, 1921.)

These narratives require a fairly high concentration of secret passages, secret rooms, secret tunnels, and extraordinary drugs. It is rather like reading a silent movie. Stories frequently conclude in a violent gun fight, during which more cartridges are fired than by the Union Army at Shiloh.

No one ever gets killed. The Gray Phantom never kills; that would smudge his rectitude. Helen can't kill; that would brand her for life. And the crooks can't kill because that would end the series.

Through these scenes of non-lethal violence flits Lieutenant Culligore. He never quite seems to understand what is going on—astonishing in a man so obviously competent and intelligent. But for the purposes of the story, to sustain its improbabilities, pad its situations, and magnify the Phantom's abilities, Culligore must seem dim. He must misunderstand when the situation would be clear to a wooden post. He must never quite do the right thing at the right time. He must never be quite good enough.

The one thing at which Culligore excels is capturing the Gray Phantom, that elusive man of mystery.

But then, everyone captures the Phantom. He is the most easily caught hero in popular literature. Your three-year old daughter could do it and never drop her dolly.

Through the action, the Gray Phantom glides, from misjudgment to blunder to oversight to folly. He fumbles blindly along, sustained only by his reputation. In spite of his uniformly dismal performance, all characters regard him with awe, none more so than the author.

The reader remains unconvinced.

He sees only too clearly that the icy planner of 1919 is the lovesick boy of 1921. Let Helen be shadowed by the slightest danger, and Vanardy comes all unstrung. His collar wilts. His trousers lose their press. A pitiful sight, he shakes and sweats.

Helen compounds his fears. She has no more instinct for self preservation than a lemming, and she gives Vanardy no easy time of it.

In "The Gray Phantom's Romance" (five-part serial, January 15 through February 12, 1921), Helen falls into the clutches of the sinister Mr. Shei. A former pupil of the Gray Phantom, Shei has purchased the Susquehanna property and adopted the Phantom's old methods.

Shei announces that seven wealthy men in New York City are to transfer half their wealth to him. He knows they are going to obey because he has injected each one with a slow-acting poison. If they don't pay for the antidote, they will die, laughing insanely, shrieking, foaming.

The plot cannot fail. But Shei feels it wise to keep the Phantom from meddling. Thus Helen becomes hostage and the Phantom again begins to shake and sweat.

However.... The Azurecrest property is built upon a tangle of secret passages and concealed rooms, none known to Shei. Through these, the Phantom enters the stronghold, there to fumble and fritter and flub.

Locates the antidote. Then blunders his advantage away.

He is beaten at every turn.

"Defeated? The Gray Phantom doesn't even know the meaning of the word."

With that defiant cry, he leaps away with Helen. Hidden doors clash shut, trapping all the criminals and the grand villain, Shei, in a dramatic climax that must be read repeatedly to be believed.

The seven-part serial, "Human Pawn" (September 30 through November 11, 1922), is a long, loose story containing enough plot for two novels. When published as a book, the serial was enriched with additional material. The end product, a rather hysterical confection, was published as *Gray Terror*.[29] It has no connection with the first Gray Phantom novelette of that name.

The central story tells how the Duke's gang kidnaps Helen away. This time, she will be held hostage until the Phantom breaks the Duke out of jail. Or else.

At one point, tension rises so high that the Phantom slugs Culligore, who is behaving more rationally than usual. Repenting his hasty action, the Phantom pledges that he will make Culligore a present of the entire gang.

He does so by entering the Duke's secret hideout while disguised as the Duke. He is dressed in the Duke's clothing, sneering the Duke's sneer, fooling the Duke's men. He even sits at the Duke's desk, along which extends a plot device—a row of pearl buttons. These have no labels, but he is able to learn the function of all save the final button.

At this point, he is recognized as an imposter. As the killers close in, he hazards all on one great gamble and places a finger on that final button.

All blench and cower.

—Surrender or I will press this button.

—Oh, do not press that button, for it is connected to a million tons of explosive and will detonate largely.

The scene illustrates one of Mr. Langdon's favorite concepts: The man bent on suicide can force others to do whatever he wishes, as long as he can take them with him.

In "The Gray Phantom's Madness" (six-part serial, May 26 through June 30, 1923; re-titled *Hands Unseen* for book publication), it would appear that the Phantom has lost his mind. He has written to ten wealthy men, demanding from each a million dollars for a special fund. As usual, blackmail is at the bottom of it all. Helen's father has been kidnapped and the Phantom has been ordered to pay ten million dollars for his release.

Now you understand. He was not mad after all.

A secondary story stirred into this confusion concerns murders in a sealed room. No secret door can be found. Yet muffled figures appear by night to jeer and mock. Men die. Culligore is positive that the Phantom is responsible and takes forceful measures for a change. Once more the Phantom is driven back and back, his position increasingly hopeless. He ends up trapped in the room with Helen, his enemies booming at the door, and only a Chinese coin and a few remaining seconds to solve the mystery. He does. And unmasks the real killer.

"The Speaking Fog" was a six-part serial, August 30 through October 4, 1924; for book publication, it was re-titled *Gray Magic*. The Fog is a silver-gray mist from which a voice purrs. Although the gimmick was used by the Phantom in 1919, he has forgotten all about it in 1924 and is, consequently, in a pitiful puzzlement.

The novel is a confusion nested within a muddle.

The Phantom wakes to find himself presumed dead, burnt up in an automobile accident. The plot has been engineered by that fiend, Rude, who holds the Phantom prisoner on an island in Maine. His captors address him as Wyndham. They know he is not Wyndham; they believe that he is an escaped convict named Allan Hoyt. The reader knows no one's identity and after a time ceases to care.

Behind this numbing tangle grins Marcus Rude. In the very finest tradition of sensational literature, Rude is into wholesale murder. He has perfected an elaborate murder technique which slaughters men on their birthdays.

Selected men: Respectable businessmen sharing a deadly secret.

Once all of them belonged to Rude's gigantic smuggling ring. To protect themselves from each other, each man signed a confession, gave this to another member.

That businessmen would be so credulous explains the Depression. Rude decides to collect the confessions and institute non-stop blackmail. That central spring powers the story.

The Phantom and Helen end sealed in an air-tight room that contains only a sarcophagus and a deadly snake. Curiously enough, Rude does not anticipate that they would find refuge in the sarcophagus. But they do, later emerging for a dramatic ending. The Phantom pounds Rude to jelly and Culligore carries the gang off to jail.

Since the plot requires a special twist, Culligore does not recognize

Wyndham as the Gray Phantom. Officially the Phantom is dead. Dead, buried, lamented, forgotten, his life of crime and struggle closed, his police record stamped "Deceased," his checking account at the bank held in trust, his serialized adventures terminated.

Life rises from death and Wyndham rises from Vanardy.

Those lingering clouds have finally blown away.

Blue skies, oh, blue skies, Phantom Man.

Helen: "...the clouds are all gone. Isn't it glorious?"

Phantom Man: "Glorious!"

Readers well steeped in the lore of the 1930s pulp magazines may be startled by the familiar plots of these 1924 Gray Phantom adventures. They are the same plots which filled year after year of *The Phantom Detective* and *G-Men,* and appeared intermittently in both *The Shadow Magazine* and the *Spider,* in the novels of the early *Clues,* and in short stories and novelettes of the detective action magazines.

The central situation is serial murder among men sharing a common secret. Once that common bond was established, the story virtually wrote itself. The major variation was that, by the 1930s, the action was lubricated with blood. People died in every column—an extravagance not practiced in 1924. The core situation persisted. But the action, ever more violent, raced across the decades toward the hills of nightmare.

Other aspects of the 1930s mystery action fiction are prefigured in Landon's Gray Phantom.

—An outlaw hero, young, wealthy, and with artistic tastes, battles enemies of society in an effort to atone for his previous crimes. In doing so, he must evade both police and criminals.

—He carries weapons and a small tool kit. At least once an adventure, he must fight a gun battle against overwhelming numbers.

—His wits are pitted against a large criminal gang led by a criminal genius of concealed identity.

—This criminal usually plots massive crimes, extortions affecting vast numbers of people, and serial murders of those he has been secretly associated with.

—The hero is supported by a responsible police official who offers tacit support. And by a heroine of such competence that she repeatedly influences the action.

—The hero and heroine are repeatedly trapped, only to escape by their wits. They intend to marry at some unspecified future time.

—The hero is so able at disguise that he can impersonate an individual, even among that person's intimates.

This later characteristic, the ability to disguise, became a fixed convention of the later single-character magazines. The primary assumption of such series as *The Phantom Detective* and *Secret Agent*

X is that the hero can routinely assume another's features and personality. Suitably disguised, aided by bluff, good luck, and intelligence, the hero can stroll unsuspected to the heart of any criminal conspiracy. Once there, his quick pistol supplements art.

The tradition of the human chameleon, as we have seen, embraces such past masters as Cleek, Nick Carter, and Colonel Clay, all from the turn of the century, all able to counterfeit a known personality. The tradition the characters represent runs straight as a chalk line from 1886 to that scene in the 1922 "Human Pawn" when the Gray Phantom successfully passes himself off as the Duke.[30]

A decade after the Gray Phantom, any popular fiction character could become any living man. (Women were almost never impersonated.) It is one of the major conventions transmitted from the 'Twenties.

Few of these elements just described—the hero's personal characteristics and his relationships to the supporting characters—were original with Landon. Like Johnston McCulley, Landon was a major conduit through which the energy and narrative devices of earlier mystery fiction were transmitted. Landon invented little that was new. He worked within a tradition already defined and elaborated by the exploits of Cleek and Jimmie Dale. These he lightly modernized and repackaged.

Rather by accident, Herman Landon seems to have formulated a prototype 1930s hero figure some ten years too early. With a trifle less sentiment, a fraction more aggression, Vanardy might have survived into the 1930s single-character magazines. The large success of The Phantom Detective (1933-1953) demonstrates how eagerly readers accepted a character embodying many of the Gray Phantom's characteristics.

By then, criminal heroes who sought that elusive bird Reform were no longer in vogue. By the mid-'Twenties that character type had hardened to cliche and was disappearing from the magazines. A few late blooming series appeared after 1925, like roses in November. In these, however, the criminal hero does not reform as a conscious act. He merely gives up crime to do something else. Frequently he becomes a detective.

8-

As did the Motor Cracksman, who appeared in *Flynn's Weekly* from mid-1925 to mid-1926. The stories were written by a Roland Johnson, probably a pen name. Mr. Johnson had learned the valuable fact that, if you wished to be published by the mid-1920s Flynn's, you should be English.

The early Flynn's was tightly packed with stories by English authors; stories purchased direct from England and featuring such names as Wallace, Christie, and Wynne; English detectives and medical men; stories set in England that were written by people who confused Northumberland with the New Jersey mountains.

A fraction of the magazine also contained American crook stories, thief stories, convict stories, all describing a variety of social losers in the act of failure.

Each front cover was illustrated by a posed photograph. These showed girls, in the remarkable clothing of the day, being menaced by men in masks, clutching hands, or shadows from beyond. The internal illustrations were rather artless line drawings, mannered and lightly sketched. All the men looked the same—young and dull or fat and humorous. All the girls were thin and held their mouths roguishly open. After some months, the illustrations reveal a certain wispy charm and what you first looked at with contempt, you eventually consider with a feeble pleasure. At best, the early *Flynn's* illustrations are an acquired taste.

The magazine writing is sound, if unexciting, narrative. The emphasis is on problem mysteries: Who killed him? Who stole it? Through the fiction pass ponderous police inspectors and sharp-eyed amateur sleuths, fool girls creeping about blackened mansions, and innumerable dead corpses, killed lifeless by a nameless fiend.

The bulk of the stories are so brazenly English that they rouse in you an insatiable desire for Brussels sprouts.

This is particularly true of the Motor Cracksman series, which is so intensely English that it was likely written in Chicago. Basil Lisle, Esquire, has been disinherited by his overbearing father, Sir Fortescue Champreys Basil Lisle of Winterton, Northumberland, that old devil.

Far back in Basil's family tree is an ancestor known by the tolerably cute name of The Laughing Highwayman. After he is cut off without a pence, Basil models his career upon that of his ancestor.

He becomes a modern highwayman. He waves a large pistol. His face is concealed by a khaki handkerchief, complete with eye slits. Not only does this look devilish, but it hides the long scar on his temple. Comes concealing night, he slips to the roadway and urgently flags down automobiles. Then points his pistol, commandeers the machine.

This was, you understand, a time of open automobiles traveling 25 to 40 miles an hour on country roads. His technique was adapted to the times. Since all the cars are insured, no one loses anything.

Well, the insurance companies do. Although when you figure how rich they are.....

The Motor Cracksman's wholesale thefts finally catch Scotland Yard's attention. Muttering sluggishly, their faces red, their eyes glassy, the authorities initiate appropriate action to counteract the depredations of this scoundrel. They are fooled with ease. "Through the Net" (July

11, 1925) tells how Basil foils the police trap by loading the stolen car into a van, then driving through police lines.

Once the machine is in Basil's hands, he delivers it to his manager, a tubby little rascal named George Stycey. This wretch turns it over to the mechanic, Waltham, for repainting. Then it is sold out of England. Or it is taken to pieces and strewn over Stycey's secondhand parts store, "one of the largest in England."

"Highwayman's Conscience" (September 12, 1925) is concerned with family matters. Basil's father, in a fine rage, is pursuing Basil's step-sister cross-country in an automobile. Father thinks that she is with a boy friend and he intends to whip the rascal with a black-snake whip. Enroute he encounters his son (unrecognizable in that khaki mask) and is marooned carless, miles from home. Basil does not steal the car, however. Only drives it a short distance away. "But to steal from one's own father—even if one is disinherited—would be the outside edge of a limit."

Numerous thrilling adventures later, Scotland Yard lumbers close, its honest face wrinkled with the effort of thought. Since his identity as The Motor Cracksman has become known, Basil changes his name and face. He retires from crime to Merrywell Hall near the village of Belford.

His manager, who has re-christened himself Alfred White, joins him in retirement. This calm interlude lasts for one breath, perhaps two. Since it is the nature of a series to add one story to another, or terminate, the adventures must continue, although the characters have all changed their names, the initial premise has been abandoned and retirement wraps our hero in its drowsy arms. Until "The Phantom Car" (September 12, 1926), at which point the series lunges off in another direction. Basil takes up investigation of problems associated with automobiles and highway travel. As his first case, he solves the problem of the mysterious white car that streaks, silently, without lights, along night roads.

Dope smuggler.

The Scotland Yard representative is amazed. Naturally he does not recognize as Basil Lisle, the notorious Motor Cracksman, this astute young man of aquiline features, who reasons coldly, as smoke from his perfecto finos cigarettes wreathes his head....

Near the end of the 1920s, the fictional criminal heroes became, at once, less elaborately presented and justified, and somehow less consistent. The writers seemed to sense massive change creeping stealthily within the fiction, a terrible cat, but were, as yet, unsure how best to modify their work.

Leslie Gordon Barnard's series about the wicked Mr. Philibus is from this period. The stories were published in *Detective Fiction Weekly* and *Detective Story Magazine* and were as erratic as a team of black

Popular Magazine (February 20, 1926). The automobile, that wonderful invention, added a modern touch to that old favorite, the chase.

snakes.

It is hard to explain the peculiar tone of the stories. In eight pages, they veer from sentimental slush, flecked with hardboiled and comic passages, to ponderous irony to vaguely stream-of consciousness narrative. You wonder why the style is so heavily facetious, like a sick man cracking jokes. Why do British phrases roll from American mouths, the dialogue frequently as stilted as a tintype and as obsolete.

And where exactly do the stories take place? London or New York? Brighton or Atlantic City? Early in 1930, Philibus does visit London— or was he there all the time? No that couldn't be; he crosses the Atlantic on a liner, but still. . . .

Philibus begins as a minor crook in minor fiction remarkable only for its lack of contact with the real world. As introduced, he is middle-aged, pudgy, ruthless. His hair is iron-gray, and he wears a pair of long mustaches. As a character, he is—well, inconsistent, for lack of a harsher word.

He is a wanted man at the opening of "Mr. Philibus' Christmas Eve" (December 22, 1928, *Detective Fiction Weekly*). As he gazes from the window of a restaurant, he sees a mean policeman nab a boy for sledding on the sidewalk. We recognize at once that Philibus' crimes are to be offset, in the reader's eyes, by the swaggering arrogance of law enforcement officials. These are cold-spirited, bungling, corrupt wretches. You disdain them. Certainly you disdain that policeman, a Scrooge in uniform, blighting that little sledder's happiness. Makes you almost feel like cheering, as Philibus trips the officer, lets the boy escape.

This good deed is observed by a starveling young man who has nothing but a British accent. He blackmails five dollars from Philibus, then returns to his starving, patient wife and his starving, good-natured children, all huddled in their miserable slum room, freezing but brave. And this on Christmas Eve. It is just awful.

You feel that something should be done. And Mr. Philibus does it. He steals the five dollars from the young man's pocket. When the young man returns to the streets, desperate, ready to commit any crime, Philibus is right there, in disguise.

He tells the young man about a particularly vulnerable safe and, having planted the seed, melts away. It is all part of his plan. He cracks the safe, leaves it gaping for the young man as a sort of inexpensive Christmas gift.

On leaving the building, he encounters the mean policeman, peering and scowling. Within a page, he has lured the officer into the building, knocked him out.

Now the young man appears to rob the safe. Instead, he encounters an officer waiting in the shadows. This shadowy person lectures the young man severely, gives him the chance to go straight, buys toys for the children. Off the young fellow goes, morally strengthened by his experience.

That shadowy official figure was Mr. Philibus, himself, dressed in the uniform of the mean officer. And very nice he feels for having done good at Christmastime.

At this point, the reader may rouse with awful cries to hurl his Christmas tree across the room, for there are among us those who react violently to incoherent plots, improbable situations, and mechanical prose. If such a reader exists, he will not enjoy other Philibus adventures, either.

He may not even enjoy "Drowned To Win" (June 22, 1929, *Detective Story Magazine*). As this story opens, Philibus has just slugged and robbed a payroll messenger:

> ...when a man resisted and put up a fight to save the payroll he was carrying, what could even a peace-loving man like Mr. Philibus do? Land him one—that was all.... It was deplorable that he could not stay to render to the poor chap first aid. Had to leave him there on the sidewalk. Very messy! Deplorable! But certainly as you can see, it was the fellow's own fault. Without a doubt, he had struck at Mr. Philibus first....[31]

From this high point, the story minces onward, full of movement but lacking direction or coherence. Philibus next takes a train ride, sees a detective, eats a clam dinner, takes a room, dyes his hair, meets an old woman. Eventually he pretends to drown, rising from the water at a distant point and, with his mustaches clipped, free of the Law's pursuit.

"Philibus' Romance" (July 20, 1929, *Detective Story Magazine*) tells how he humiliates mean detective Gracey. Philibus plans robbery of an old rich woman who wears about fifty pounds of jewelry to the Yacht Club Masked Carnival. She loses it all, after immense confusion about two plain clothesmen stalking Philibus, mocking notes, costume switches, and enough coincidence to make you faintly ill.

Coincidence is worked overtime in "Mr. Philibus Goes Ratting" (August 3, 1929, *Detective Story Magazine*). Believing Philibus to be a detective, wharf thugs knock him on the head, tie him to an iron bar, and toss him into the bay, which seems a reasonable solution for thugs and reader alike. It is painful to report that Philibus is saved when a tug boat snags his bonds.

He returns to the crooks' hideout carrying a cage full of rats—got Lord knows where. He releases these, shouting "Plague!" While the criminals bounce around screaming, he snatches up their machine gun and escapes out one door as the police pour in the other.

"The Pond Lily" (February 8, 1930, *Detective Story Magazine*) refers to a beautiful, fragile, young, tender fluff of a girl who is riding the ocean liner between New York City and London. She deftly cons every male character in the story, including Philibus and his associate, Hot-dog Ryan.

Hot-dog is the exuberant second banana. He seems to have appeared first in early 1930, a lean, tall fellow dressed in vivid bad taste, and speaking that vivid patois used by right-hand pals since the days of Red Raven. He is crude, loud, inept, and Philibus tries hard to send him on his way. But Hot-dog hangs on, is accepted as a partner by 1932, and remains until the series terminates around 1935.

Hot-dog functions as the dumb foil who creates complexities. In his presence, the simplest plan becomes a corkscrewing marvel, reeling giddily about itself. He talks too much. He acts before thinking. You may depend on him to be in the wrong place at the wrong time for the wrong reason. He is an ideal character for the transformation of a fragile little idea, wispy and thin, to a story of complex confusion.

As soon as Mr. Ryan enters the series, the stories lighten. Barnard's ponderous strivings for humor are touched by comic flashes. It is obvious, rude comedy, but rude comedy has its uses. It interrupts the otherwise unrelenting archness that was characteristic of the series to this point.

As in the matter of the death of Mr. Philibus' father.

In "The Pond Lily," we learn that Mr. Philibus, Senior, an altogether worthless wretch, slipped on a banana peel after shooting a policeman, was captured, was hanged.

This simple statement of crime and punishment is puffed up grandly and presented, radiating spurious elegance, after the manner of Mr. W. C. Fields:

> The accident (his father's death), Mr. Philibus did not go on to state, was due to a banana peel on which his father, fleeing from an affray in shooting a policeman, slipped, and was pounced upon by another representative of the law, and in due course led to an eminence and let down suddenly on the end of a rope.[32]

Since little can be done to medicine such prose, short of purification by fire, let us turn to "Mr. Philibus—Thousand Dollar Man" (June 14, 1930). In this, Philibus steals the reward offered for him by a crooked businessman. In doing so, he bamboozles a hotel detective, a private citizen, and the business man, all fools. The March 12, 1932, "Mr. Philibus' Unwanted Partner," tells how he plans a simulated robbery; unfortunately, Hot-dog blabs the plan to a crook friend, who carries off Hot-dog's clothing and robs Philibus for real.

By mid-1935, private detectives were the fictional rage. Philibus adapts to the times and opens his own agency. "Winner Takes All" (August 25, 1935, *Detective Story Magazine*) tells how he meets the challenge of crook Jerry Jarman. Mr. Jarman bets 10 g's he can make a monkey out of Philibus "in a fortnight or less." Which is just the phrase we would expect from a New York thug.

Into Philibus' office comes a mysterious woman. Regarding this lady, Hot-dog comments: "Say, are all your clients as flossy bits of the nether sex as the Jane I've been meeting here the last two or three times?"

Believing Hot-dog to be Philibus, the flossy Jane leads him into a murder frame-up. Philibus, rousing to the rescue, is captured, escapes by setting a building aflame. He then captures Jarman with a mass of stolen furs. And wins the bet, obviously.

This is the kind of fiction that compromised the reputation of the pulp magazines. To think that it shamelessly displayed itself in *Detective Story,* the same magazine which would soon publish two of Ellery Queen's polished and wickedly sly adventures.

9-

Light fiction is not intended to bear load. Like a bridge of meringue, it exists to delight and amuse, to be decorated in gay colors and lighted fancifully. But under no circumstances to be walked upon.

This is hardly a fault. There are innumerable gradations in fiction, each with its own merit and its own yield point. To define one form of fiction as the best, codifying rules and regularizing merit, is to impoverish yourself. This world has room for both Tolstoy and McCulley, and sufficient opportunity to enjoy both, if you will. Or neither.

Light fiction is to be met on its own terms. It will delight and amuse. Less frequently, it may illuminate a character and his world. Rarely, only rarely, does it examine the issues implicit within that world. Such weighty matters are for more sober publications in which the heartbeat of the fiction shivers with that ecstasy of multi-level interpersonal interactions and awareness shifts from one mode of desperation to the next.

Detective fiction, mystery-adventure, being frequently light fiction, aspires to less formidable heights. Not for *Flynn's Weekly* or *Detective Story Magazine* those cliffs scoured by spiritual storm. These magazines sought the lower meadows that gleamed with problem stories, like bright little flowers. Who robbed away the jade Buddah? they cry eagerly. Who crept murderously through the dark? Who tied and kissed the unfortunate girl?

It is not usually difficult literature, save for the effort the problem requires. Each problem is a story. Resolve the problem and the story ends. The reader, lightly entertained, rustles over the page to the next problem, as skillfully embedded in narrative drama as the stone is embedded in a peach.

The people met in this chapter stand at the edge of the light mystery story. They may solve an occasional mystery problem. Still their attention is fixed elsewhere. Their destiny is to solve procedural problems, to reach a specific goal that has been armored by difficulties. They must punish greedy financiers. Or assemble the amulet. Or avenge the father, the brother, the sister betrayed and forlorn.

These series characters, criminals in name only, are adventurers, first of all, not detectives. They must balance their need to correct wrongs and protect the innocent against their ability to stay out of jail. For their methods are not legal, be their motives ever so pure.

They are criminals, at least for the duration of the story. It does not matter that they pursue limited objectives or strive to give up their old, bad ways. They are criminals as they adventure through the urban jungle. How their eyes shine as they feint and dart. Your heart glows with pleasure.

Because they work toward a single goal, their series are short. A cut fuse soon burns out. After two stories or a dozen, the clouds roll away, the costume smolders to ash, the terminal corned beef and cabbage fumes on the table. Their brief interlude of criminal activity is complete. Now a different life beckons with golden fingers.

Few characters return for a second series. When they do, they are fundamentally changed. They turn from justified crime to pure adventuring or detection, changes inspired as much by the needs of the fiction market, as by the character's moral regeneration.

The history of magazine series characters is long. Much shorter is the history of the temporary criminal and the criminal who, in a tremble of self improvement, determined to reform. Their stories appeared and peaked during the late 'Teens. By the mid-'Twenties, the flames had burned to ash. They did not entirely die. Through the decades into the present, the old ashes yielded infrequent sparks. But after 1924, these series characters, as a type, had lost their high appeal.

Most of the people in this chapter are variations on that grand old theme of the Bent Hero. Most wonderfully various are the Bent Heroes, and for how many reasons did they practice innocent crime for the benefit of society.[33]

Some were falsely accused. They must struggle under the twin burdens of police pursuit and a concealed plot against their person. That they could regain their reputation seems impossible.

Others willfully transgressed the law. Some did so in the abstract name of justice, righting wrongs recognized in no courts. Others, loving the excitement of crime, accepted the challenge of outwitting the world, with the stakes given to charity. After expenses.

And some few rogues preyed cheerfully upon criminals, stripping them of their soiled gains and, in the process, having a rousing good time for themselves.

VI—MORE ROGUES AND BENT HEROES

1-

A "picaroon," derived from the Spanish *picaron*, is a rogue, thief, rascal, and brigand. He may also be a pirate, that upsetting profession. A picaroon is, in short, a hazard to private property; he regards this as his own and comes to take it away at inconvenient times.

The Picaroon was one of *Detective Story Magazine's* most enticing bad boys. His adventures were written by Herman Landon and began perhaps two years after the Gray Phantom, in mid-1921. Certain differences separate the two characters. Unlike the Phantom, the Picaroon is a loner who never pillaged a town, never managed a gang, never had wide gangland contacts, never wished to reform, and never never never recast his life for a good woman.

It is disturbing to admit, but The Picaroon is a common thief. He is not even a cracksman, a title suggesting some form of distinction in crime. The Picaroon lacks the technical skill to open safes, unless these are positive cheese-boxes. He is merely a thief.

And, with becoming impartiality, The Picaroon will steal anything of value—money, jewels, bonds, paintings, tapestries, ornamental beams and ironwork. The Picaroon whisks them all away, leaving his card behind:

I trust you will pardon my little jest and excuse the liberties I have taken with your valuables. They will be returned to you promptly as soon as you have donated ten per cent of their value to the Society for the Protection of Animals.

THE BENEVOLENT PICAROON[1]

He is certainly not stealing for profit. He lives on his investments. Nor does he particularly care that blessings on him rise, a heady perfume, from legions of homeless dogs and cats. Not at all. The Picaroon steals for only one reason—he is out for excitement. And just a trifle of revenge.

> "...when The Benevolent Picaroon was a mere youth, he was unjustly convicted of a crime he never committed. He served several years in prison, and when he came out, he was naturally an embittered man, hostile toward the authorities and none too respectful of the law that had wronged him. Ever since he has been getting even by playing unmerciful jests on the police."[2]

It is hard on those losing valuables. Still, you may be sure that most victims are dishonest. It is that fine old technique of blackening the victims so that the hero criminal takes on a pale golden glimmer, agreeably salving the reader's conscience.

As to other details, The Picaroon is the alter ego of Martin Dale, an idle society lounger, clubman, horse and art fancier. As described by the heroine of the first story, Martin Dale is

> "Tall, well-proportioned, strong, but not exactly athletic. He really should be doing a man's work in the world, but instead he prefers to live the life of a genteel loafer....his features are striking rather than handsome. He appeals to women, but he is not the kind of man who is easily spoiled by them...
>
> "...he is rather dark. There's a brownish gloss to his short-cropped hair. His eyes are strong, sharp, and restless. When he smiles, which isn't often, his smile goes clear through one. His nose is rather too prominent, but he has a good mouth and a rather resolute chin."[3]

Tended only by the faithful Bilkins, who looks like a thug (in the tradition of valets to criminal heroes), Dale lives luxuriously in a brownstone on Forty-Eighth Street. His home is packed with art treasures and "rare contraband wines"—these being the dry years. The elegance is salted by bizarre touches—the etching of a French Apache, the skull of a world-famous swindler. But genius may be forgiven its private amusements.

At some distance from this plush nest are the seedy rooms of The Picaroon. It is the Jimmie Dale-Larry the Bat separation popularized by Frank Packard. The Picaroon has a life meticulously isolated from his real identity. At the beginning of the series, The Picaroon occupies a broken-down house on West Third Street, "an unsightly thoroughfare whose hideousness was accentuated by the roar of elevated trains and the presence of junk shops, reeky basement restaurants and garages and horse stables."

In later times, The Picaroon will occupy temporary quarters secreted about town. As do other gentlemen of secret identity, past and future, The Picaroon has a strong Chinese connection. When the police scowl, when the heat rises, when danger sniffs after him, The Picaroon will vanish into certain hidden basement rooms in Chinatown. One is at Wuh Chung's; another under Sam Ling's laundry.

On more relaxed occasions, he occupies the house on West Third Street. Inside the slatternly structure, bookshelves tower up. Heaps of books and papers pile in the dust. The rugs and furniture show hard wear. It seems clearly the home of a poor, and none too particular, scholar.

You should look further. Behind a secret door in a closet lie less innocent items. Here is stored that stolen property not yet redeemed and here are certain other items, equally interesting, from which the figure of The Picaroon is conjured up.

About half an hour is required to transform Martin Dale into The Picaroon. Over the years, details alter slightly. The basic figure is that of a stooped, sallow man, perhaps fifteen years older than Dale. He dresses in shabby gray. Large horn rimmed glasses cover his eyes. At first glance, he looks like a failed professor, mild, timid, his voice softly hesitant. He walks with a pronounced limp.

His altered appearance was not due to disguise of which there was very little, but rather to the easy familiarity with which he entered into another role. (Included) certain gestures and manners giving. . . . The Picaroon an individuality and a character that, together with the change in voice, made him a vastly different being from Martin Dale.[4]

These assurances to the contrary, Dale seems to have used some grease paint. However it is handled, the disguise seems effective, Even Captain Summers, who knows both Dale and The Picaroon, is not quite sure that the two are one.

That is Captain Summers of the detective bureau. He is the series cop, a heavy-set man with very short legs, a pear-shaped head, and immense ability. Summers is not a Johnston McCulley buffoon. A competent officer and a dangerous opponent, he enjoys a mild friendship with Dale. Almost at once, he suspects that Dale knows something about The Picaroon. That suspicion soon hardens to certainty.

He is never quite able to prove it. Two dozen times, Summers has The Picaroon caught, handcuffed, ready for booking. It is a rule of this particular world that, whenever The Picaroon walks out a door, he meets Captain Summers walking in, gun first. It seems incredible. Summers captures The Picaroon once or twice a story and never once manages to hold him.

But there never lived a being as slippery as The Benevolent Picaroon. Or one so full of tricks and astonishments.

It is like something you would read in cheap fiction. Enter Summers with cocked pistol. The Picaroon, diffident and gentle, walks into the pistol and takes it away. Or he pretends to strangle himself with a necktie, then snatches the pistol. Or pretends to become unconscious from poison, only to flit off when Summer's back is turned.

So childish are the tricks, so easily is Summers duped, that you must conclude the officer is practicing a little benevolence of his own.

The Picaroon enjoyed a mighty run in *Detective Story Magazine*. The stories appeared for slightly more than a decade, from 1921 to at least 1932, including more than thirty novelettes and serials. From this material, three books were assembled: *The Green Shadow* (1927), *The Picaroon Resumes Practice* (1931), and *The Picaroon, Knight Errant* (1933).

First of the series was "The Benevolent Picaroon," *Detective Story Magazine*, July 16, 1921. During the course of one of his little jokes, The Picaroon carried off a jade brooch. Now everyone wants it: the girl who has guessed Dale's dual identity, her plotting father, the crooked private detective. The brooch's secret eludes The Picaroon, and he is hard pressed to dodge Summers, who stands behind every door and peers through every window.

After complications wonderful to consider, it is Martin Dale who must save the girl and restore the brooch to her. In doing so, he gets mildly shot. Perhaps for that reason, Summers does not inquire too closely into certain technical irregularities—such as how Dale got possession of that pistol The Picaroon took from Summers.

That brooch is the first of many jade pieces. The cool shine of jade irradiates the series. Jade objects provide something to be chased after and struggled for, each piece having a different secret.

"The Picaroon and the Black Bag" (February 11, 1922) does not show Dale at his best. During a casual little robbery, he is caught, knocked out, tied up, and his fingerprints placed on The Picaroon's card. Blackmail is then applied. Services, not money, are wanted. The blackmailer, another crooked millionaire, wishes to be rid of his insane partner, and the Picaroon is to provide the final solution.

You may think The Picaroon ineffectually mild. He is not. In a crisis, he simply hurls plans in all directions, a hurricane of deceit. Wearing a simple disguise, he tricks the millionaire. A faked death scene tricks Summers. (Ah, poor Summers.) But it is luck luck luck that wins The Picaroon the millionaire's bag, fat with money, and the tell-tale card of fingerprints, too.

The Picaroon's illegal amusements constantly embroil him in problems. That situation launches most of the early stories. From that point, with a loud mechanical clicking, other familiar elements troop in procession. Girls must be assisted from deadly circling webs. Murderers and devious plotters must be exposed. The Picaroon's real identity must be shielded, and the unfortunate Summers must be circumvented one more time.

Dale's alternate identity is a fragile enough secret. He might as well wear a sign proclaiming him The Picaroon. During the first breath of the series, a hostile girl guesses the secret immediately, deducing it by the way Dale jumps and looks uneasily about when the Picaroon's crimes are discussed. From that point, matters deteriorate.

Even Summers catches on. Thereafter it is Summers, Summers, everywhere Summers, scowling, grim, handcuffs extended. He is such a bother.

In "The Picaroon Framed" (December 16, 1922), Dale's life is again complicated by one of The Picaroon's cards. Summers finds it by a murdered man. He also finds a small topaz from Dale's stickpin close by. Not wishing to explain such evidence, Dale bolts, stealing a fire chief's car and whirling off spectacularly.

Escape is hardly enough. His name must be cleansed and The Picaroon's reputation re-polished. Out he sallies to investigate, with predictable results. Summers instantly captures and handcuffs him.

It is only a minor matter. At some earlier time, when the reader was not paying attention, The Picaroon had planted his own handcuffs on Summers. These he opens with ease and bounds away, off to trap the real murderer. Who is, at this very moment, snuffling about the murder apartment, mopping up clues.

Confrontation. Drama, And Summers, reappearing like the knell of doom, captures the real killer, as The Picaroon melts away.

"The Green Shadow" (six-part serial, November 27, 1926, through January 1, 1927) combines all these familiar ingredients into another familiar story, only longer. An unknown blackmailer plies his wickedness in a room glaring with green light. A woman is murdered and her pearls vanish. A blurry being, glowing bright green, comes to Dale by night. Summers, forever in error, arrests Dale for the woman's murder. (And promptly loses him.) As the blackmailer threatens the wretched heroine. As Dale is again arrested. As the voice of a dead woman accuses him of murder. . . .

After this, the action gets underway.

The role of jade as a central device in these stories is challenged only by handcuffs. Of handcuffs, there are more than enough. Once a story, The Picaroon gets handcuffed and must clink around, hands shackled together. We expect nothing less. A variation on this familiar theme is played in "The Picaroon's Iron Band" (three-part serial, January 25 through February 8, 1930). As the story opens, The Picaroon is wearing an iron band about his wrist. It has been fastened there by the fierce Caeser Pym, gangster lord. The band symbolizes subjugation.

It is embarrassing to wear another man's band, particularly when Summers sees it on Dale's wrist. So many difficult questions to answer. But Dale is determined not to remove it. Pym must do that. And so, into the thick of the gangsters, comes The Picaroon to intrigue and scheme and trick among the blood-thirsting types. And Pym finally removes the band—either that or The Picaroon will reveal that Pym is holding out a large percentage of the gang's loot.

(Al Capone would certainly have loved that part.)

The 1930s Picaroon has sensibly altered from the original concept. In the furnace of time, that light-hearted burglar, whose adventures arise from his crimes, has become an amateur Robin Hood, whose adventures are thrust upon him. Every girl he meets has a dangerous problem. And, being a gentleman, he must help all of them.

In "The Picaroon Handcuffed" (four part serial, January 3 through 24, 1931), the lady in distress has stolen a jade brooch. No sooner has she passed it to Dale for safekeeping than it is stolen again. She must have it back. And also the chip from it.

Before these can be recovered, The Picaroon wades into neck-deep trouble.

Mysterious blackmailers menace the heroine.

Illiterate men lie dead before letters written in French to a non-existent Mimi, each letter mentioning a mansion in the sky and a green door.

All is mystery. All is confusion.

Through bristling clusters of pistols, The Picaroon presses onward. He is captured by Summers. He is handcuffed. He escapes by a trick. He...

The Picaroon worked within the convention of the Bent Hero, borrowing from the shadowy figure of Jimmie Dale and the more immediate figure of the Gray Phantom. To that convention, he added a few footnotes: A disguise as perfect as ever worn by Nick Carter to protect the secret identity. A separate operating base more elaborate than Dale's Sanctuary, that grimy room in a tenement. And a friendly policeman whose duty it was to jail The Picaroon:

Dale: "The Picaroon has had another pleasant fling, and now, for awhile, he fades out of the picture."
Summers: "Wish he would stay out. He did me a good turn this time, but duty is duty. When my chance comes—"[5]

Four years later, you would find identical conversations between Richard Wentworth, the Spider, and his friendly enemy, Police Commissioner Kirkpatrick.

The Spider's time was not yet. Not quite. It was 1932 when the final Picaroon adventure appeared. *The Shadow, A Detective Magazine* had been published less than a year before, the first of the single-character magazines which, by 1933, would swarm in the market place. A twenty-year span of blood and violence was opening. In that lurid glare, the mild Picaroon, apologetic and gentle, would fade away. His contribution was made, his lesson taught. He had helped alter 1920s fiction. The time had come for harsher faces.[6]

2-

While the Gray Phantom sought to retire, and The Picaroon evaded Summers, and Johnston McCulley exploited the American taste for costumed simplicities, across the Atlantic the last great, gentleman burglar made his appearance before English audiences.

Blackshirt was the name.

The first Blackshirt story, 10,000 words long, was published in the 1923 *New Magazine*. Forty-six years later, in 1969, the final novel of the series was published, *Blackshirt Stirs Things Up*. During that time span lie thirty-two books, twelve written by Graham Montague Jeffries (under the name Bruce Graeme), and twenty written by his son, Roderic Jefferies (under the name Roderic Graeme).

The length of this series is astounding. It extends like the fabric of history, itself, from the Jazz Age to the Space Age, encompassing such absorbing events as a major depression, a major war, half a dozen minor wars, a non-stop retreat from the British Empire, a nonstop flight across the Atlantic, and a trip to the moon.

Through all this turmoil of event, Blackshirt persisted. He began as a Raffles figure, met a mystery woman, reformed and returned his loot, had a son who continued his father's criminal career. In 1952, Blackshirt returned as his old self, stripped of twenty-five years and a lot of accumulated history, a fully contemporary rogue. He was of first importance in the evolution of the English lawless hero.

For our purposes, this giant will be treated briefly, if with respect. His influence on American series characters seems less than on his English counterparts. In some measure, this was a matter of distribution. Even feverish scratching would hardly turn up a copy of the *New Magazine* west of the Hudson River, and the first book, *Blackshirt*, a collection of short stories, was not published until 1925.

A more severe handicap was the rise of new character types in the 1920s American pulps. By 1923, the year of Blackshirt's birth, readers in the United States had been saturated with daring cracksman wishing to reform. Jimmie Dale and the Lone Wolf retained their devoted following; their imitators, in all their frenzied hordes, had withered away, being replaced by cute street criminals, master criminals in hoods, limited-objective crook heroes, and those wonderful others whose adventures have occupied these many chapters.

While Americans embraced new themes, the English celebrated the old. Strong for tradition the English are.

"Imagine," (wrote Graeme) "a criminal—no, a gentleman cracksman after the style of my favorite character Raffles—dressed in black and working on his own."[7]

The outfit is distinctive: Black shoes and socks, black trousers and coat, black shirt and tie, black gloves, and a black mask that completely hides his face. He carries no weapons.

The costume has a double purpose. When wandering London streets by night, he could appear as a gentleman in evening dress, the black shirt concealed by his muffler (black) and cape. When proceeding to professional business, he had merely to stow away the collapsed top hat, and add the mask. Thus blackened out, he could melt without a trace into the darkness, as did generations of hooded, masked, encaped figures before him.[8]

His name is Richard Verrell.

He looked not more than twenty-seven or twenty-eight, though he was in reality thirty years old. His complexion was healthy, his features regular. As a whole his face was striking in its pleasantness. It was not that it was handsome.... The secret was that, paradoxically, it spelled that it belonged to a man—a gentleman.... Individually his features all merged into insignificance compared to his eyes...

They were large, brown eyes, eyes which danced and shimmered with delight at the bidding of the little devil behind, revealing every passing thought and motion except when on his guard.[9]

Besides looking wonderful, Richard Verrell is a successful novelist. He writes sentimental mystery stories for which there is unending enthusiasm. He is coining money by the carload.

Why then did he become a cracksman?

For the usual reason:

...he adored every moment when he was engaged in his nefarious enterprises. To him it was the thrill of danger which counted, not the amount of the haul. He would more willingly open a safe which contained only sixpence, if that particular safe were well-guarded, than he would abstract a casket of precious stones from an empty house.

His heart bubbled over with joy while he was at work. His ears alert for the slightest sound, his nerves taut to make an immediate move, it was his delight to invade a supposedly impregnable house or flat.

His amusement was to pit his wits against those of the police...and he always won. When in a ticklish situation, his ingenuity, his cunning, were superb, and none appreciated this fact more than his opponents....[10]

Later in the book, Graeme gives an elaborate justification for Blackshirt's behavior. It is along certain familiar lines already laid down by Cleek and the Lone Wolf—he had a perfectly awful boyhood, was brought up crooked, and was gnawed by the need for excitement. (In the course of these remarks, he gets off a dainty little slap at the likes of Jimmie Dale: "If he were born and bred a gentleman, with plenty of money, who then turned to crime for crime's sake, there would be no excuse.") The Blackshirt situation is different, of course. It's always different.

Verrell had been found wandering in the street when he was only a child. As Mr. Graeme puts it, "he knew not whom he was."

He is found by as sordid a couple as appear in literature, unwashed, drunken sorts who make Fagin look benign. They gather up the child, teach him thievery. Whatever he steals goes down their throats. When they are not drinking, they are beating the poor waif.

It is a pathetic story. With a background like that, it's no wonder young Verrell grew up with all his moral values askew.

Fate, with trifling help from Graeme, kills both these people in an accident. Thereafter, Verrell educates himself. He creates a new personality upon his unpromising beginnings. Becomes an author at twenty-two. Becomes a war hero a few years later, decorated, renowned. After the Armistice, he returns to London, writes his first novel, sees it streak gaudily into the upper air to flare success and reputation over him.

Nine months after the Armistice, Blackshirt appeared.

Why was he what he was? How was it that he lived a double life—on one hand a gentleman, a respected member of society; and on the other an outlaw, a thief of the night?

...he abhorred hypocrisy—he that lived a life of hypocrisy, his one life a living lie to the other. He himself knew not why, why he was thus, a man of dual personality, but one who could have known him well would have instantly laid his finger on the root of the trouble. His hidden life was nothing more or less than his excessive craving for excitement, an outlet of his dynamic forces, an opportunity to play a living game of chess. As a thief he was superb; as a detective he would have been prominent; but Fate had cast him on the wrong side of the law....[11]

In the face of such a perfect representative of the Bent Hero, we can only stand in solemn respect, hat in hand, eyes gravely lowered. Just one thing is lacking. A beautiful woman must now appear to stimulate his moral conversion.... Since Verrell lacks the intellectual strength of the Lone Wolf, he must be blackmailed into the paths of light, as Jimmie Dale before him.

Dale received letters. Verrell, being a 1920s figure, received telephone calls.

Not halfway through the initial story, just as Blackshirt is lolling in his room, admiring the pearls he has stolen, the telephone rings. At the other end speaks an unidentified young lady with a strong American accent and a bright command of American slang:

"Hello, is that Blackshirt speaking?"

From that point on, his life is not his own.

Somehow she knows all about him. She knows when he comes in and when he goes out. She knows what he has done and, worse, she proceeds to direct his life.

He must return the pearls. (And so he does, slipping through a house clumping with detectives.) He must then rob the arrogant Ronald McTavish, whose home is crammed with electrical devices that could detect the most cautious mouse. (And again he succeeds, creating an enemy who will pursue him ruthlessly.)

He must even return to the mansion of Sir Allen Dunn, scene of that initial pearl theft. By direction, Blackshirt must steal the opal ring of Sir Allen's daughter, Bobbie.

And so one thing leads to another. Through a series of connected adventures, Verrell gradually falls in love with Bobbie. Unfortunately for his peace of mind, he also falls in love with that jaunty American voice, His Lady of the Telephone—he believes her to be Jean McTavish.

While crime prances and love matures, McTavish has neither forgotten nor forgiven. He plots a trap of great complexity. Into this Verrell tumbles, escaping only by the author's considerable assistance. McTavish is accidentally killed while attempting to murder Blackshirt. It was his own fault, the wicked thing. Blackshirt is innocent.

And, shortly, Blackshirt is astounded. For he learns that his Lady of the Telephone is Bobbie.

Blackshirt, he assures her, is no more; they are to be married; the book closes in a flutter of cupids.

But there is no sense in wasting a superior Bent Hero on marriage. *The Return of Blackshirt* (1927) solves the problem of un-reforming the hero in a manner familiar to every soap opera aficionado. On their wedding day, the Verrells are involved in a train accident. Verrell believes Bobby killed. He has also received such a hit on the head that the past months vanish from his mind. As a natural consequence, he takes up Blackshirting again, vigorously as ever.

You will be pleased to learn that Bobby has not died. But she must locate Verrell, woo him, reform him all over again—this time without the advantage of being able to see directly into his room with a telescope, which is why she knew so much about Blackshirt to begin with.

Blackshirt Again (1929) recounts earlier adventures before he fell into the clutches of Miss Bobbie Dunn. During this novel, Blackshirt steals every jewel from members of a large house party. Then, because a beautiful girl is suspected of the crime, he must return them. After which, someone else steals them and he must spend the balance of the book recovering the things.

When they are finally restored and everyone is gloriously happy, Blackshirt steals them all over again. Such a merry rogue.

It is doubtful that any secret identity was more thoroughly known than that of Blackshirt. Every character who comes near Verrell suspects the truth. Bobbie knows, of course, and McTavish, as long as he lives, and retired Superintendent Marshall, and a newspaper man, and a crook, and....

Much of the story suspense turns on Verrell's attempts to divert suspicion, to prove that he is not Blackshirt by appearing in two places at once, to slip away from a constant stream of watchers and followers. He is singularly adroit. Still, Blackshirt's identity is one of the least well-kept secrets of the British Empire. Compared to him, The Picaroon was a mystery man.

Blackshirt represents the 1920s last major fling with the cracksman figure. The character is completely mainstream, a blend of Raffles, Jimmie Dale, and the Lone Wolf. Verrell is, however, more than the sum of these borrowings. He is his own unique man.

He is bold, even beyond the limits of good sense. An indulgent author favors him. The public adored him. So plated against adversity, he pushed his luck to the limit. "He had" (Graeme remarks), "so often left his coups to fate that he was beginning to be superstitious enough to believe himself lucky."

Coddled is a more accurate word. Let his nerves throb with anticipation, his body heat with impending excitement, and he is out in the night, rambling blindly. Selecting at random some house to enter and glide about in and be merry, in his own fashion.

This "Don't Plan/Strike At Once" attitude is characteristic of the early 1920s elan. Be bold and audacious. Make the large gesture, the astounding effort. Relish today and party tonight. Tomorrow is soon enough here.

English fiction first reflected these tinsel glitterings, a state of mind apparently carried over from the war in France where planning for tomorrow was wasted effort, considering that another bayonet charge against massed machine guns was scheduled for the morning. The attitude swiftly seeped into American letters. Popular fiction, that hungry exploiter of fads and attitudes, followed swiftly. Out in the real world, elan was a symptom of emotional bankruptcy. In fiction, where extreme attitudes enabled easy narrative drama, elan was the mark of a superior mind which saw *nada* and *nada* and again *nada* behind the world's crystal shell. So in the looser forms of 1920s fiction, rational despair was perverted to posturing. There was enough rational despair for all purposes.

The 1920s opened with customary social values under intensifying scrutiny. The alienation expressed in T. S. Eliot's "The Waste Land" (1922) and Ernest Hemingway's paragraphs between the stories of *In Our Time* (1924) could be seen, much diluted, grinning from behind the adventures of Blackshirt. In the face of that alienation, the large gesture is essential.

It is easier to make a gesture if you are an athlete dressed entirely in black. You may then scorn personal danger. You can clamber down a drainpipe carrying a helpless victim from a flaming building; then climb back into the blaze to make your daring escape. In even more emotional circumstances, you may carry a weeping child away from the body of its murdered parent. Even if this reveals your presence. Even if it causes others to suspect that you might be Blackshirt.

These gestures emphasize the excellence of the man. They reaffirm the persistence of stable values in a world where too many had died for reasons that grew increasingly nebulous as the years fled. The values may not exist. But it is essential to behave as if they did.

Attitudes alter over the decades. The shock of World War I was blurred by a continuing series of shocks. There was no lack of these. As post-war posturing faded into time, and Jazz Age elan grew so pallid that Scott Fitzgerald found himself a stranger in his own generation, change also worked its way with popular series characters. Blackshirt gave up his boisterous past—except at those frequent intervals when he must dress in black to defend his country against spy rings. Of which there were a goodly many through the years into the 'Thirties.

At the end of 1939, ten books into the Blackshirt series, Graeme found ideas growing thin. Perhaps there was also an element of slumping sales. He records that, at this time, he met a young girl who remarked that she had been a Blackshirt fan.

"When she said that she was no longer one, I asked her why. He is too old by now,' was her reply.... 'Couldn't you write books about the son of Blackshirt?' "[12]

Graeme could and did. He created a full grown son, Anthony Verrell, an RAF hero, who entered the series in the 1941 *Son of Blackshirt*. By normal calendars, Anthony would have been no more than seventeen in 1941. However, time in fiction is independent of earthly clocks, as Edgar Rice Burroughs had previously demonstrated with the son of Tarzan. Although the son of Blackshirt made a chronological shambles of the past ten books, no one seemed to object to the discrepancy.

They did not even object to a book dated 1941 that skipped the Second World War entirely and began as that war ended.

Anthony Verrell goes on to wonderful experiences and amazing discoveries. During his first adventure, a complicated series of events leads him to temporary imprisonment in a priest's hole. This is concealed in the home of the widow of the first Earl of Redbrook. Anthony discovers that the Earl's private diaries are stored in this hidden place. No wonder. As he reads through them, he learns that his father, Richard Verrell, is really the lost son of the Earl.

And why had the Earl never recognized Verrell? Because he had hired a private detective to locate that lost son. The detective succeeded all too well. He discovered Verrell. And he also discovered Verrell to be Blackshirt. (It *was* a most transparent secret identity.) Reeling with shock, the Earl chose to suppress the whole matter.

Anthony, however, ignites gloriously. He is soon Blackshirting in the family tradition. And so the series continues with Anthony through *Calling Lord Blackshirt* (1943). The original Blackshirt does not appear in his son's adventures.

Graham Montague Jeffries (Bruce Graeme) had retired from the series. Eight years later entered his son, Roderic Jeffries (Roderic Graeme), restarting the series with *Blackshirt Helps Himself* (1951). At this point, Anthony is dropped and the original Blackshirt steps forth, modernized, newly polished, strangely changed to suit the 1950s.

From these fascinating digressions, we must be excused. Blackshirt had coaxed us far from the 1920s, that mythic time when the soul of the pulp era was being forged. We turn again to that period when Richard Verrell, unknowing of his birthright, walked among the Sirs and Lords and Earls as a guest, a successful author. Under his upper-class manners and wealth lay the talented young thief. Throughout the initial novels he remains so—the outsider, smiling and so amusing as he plans his next raid on the cornucopia.

In Johnston McCulley's fiction, the wealthy upper classes, extensively criminal, are punished by thorough looting—and by a member of their class, afflicted with a sense of justice. Aggression was not directed against the person but against wealth. The most grievous punishment was to take away wealth.

Graeme's Blackshirt spurns even this tenuous justification. He is, in his early stages, an adventurer, a little boy who slips over the wall to rob the apple tree. It is defended by burly caretakers and fierce dogs; yet rob it he does, with zeal and imagination, retiring over the wall, his black shirt loaded with apples.

It is play. It is joy and high elan. Blackshirt is not punishing wealthy criminals; he is merely stealing from the wealthy, a different matter entirely. He provided a satisfying figure for readers who had fought a war and discovered, at the end, that death, unemployment, and high prices seemed the only tangible result. If jeweled women and wealthy men suffered at Blackshirt's hands, what real crime is that? High prices and a depressed job market harden readers toward the losses of those reveling in conspicuous consumption.

3-

One year before Blackshirt opened his joyous career, Johnston McCulley added still another link to the prospering chain of costumed heroes. It was late 1921. The Thunderbolt had not yet returned from his honeymoon, and there was McCulley, scouring away at the Thunderbolt character with wire brush and polish.

From his efforts in the armory of his imagination came two characters: The Man in Purple, a direct continuation of The Thunderbolt, and The Crimson Clown, a full-scale elaboration of The Man in Purple with incidental borrowing from Black Star.

The Man in Purple continues The Thunderbolt saga with modestly revised nomenclature. New costume. Different names. Minor descriptive variations. Same structural ideas:

> The man...had on purple coveralls, purple gloves, a purple mask, and a soft hat drawn down on his forehead. Through slits in the mask (he) could see the eyes glittering, and the sight did not bring a feeling of comfort to him. And the muzzle of an automatic was directed straight at (his) head.[13]

As usual, this costumed hero preys on crooked businessmen, all of whom cheated widows and fatherless children.

The Man in Purple: "But I am not the usual thief. I am merely a man who rights wrongs, a collector of back pay for the swindled. You will never hear of me robbing an honest man, no matter how wealthy he may be."[14]

As he elsewhere remarks:

"We steal only from men who have stolen themselves. We rob swindling financiers, profiteering merchants, and folks like that. We steal from the rich and give it to the poor."[15]

Laudable guidelines, Behind the words you detect the public outcry at those profiteers who made, it was thundered from the newspapers, vast fortunes during the First World War. In the tight little world of *Detective Story Magazine,* it was an article of faith that businessmen and financiers got rich in ways other than saving their pennies in a little tin box. Immediately after the war, the country endured a severe money pinch and severe unemployment. It might have been more accurate to blame hard times on the sudden cancellation of government war contracts. But then, as now, it satisfied felt simplicities to blame crooked financiers for all social woes. It was more comforting than to blame abstract policies.

Financiers smirked fatly on their money bags, even as the working man walked barren streets. That image focused your discontent. If then a hooded terror or a man draped in purple separated these rich criminals from their spoils, the tears shed wouldn't water an ant farm.

The concept of The Man in Purple belonged neither to Mr. McCulley or the Man, himself. It was thought up by Betty Hayler, a society beauty, wealthy in her own right. (The possession of wealth is somehow equated, in popular fiction, with the right to exceed customary laws.) Dark-haired, clever, Betty longs for danger:

Betty (To the Man in Purple): "I am in this as much as you. I crave adventure and excitement as much as you do, sir. And it was my plan from the beginning to take from thieving swindling financiers and give what we got to charity."[16]

Somehow it all seems right when a rich beautiful society girl speaks those piratical sentiments.

Richard Staegal agrees with her completely. He is Betty's fiance and the conventional hero figure. Neither as devious nor as cautious as The Thunderbolt, Richard is equally tall, broad-shouldered, and daring. He is the conventional figure of the unconventional young man who shines in society, has worked on a whaler, fist fights like a demon, rides to the hounds, and needs excitement like air, an implausible mixture of high talents and low.

Richard is, on formal occasions, The Man in Purple.

Details of his costume vary slightly. The purple coveralls and soft hat of the first story alter immediately to a purple coat, trousers, gloves, "and a sort of purple hood over his head."

This costume was made from a "peculiar" cloth purchased in the Orient. "Peculiar" is hardly the word. "Dangerous" is more like it. The stuff fumes away entirely when touched by acid. Richard is always equipped with a small vial of acid. After each appearance of The Man, he strips off the garments, pours on the acid, watches the evidence fume to ash.

It is not really wasteful. Richard owns purple suits beyond counting. Some are concealed in a secret compartment beneath the rear seat of his limousine. (It is the same location as The Thunderbolt's secret compartment, and that of The Shadow, a decade later.) A half dozen additional suits hang concealed in Staegal's apartment bedroom, together with his automatic, flashlight, and such loot as hasn't been fenced.

All things being equal, a costumed hero requires a determined detective to snort after him and a faithful reformed crook, of some personal peculiarity, to serve him.

In this brief series, Detective Troman, "the best man on the Force," is assigned the unrewarding job of pounding after that elusive Man in Purple. A tough, clever fellow is Troman. How amusing is his face when The Man in Purple sends him a gift box of purple sweet peas. Hear his teeth grit together. Arsene Lupin and Cleek, both of whom sent little gifts to the police, may have approved. Although you suspect Staegal's sense of humor to be that type which enjoys poking hornets' nests to hear them hum.

The series' resident Adorable Crook Aide is named Broph. Where The Thunderbolt's man was an ugly, incompetent crook, Broph is a fragile, little, incompetent crook. Barely five feet tall, weighing a trifle over 100 pounds, he is braver than other McCulley valets, more intelligent, lots more eager.

Broph is introduced immediately. As in The Thunderbolt series, the costumed hero steps from nowhere, unveils himself to a sure loser, lays himself open to blackmail and arrest—all to recruit an assistant who is eighty-percent liability. Broph is tapped for service in the second chapter of "The Man in Purple," becomes a chauffeur by day, an accomplice by night.

The Man in Purple series is so brief that it hardly classes as a series at all. Two stories are known from late 1921 and it is remotely possible that more were added in 1922. The first story, "The Man in Purple" (*Detective Story Magazine*, October 1, 1921), is a bare-faced redo of "Master and Man," the first Thunderbolt novelette.

An unsuccessful crook, Broph, is saved from the harassment of three thugs by Richard Staegal. Later than night Broph is visited by the mysterious Man in Purple, a criminal who began operations only a few weeks earlier. He has already robbed three rich men. The Man in Purple tells Broph that he wants him to become an assistant. Scorning consequences, he then spills the whole Man In Purple secret, including Betty Halyer's involvement. He babbles without caution, driven by the reader's need to know.

His crimes are conducted in the same way. Charge right in, expending no visible thought.

At once he decides to steal the Carlen diamond necklace, since this had been purchased "with money stolen from widows who had been swindled by Jasper Carlen."

The theft will occur during the fancy dress ball at the Carlen mansion. Staegal attends dressed at The Man in Purple. He identifies himself to Detective Troman, explaining that he wishes to play a trick on Carlen—he wishes to conduct a fake holdup.

As stupidly cooperative as any McCulley detective, Troman agrees not to interfere. Thus The Man in Purple appears, strikes, vanishes while the police yawn. Upstairs, Betty hastily binds Richard tight. When he is found, his story is that The Man in Purple leaped upon him, "took out a sponge with some confounded stuff on it," and lights out.

The police do not hesitate. They gulp down this confounded story whole.

Success is not yet. The diamond necklace turns out to be paste. And that very night, once again, The Man in Purple appears at the Carlen mansion to steal the real stones. Betty, also decked out in purple togs, rides along to enjoy the sport.

Once confronted by The Man in Purple, Carlen comes apart with fear. No Johnston McCulley millionaire ever did less. In that way, the hero doesn't dirty his costume forcing open the safe. All things are easy for a costumed hero. No one falls down laughing at his odd appearance. Detectives obligingly allow themselves to be surprised and tied up. Even Troman, who arrives unexpectedly, presents his head to be knocked.

Exit hero and heroine into the night.

Such slovenly operations could hardly survive without gross good luck. "The Man in Purple Meets a Man in Blue" (November 5, 1921) tells how the luck almost runs out.

To the usual millionaire, Hannibal Carle, appears The Man in Purple, who announces that he will rob the cowardly fellow during his *third* visit. Carle's crooked private secretary, Raite, disguises himself in purple pajamas, and attempts to rob his employer first.

His activities are interrupted by the untimely arrival of The Man. Who is, in turn, interrupted by the more untimely arrival of Detective Troman.

Away The Man darts, the police raging behind. Whenever a McCulley hero darts out, you may be sure that he will dart back, and so it happens that The Man doubles back and reappears to rob Carle. Visit number three.

That done, The Man in Purple melts off into the night. Only to blunder directly into the arms of the beat cop. As the dire handcuffs impend, Broph slugs the unfortunate officer and away our miscreants toddle.

This act of violence introduces a dim glow of reason into the series. Shortly afterward, Staegal gives up his amusing hobby. As McCulley tells us: "The Man in Purple has served his turn and now is a law-abiding citizen and a sedate householder, a man of family, if you please."[17]

Crime pays after all—particularly when no profit is taken.

4-

The defection of The Man in Purple reduced McCulley's list of active costumed heroes to Black Star and Zorro. His interest in costumed characters remained, although that of Frank Blackwell, editor of *Detective Story Magazine,* seems to have burnt less enthusiastically. Not until 1926 did McCulley introduce another costume series. Then, with The Crimson Clown, the ghosts of past series dressed in new prose and walked once more.

> The enigma in crimson was a strange, masked figure whose face had never been seen by the police department, whom he completely mystified, or by the underworld whom he terrorized. For "The Crimson Clown" preyed on crooks!"[18]

The Crimson Clown adventures have a lot in common with the hot swing bands of the later 1930. Once settled down to pounding out a phrase, with microscopic variations, they generated enough heat to melt I-beams.

As does The Crimson Clown series. His stories ride a single riff. Titles vary. Locales change. The story remains essentially the same. Granting normal variations, it is as follows:

A dishonest rich man is hosting an ostentatious social function. Among the glittering crowd is Delton Prouse, wealthy socialite and man about town. He is The Crimson Clown. During the festivities, Prouse dons The Clown's costume, holds up the rich man, forces him to disgorge his ill-got wealth. Before the robbery is complete, The Clown is interrupted by Dave Donler, Headquarters detective on special assignment to capture The Clown. Hue is raised and cry. To no avail. The Clown slips through Donler's fingers, leaving behind heaps of people drugged to unconsciousness. Including Mr. Prouse.

The series ran from 1926 through 1931. About half the stories were collected in two books: *The Crimson Clown* (1927) and *The Crimson Clown Again* (1928). After a long absence, "The Crimson Clown" was reprinted in the September 1936 *Best Detective Magazine*. And finally a single new story appeared in the October 1944 *Popular Detective*. By then, The Clown's time was done and no other stories materialized.

The Crimson Clown borrows heavily from McCulley's earlier series characters, The Thunderbolt, and, particularly, The Man in Purple. Once again we are joyed by the acid-sensitive costume, and the same alibi construction, dull policemen, and crime-stained victims. McCulley was never afraid to borrow from himself. Without apology, The Clown took over The Man in Purple's habit of terrorizing cowardly millionaires:

> "Not a sound, Mr. Curton, or you die."[19]

Of splitting the loot with charity:

> "Fifty per cent of what I get from you will go to the (free milk) fund, and I'll keep the other half for my trouble and risk."

Of costume:

> He wrapped the overcoat closely about him, then shook out the silk clown suit and got into it, pulled up the hood, and fastened the mask across his face...
> The clown suit enveloped him completely. The sleeves ended in thin silk gloves. His shoes slipped down into pockets arranged for them.

And of costume destruction:

> He ripped off the clown suit and piled it in one corner of the room, false finger tips, too. From a pocket he took a small vial filled with a colorless liquid. Following his usual method, he poured the contents of the vial upon the thin silk. Tiny spirals of smoke arose. The acid commenced eating away the silk.

Like all of McCulley's series heroes, Delton Prouse is a rich bachelor and socialite. Tall, athletic, with the face "of a patrician, and inscrutable," he is an ex-combat man, a big-game hunter, a North Pole explorer, and all those grand things which magnify a man in the telling.

Unlike his prototypes, Prouse has no humorous valet or steady girl friend. The life of The Crimson Clown is quite solitary.

It is Prouse's peculiar fortune to run afoul of The Clown time after time, always to his disadvantage. "Some ruffian in a crazy costume assaulted me...."

The frequent proximity of Prouse to The Clown's activities soon rouses the suspicions of Detective Dave Donler, the series official.

Donler is a burly big fellow who looks more like a business man than a detective. His record is brilliant, his methods individualistic. The Chief of Police has given him a freedom to chase The Clown that would stun the boys of the 87th Precinct. Donler has totally independent action. Administration must often have snarled over his time card.

But Donler's assignment is clear and specific: Go out there and bring The Clown in.

He often gets close. For a brief period in 1926, he suspects Prouse. Then he does not suspect Prouse and becomes warmly friendly with him. Later, during 1928, he becomes steadily more hostile, setting watchers on Prouse. It is the same thing that a colleague once did when faced by The Avenging Twins. Donler has no more success, either.

His luck is never quite good enough. On certain spectacular occasions, he enters a room to discover the shapeless crimson figure of The Clown standing before him. The advantage never remains with Donler. Always he gets slicked. Given the least advantage and The Clown is gone glimmering into the air. No costume, no loot, no gun. Gone.

The festivities begin promptly. "The Crimson Clown" (*Detective Story Magazine,* July 31, 1926) scuttles about with great vigor. A note dropped by a mysterious girl leads Delton Prouse to imprisonment in the house of the fake mystic, Yogi Ra. He is to be used as bait to trap The Crimson Clown.

Yogi Ra: (The Crimson Clown) has become a terror to criminals. They fear him more than they do the police. He does not deal with small fry, this Crimson Clown. He waits until clever men and women make a haul, and then he demands half of the swag. He claims that he retains half his receipts and donates the other half to charity. He seems to know everything. He knows when a big trick is turned. And he knows who turns it."[20]

The Clown is coming to get half the diamonds that Yogi Ra and gang have just stolen. The Yogi, pretending to be a traitor, has promised to deliver himself, all tied up, to The Clown. Instead he plans to deliver an innocent passerby, tightly tied, in his place, then ambush and kill The Clown and innocent alike.

The plan immediately falls apart. Prouse is tied but not helpless, for he places his reliance on Johnston McCulley. And Yogi Ra, as inept as all McCulley's lesser criminals, leaves Prouse tied up near a sword cane and his hat, which contains a gun strapped inside the crown.

In a few paragraphs, Prouse is free, dressed as The Clown, and riding a wave of frothing action, of death traps and captures and escapes, the police bumping in and out, Prouse appearing and reappearing, The Clown vanishing, only to return, a struggling tumble of criminals and diamonds and cops and Clowns, as if the final five minutes of a silent movie farce had been rendered into prose.

Prouse, pretending concussion and with the diamonds in his pocket, is sent to the hospital under police guard, injects the officer with sleeping drug, and is away.

After that first story, The Clown forgets all that foolishness about robbing criminals of half their loot. The series gives a little shudder, like the hide of a horse bothered by flies, and turns unerringly to McCulley's favorite story—the robbing of wicked rich men. It begins at once.

"The Crimson Clown Cornered" (August 12, 1926) brims with the joyous foolishness that is so much a part of the series. It establishes, in fact, the pattern for the rest of The Clown's published life.

To the Manborough Arms, at 2:15 am, wanders Mr. Delton Prouse, driveling pseudo-English nonsense like a man possessed by the sacred mushrooms.

> *Prouse (to the Night Clerk):* "I feel sure that you will pardon this intrusion. I know that it is rather a silly hour for me to drop in. But I so often do unusual things....
>
> "I attended the theater and saw a miserable performance. Why are there no good shows? Afterward I spent a short time at a supper club. Got rather bored there. Splendid evening, so I thought that I would walk to my rooms instead of motoring. Rather a fad of mine—prowling the streets at all hours of the night."[21]

He opens proceedings by feeding the clerk drugged candy and injecting the elevator operator with a sleeping drug. That done he enters the apartment of Hagley Curton, Milk King.

From beneath his overcoat, Prouse removes the garments of The Crimson Clown. (In "The Crimson Clown" the outfit was worn under all his clothing, wrapped around his body.) He steps into the outfit like a man getting into a sack. After his hands are in the silk gloves, he slips over each fingertip, thin rubber finger-stalls which bear forged fingerprints. These would not, perhaps, fool Dr. Thorndyke, but he is far away.

Entering the bedroom, he awakes the milk czar. As per specification, the fellow goes all sticky with sweat. At this point, it will be usual for The Clown to deliver himself of a brief oration, establishing that the selected victim is a large-scale scoundrel. Thus:

Clown: "Curton, you've been raising the price of milk again. And you're making a confounded big profit already...

"I have investigated fully. This sudden lift in the price of milk is unnecessary. You simply want to buy a new yacht or something like that, and make the public pay the bill. And your milk isn't pure, either. It's diluted, adulterated, and doped, and grafting officials let you get away with it."[22]

Having assured the reader that crime stains the highest positions of the land, and that The Clown is on the side of justice, since he is making the wretches pay, McCulley now leads us step by step through the great robbery. Which takes forever. Terrible, scorching blue threats force Curton to open his safe:

Clown: "I feel nervous vibrations in the air. Confound it, I suppose that my trigger finger will be contracting in a moment or so. I always hate to shoot a man. It is so messy, and creates such a stir...

"But I am going to see (your safe open) very soon, or else I am going to see you down on the floor, writhing nicely, crimson fluid flowing from a wound and over your expensive imported rug—"[23]

The safe is opened; the safe's secret compartment is opened. While Curton cowers, The Clown ostentatiously coats every available surface with spurious fingerprints. But down in the lobby, menace stirs. Detective Donler has wandered into the apartment house. Surely you expected him, knowing that a story lives by the amount of internal tension generated.

Donler finds trouble. There sprawl the desk clerk and the elevator boy, obviously unconscious.

Donler suspects foul play. Summoning vans of police, he has the apartment house surrounded, fills it to bursting with bluecoats. then begins telephoning each resident to discover if they are all right.

The Clown hears the telephones ringing and understands what is happening. He promptly injects Curton with a hypodermic of sleep drug. And now he telephones to the lobby: "Help! Send police! The Crimson Clown is here! The..." Terminating dramatically.

Up rush Donler and the building superintendent, children in the face of The Clown's strategy. Which is to divide and immobilize the police and flee to an empty apartment. With no difficulty he ambushes the pair, robs Donler, and pours on the sarcasm:

"Oh, you'll not be able to identify me if you see me again! Rather a complete disguise, what? And my voice is disguised, also, of course. This little affair will probably infuriate you, Mr. Detective, and cause you to swear that you'll capture me some day. It will be rare sport to have such a capable officer on my trail. Possibly it will give me a thrill."[24]

As they foam and rave and look pale, he blinds them with tear gas. Slipping away to an empty apartment, he destroys the costume and ties himself up. When the police eventually come lumbering in, he is a pathetic picture.

At this point, the career of The Crimson Clown should have ended. A man self tied looks like a man self tied. Except in certain types of sensational fiction.

In this sensational fiction, Donler notices nothing. Even when the desk clerk and elevator operator point wrathful fingers at Prouse, the police are not aroused. Prouse explains, quite reasonably, that he is obviously suspected in error.

Might as well believe him. His fingerprints do not match those of The Crimson Clown. And Clown, costume, loot are gone. Quite gone.

In appreciation for a thrilling evening, Prouse leases the seventh-floor apartment in which he was found. (He has concealed the stolen valuables in the refrigerator.)

Had any of our later series police been present, the apartment would have been searched and Mr. Prouse would have spent the first of many nights behind those unsympathetic bars. We are, however, in McCulleyland. Donler fails. Prouse sets up housekeeping in his apartment for a few months, then moves to the second floor. There he creates a luxurious bachelor establishment from which he ranges on years of delightful adventuring.

Over the seasons' slow coursing, a few of these details change. Not many. During the course of "The Crimson Clown Cornered," The Clown terrorized his victim with a dreadful chuckle:

"...that chuckle had a certain quality in it that caused Curton to shiver anew. That chuckle was a greater threat than could have been expressed in words."[25]

In later stories, that sinister chuckle becomes a "gale of mocking laughter." When he is trapped or defiant, he pours out "laughter that caused a chill to run up and down Dave Donler's spine."

The Clown also begins sending Donler little notes written in red pencil or red ink. These tell him where The Clown plans to strike next, another faint echo of Cleek, The Vanishing Cracksman, in this modern series.

So do your worst, dear old detective and make the game interesting.

THE CRIMSON CLOWN

By late 1928, The Clown's tear gas pistol has modified to the gas

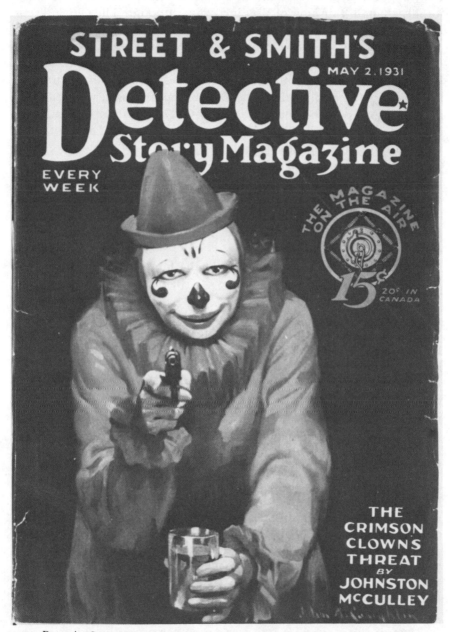

Detective Story Magazine (May 2, 1931). The Crimson Clown, shown inaccurately in clown facial makeup, was the final, major costumed figure of the 1920s.

gun, the same type of weapon used by Black Star. The gas acts more rapidly than an injection of sleeping drug, although The Clown keeps his hypodermic and vial constantly with him.

Not all The Clown's exploits occur in the city. "The Crimson Clown's Treasure Hunt" (June 18, 1927) occurs at a millionaire's summer place by a lake near the Canadian border. There guests play a game of treasure hunt. During these pleasures, The Clown appears inside a boat house, drugging four people—and Mr. Prouse. Only later does Donler (there on vacation) discover that The Clown has intercepted and made off with a shipment of smuggled jewels.

"The Crimson Clown's Winged Loot" (February 11, 1928) tells how he robs two crooked businessmen of their rare rubies. It all happens at a fashionable party with one hundred people present. This time, Donler catches The Clown in the act but is so ineffective that the rascal escapes. His mocking voice is heard from a locked room. Then a shattering explosion.

When the room is entered, behold the familiar scene. There sags Mr. Prouse, all drugged. Of the rubies there is no trace. (Prose sent them away via carrier pigeon.)

Even a detective as thick as Donler can not be fooled forever. As "The Crimson Clown Scores with a Snore" (November 3, 1928) opens, Prouse finds himself "Surrounded. Trapped, and all that sort of silly rot! Beleaguered and besieged."

That is because Donler has filled the streets with comic page detectives, all peering after Prouse while their cigars burn to their finger joints. In spite of these annoyances, The Clown steals a fortune in jewels for which an evil rich man has ruined a friend. And what about Prouse's alibi? A lurking detective listened to him snoring the whole night through. You would think that the police would remember that The Thunderbolt once stung them with a snoring record. However...

Those alertly following the discussion so far will note that the only place the underworld has appeared was at the beginning of the series. One further encounter occurs during the five-part serial titled "Thubway Tham Meets The Crimson Clown" (November 11 through December 9, 1928). Other than this adventure, The Clown had little contact with the lesser world of crime. He preferred millionaires. Any terrorizing of the underworld was left for The Shadow, who would begin his violent activities in about two and a half years.

"The Crimson Clown's Threat" (May 2, 1931) continues the formula. The Clown ambitiously drugs every last person at a penthouse party. For the entire story, he flits in out around, drugging, injecting, almost caught, barely escaping, in out around. Caught from behind, he bluffs the policeman into dropping his gun by threatening to kill the rich man. If the reader is depressed by these antics, he will go into convulsions when the stolen property is removed from the premises in a vase; Donler carries it out as a favor to Prouse.

"The Crimson Clown's Romance" (May 16, 1931) is a rather more interesting story, moving slightly from the formula which grips the series like an ice age. It seems also to be the final Clown story published in *Detective Story Magazine*.

During these concluding moments, The Clown exposes a rich man's crime. He reveals a concealed love letter by Napoleon and a hidden will, the suppression of which allowed the rich old devil to steal his niece's inheritance. Parts of the story harken back to that Avenging Twins yarn about the millionaire who kept a stolen old master behind a panel in his bedroom. On the whole, this Crimson Clown adventure is, relatively speaking, a dazzling departure from the usual stuff.

Thereafter, the series guttered out, save for that reprint in *Best Detective Magazine*, September 1936.

More than a generation later, a curious coda to the series sparked up in *Popular Detective*, October 1944. "The Crimson Clown Returns" brought our 1920s hero forward to wartime America, coldly bright. The story rated a cover illustration. The Clown, shown in white face, holds a .45 at the heart of a girl-abusing tough. Like other vintage covers, this one has little to do with the story contents. In the novelette, The Clown uses his vapor gun exclusively.

The years have left few marks. In addition to the usual clown suit, Prouse now wears a white mask covering his entire head and white silk gloves. During that period carelessly left unrecorded by Mr. McCulley, The Clown has turned back to robbing criminals and turning part of the money over to the police. Until this issue of *Popular Detective*, he has operated quietly. But now he appears to Inspector Thad Blurney, announcing that he has returned to practice his art, once more. The town is filled with big-time criminals who are taking advantage of the war workers. The Clown, distressed, intends to put an end to this.

What great sport there is to be: "Dodging police and crooks both at the same time—that's a great game."

We begin at the beginning. A crooked carnival man is promoting a big society circus and bazaar to raise funds for the War Orphans' Relief. He plans to skim 90% of the receipts for himself. The Clown plans to skim the skimmer. Before he is able to do this, he must clear himself of a backstage murder, trap a gang of jewel thieves, and evade a massive police trap. He does so, performing with untarnished grace. And Blurney, all unconscious of the past, aids Prouse by carrying out a box for him past the police guards. The box is, obviously, stuffed with stolen money.

The story bounds along, full of old-time touches and old-time vigor. Prouse's background is elaborated in some detail—we learn that he had been an Intelligence Officer in World War I—and his character is developed deftly. We learn more about Prouse in two pages than in all the original series.[26]

The Crimson Clown is the final major costumed character of the 1920s. After him, the mood darkened. Guns began speaking and bodies fell and the secret heroes of dual identity became fierce in ways the 1920s would not have understood.

For the next decade, the magazines would fill with lead characters whose nature was harmful. Terrible tasks faced them. Terrible odds. That lightness of spirit characterizing the earlier fiction boiled away. Tasks of the 1930s were grim and dangerous. Success was achieved only at a human cost which, even at the time, seemed excessive.

All most alien to playful fiction about The Crimson Clown. Through these stories, the sunshine still falls. They are sober-faced little farces of no depth, charming in small quantities. The stories closely resemble those improvised by children to amuse themselves during that interval between dinner and bedtime, when twilight melts the familiar street and, in the shadowed blurring, all things become possible. The children laugh and leap. Now chased, now chasing. "Look at me. Look at me. I'm the bad guy. You shoot me. I fall down. Ahhhhh!"

In The Crimson Clown stories, the characters wear adult masks and speak importantly. Beneath the masks, the faces are the faces of children. They shine as they whirl through their shallow, merry games. Through the stories, children's laughter shrills.

5-

Of rogues and bent heroes there is unending supply. They persist in popular literature, as indispensable as periods to prose. For all their permanence, they are not immutable. They alter as tastes in fiction alter, a gentle reworking of their surface characteristics. Their haircuts change. Their clothing and automobiles and taste in drinks reflect the latest styles. Their adventuring techniques adapt to the latest and newest of the newest, latest modern world.

They star in television series or long runs of paperback adventures. The polished surface of their exploits reflects 1970s brightness and 1980s wonder. Only the inner characters remain unchanged. Wealthy young men thirsted for adventure in 1914 fiction. As they thirst today, amid their wealth and social polish, their charming girl associates, their rough-hewn pals, their sleek opponents, and their curiously obtuse official friends.[27] The eyes of 1921 sparkle in 1990 faces.

Above this bedrock, new grasses grow. By luck, you can sometimes find a series making the transition from old stems to new leaves. Such as the John Doe series, decidedly transitional, during which a 1920s character modifies to 1930s rigor. The series began in the 1928 *Detective Story Magazine,* even at that late date publishing fiction about a bored young man who took up stealing to amuse himself. Two years later, in 1930, it ended amid violence and gunfire, the bored young man reshaped to a justice figure of sorts.

We begin in familiar fields:

> Dale Worthington's great grandfather had started as a confidence man, and had ended as a bibliophile and the largest taxpayer in the state. Dale's father had made and thrown away a dozen fortunes, and then, from sheer boredom, had taken an overdose of chloral.[28]

Dale Worthington, himself, is subject to the black devils. Easily depressed, sliding aimlessly from city to city, he is constantly alone. He is a voluntary loner, having applied the philosophy of Michael Lanyard, the Lone Wolf, to his own life.

> He had no secretary or valet. He had his own reasons for traveling alone. Moreover, he made no friends and few enemies; you can't dislike a man whom you don't know; a shadow man, a John Doe, even if he robs you...[29]

Isn't it regrettable. Poor Dale Worthington, Mr. John Doe, solitary, rootless, and bored, must amuse himself by stealing. It was the "one game in the world that could really interest and thrill him...." As usual, the moral issues are begged; he robs only those reveling in crooked money. He does it more for amusement than wealth, that old, familiar excuse.

His mind jiggles with unrealized potential. He can hardly plea stupidity for his hollow life. Once, when he was twenty years old, he played the Grandmaster of chess, Harrowitz (a name unaccountably not in the records) and successfully drew the game. He still enjoys chess. But it does fail to hold his attention for long. It is the penalty one pays for intellectual superiority in 1928.

This young man with a low threshold of boredom is lean, handsome, with "enameled gray eyes" and an athlete's muscles and agility. He is twenty-four years old as the series opens. His manners shine. He dresses supremely well and his knowledge of life's good things—"art, literature, jewels"—is tuned as finely as that of the Lone Wolf or Jimmie Dale, two primary sources. His alter ego, John Doe, is virtually a separate personality:

A subtle but unmistakable change was coming over (Dale's) face.... The eyes grew narrower and harder, the set of the flexible lips changed, the very modeling and lighting of the features underwent a mysterious alteration. (Dale's wife) felt that she was hardly acquainted with her husband's secondary self, this Mr. X who emerged from the sub-basement of his personality.[30]

Wife? Husband? Why, yes. Before the series really gets underway, that incorrigible loner, Dale Worthington, marries. More amazingly, his wife defies all rules of fiction and lives.

But to begin at the beginning. The first John Doe story was published in mid-June 1928, the series continuing until mid-1930. It was written by Paul Ellsworth Triem who was, at the same time, writing a good deal else. The pages of *Detective Story Magazine* are dense with his fiction. All the John Doe stories appeared in this magazine.

In the initial story, "Enter—John Doe" (June 9, 1928), Worthington plays the role of the romantic criminal hero. He saves a kidnapped girl from the sexually uninhibited ideas of a wealthy young scoundrel. Worse, he robs that unsuccessful hedonist. In doing so, John Doe earns the malific attention of the young man's father, Anthony Craig. This relentless fellow (like the millionaire who gave Sanderson so much trouble) has a hard face, cynical eyes, merciless mouth, rather like a spokesman for the utilities company. He is piercingly intelligent. The affront to his son sends him into a red seethe of rage and he will pour out his fortune to land John Doe behind bars.

He begins immediately by plotting with Dalton, a vulgar, rich stockbroker, to bait Doe with the family jewels, then trap him, jail him, have a hearty cackle.

The trap clicks shut at the Dalton country chateau. But not on Mr. Worthington. Instead it catches Molly Derringer, chambermaid to Mrs. Dalton. It is not much of a trap. Out the window goes Molly, pearls in hand. She climbs a sheer wall high above the ground, and escapes, having concealed the pearls on the roof. After her howls a mob of servants and detectives.

Worthington has observed her flight. Now he cuts off the lights, creating an additional row, and quietly recovers the pearls, stashing them in the detectives' automobile, from which he will lift them later. He exits. The would-be trappers remain behind to snarl and scowl and blue the air.

After a few weeks, the heat dies down. Molly suddenly appears in Doe's room, pistol first. She has figured out that he hijacked her pearls and has come to demand a share of the proceeds.

Worthington is enchanted. Not only does she get her cut but, soon after, his hand in marriage.

And why, may you ask, is the lovely Molly out stealing jewels?

The usual reason—she desires hazard, danger, excitement. She caught the fever when her brother, Red, got bumped off in a gang feud. She avenged his death, in ways not stated. That sisterly duty performed, she skipped town for a life of adventure.

As Mrs. Worthington/Doe, adventure is what she gets.

Once married, the Worthington's again get to fiddling around with Craig. During the course of a robbery, Molly leaves her fingerprints on a silver hair brush and great is the excitement until John Doe recovers this. He also forces Craig to cough up a substantial sum in gold.

In high irritation, Craig shoots Doe right through the body.

The verities sustaining the 1920s crook story seem to reel. The hero shot? An incredible event. How could it be? Heroes got shot at. By the rules of fiction, a bullet often flicked skin from their cheek, very dramatic. More seriously, they got lightly grazed on the right arm but bore up wonderfully. Dale Worthington, however, is squarely shot and bleeds and bleeds, hardly escaping with the gold. Afterward he languishes for chapters, feverish and pallid.

So early in the series, a strange fermentation stirs the prose. The characters and situations are standard elements of that great pulp paper plot in the sky. The conventional themes and justifications of the crook story are all in place. But new yeast works in this familiar must. There is unanticipated change. The hero is seriously wounded; the heroine is competent, aggressive, of almost equal weight as a character; the villain is of biting intelligence. And more variation is to come.

Matters continue to reel awry for the Worthingtons. "John Doe's Crimson Catch" (August 18, 1928) tells how Craig bribes a hardboiled nurse to drug Molly. After a lingering illness, she is suitably limp. He kidnaps her. She is imprisoned out in the country, guarded by the nurse and two enormous hounds, possibly secured from the Baskerville Kennels.

Craig comes to lay his heart at Molly's feet. He loves her. Oh, of course she is married, but likely not for long. For Craig has blackmailed Doe into stealing a priceless ruby, using Molly's safety as the whip. The ruby is merely a device for drawing Doe into a lethal trap. So much simpler than divorce.

Even the nimblest plot may stumble over the human heart. Molly spurns Craig's blandishments and off he stomps, puffed with rage. After which she escapes by an exhausting, extended effort that is violent enough to compare with later action magazine-fiction. Away Molly bolts to warn Worthington. Not that it was necessary. He has just evaded Craig's trap. The ruby is collected and they depart rejoicing, as is only proper.

"John Doe Kidnapped" (November 17, 1928) begins with Craig in a pet at having lost so many encounters to Doe. Rage clouds his judgment. He authorizes Shang Boyer, killer, to eliminate Doe the direct way, with a bullet. Shang produces his own variation to this familiar song: First he will kidnap Doe, collect a large ransom, *then* kill him. Which explains why the Worthingtons find their car forced off a country road while four sawed-off shotguns glare at them. Doe is hauled off to a house boat, there to be tied and taped and threatened within an inch of his life, while Molly, quite pallid, wrings her hands at home.

Or so it appears.

But you can't believe everything you see. Particularly since Doe has understood the plot from its inception and is now playing a remarkable game of substitution. A friend, disguised as Doe, lies tied and helpless; our hero lurks outside the house boat, imitating a ghost and otherwise keeping crime upset until the story has been padded to novelette length. And until Doe has thought of a way to screw more thousands from Craig.

It ends happily. The friend does not get his throat cut. Shang and Craig are seen on the final page, so tied up that even their hair can't move. The Worthington's exit gracefully with $10,000 from Craig's pocket—the unpaid fee for Doe's murder.

The friend who endured so much receives half that amount and so into the sunset. Made doubly beautiful by the muffled shrieks of outraged evil.

"John Doe's Funeral" (March 9, 1929) presents the probability that Mr. Worthington has been killed during a hair-brained raid on a fence's secret cavern of wealth. Molly carries on the good work alone, tears streaking her cheeks, her tawny eyes hard with resolution. Her ordeal is not in vain. At the end, Doe returns from the dead and together they make off with the spoils.

Graver combats are to come. In the May 4, 1929, "John Doe's Dummy," he plunges into battle with the "Big Five"—four crooked police commissioners and a corrupt Chief of Police. They have taken over a city and stolen everything but the jail doors. Doe's struggle against them continues through most of 1929. He goes to work in the best tradition of the Bent Hero. In "John Doe Strikes from Ambush" (June 8) and "Black Magic" (August 3) he methodically plunders the Big Five and publishes first-hand accounts of his exploits in the newspaper.

Finding Doe an intolerable nuisance, the "Big Five" attempt to frame him for murder ("John Doe's Third Degree," September 28). He gets out of this, twisting agilely. As usual, his escape is part luck, part skill, part concentrated assistance from his wife and friends. These excitements end with "John Doe's Plant" (October 26). The Police Chief attempts to steal big before he flees town. The blame will be shifted onto John Doe, impersonated by a look-alike. It does not happen that way. The Chief is captured in the act of stealing and the Big Five become extinct.

Through these intense activities prances Mr. Doe, light-hearted, astute, his mind shining with plans. He needs every atom of ability. Constantly he is faced by tasks at the limit of his strength. He faces hulking forces far more powerful than the Worthingtons. The stories gradually fill with guns and killing hate. Black savagery is loose. It is war.

It is war concealed. Society barely notices the deadly struggle at its heart. Rarely are the police involved. These private battles proceed at levels of violence foreign to past criminal hero fiction. The prose reads with a certain flat detachment. But the hero feels every blow.

A pistol barked, and John Doe felt the rip of a bullet through his coat and vest. Three inches to the right and the marksman would have drilled him through the heart! But Doe had seen the skulking figure, and now in an instant his own gun swung up and he pressed the trigger.

...Doe was no killer, by nature, but now he took a savage delight in shooting down these ruffians who had laid their hands on Molly.

The fire roared, and the room was filling with smoke. Doe fought his way forward. Apparently, the enemy had run out of ammunition. They came at him, swinging blackjacks or trying to strike him down with their empty pistols.

And Doe dropped them bare-handed. His fists were hard as rock, and were driven by muscles of steel. Each blow landed with an audible crack, as if he had struck a plank with a stick.[31]

We have already seen that Worthington is physically vulnerable. He is also vulnerable in ways unknown to criminal heroes of earlier series. He is frequently confused, often desperate. He blunders about clutching for a plan. At least once, his luck sours. His hotel locks him out for non-payment of rent. His clothing frays. He fears arrest and the thought of prison lies, a horrible cold sourness, in him.

The love of action drags him on, long after some dark magic has sucked the joy from crime. He faces unrelenting struggle. He is slugged and tied. Molly is abducted. He reels through frantic streets. When, after enervating struggle, his efforts succeed, success is not always clean and sweet and final. He cannot entirely control the shape of his adventures. The Avenging Twins, the Crimson Clown could generally direct the course of the action. But it is not part of John Doe's destiny to flicker lightly about, punishing fat millionaires, fooling the police, being witty, jesting, merry. Not in John Doe's world, where wounds bleed and evil is so very strong.

Through this black air, dragons hunt. The Worthingtons know too well the smothering weight of despair. He loves Molly and she loves him. But she becomes sick. She languishes. Her finger prints are found in unlawful places. Worthington is believed dead. The forces of evil mass grinning in the streets. Molly's head sags to the table and grief shakes her. Shakes but does not incapacitate. She wipes her face and rises to the fight, her heart worn high.

That human feelings tint these stories is pleasing, if unexpected. Between the criminal hero and his audience is usually interposed a sheet of transparent steel that eliminates all feeling, save such small change as apprehension and cool amusement. That barrier is partially removed during the John Doe series. To our amazement, human feelings rise within the melodrama, flowers among the rocks.

Even the villains of these pieces unbend briefly to show feelings other than greed. These are difficult people. They are not the usual 1920s dunderhead whose cowardice and stupidity make possible the smooth unrolling of the plot, in direct opposition to everything experience has taught us about the inability of any plan to stand without frantic propping. John Doe's opponents radiate equal parts of intelligence, vindictiveness, flinty hearts, and, infrequently and briefly, regret. They are, however, no more safe to toy with than a basket of puff adders. All are dangerous, all terribly strong.

And all are served by small armies of thugs and gunmen, eager killers. These minions do not really reflect the figures of the Prohibition gangs, although suggested by them. They are the vanguard of the homicidal swarms infesting 1930s pulp pages. They are updated versions of the gang members shouting after Nick Carter and Jimmie Dale, brothers of the wharf rats that tormented Blue Jean Billy's nights, children of the newspaper headlines that shouted *Gang Killing* at the heart of the 1920s. These shadowless figures stalk the John Doe pages, dehumanized criminals, grinning and murdering with both hands. As individuals they are nothing, ciphers to be slugged or shot as required for narrative suspense. *En masse* they represent the larger menace of gangland, that terrible thing, which would soon replace greedy millionaires and foolish police as a threat to the hero of mystery-adventure fiction.

"John Doe's Flying Loot" (December 14, 1929) is about a particularly ferocious blackmailer, Alonzo Shane. His cache of blackmail materials is destroyed by Mr. Doe. Fretting with a sense of injury, Alonzo confers with his brother, the killer. Together they whip up a trap for Doe, baited with a black pearl and a chess master. Unfortunately for the Shane brothers, Doe turns the trap inside out. Alonzo ends shooting his brother in a moment of annoyance. Then he's off to confront Molly, who calmly outwits him.

"Fugitive Finger Prints" (February 1, 1930) features Alvin Cairus, a singularly revolting old man who plans to marry his niece and ward, Nancy, for her inheritance. His hired thugs batter Nancy's young man. Worse, they carry off Molly.

It is a tactical blunder. John Doe prowls the underworld for information. By a wonderful coincidence, which speeds the story considerably, he meets an old friend who knows all about everything—that Nancy's fiance is to be framed, that Cairus has planned it, why Carius is doing all this wicked stuff.

John Doe and friend pounce upon Carius while he is drunk. They lug him off through the night to plant his fingerprints on a rifled safe. Immediately (in the only effective police work of the series), the man is arrested and jailed. Unfortunately, however, only Carius knows where Molly is being held captive. That being the case, Doe must now break the wretch out of jail.

While Doe maneuvers wildly, Molly is getting that adventure she thirsted for. She is tied up, helpless and alone, in an ancient house, Lord knows where. Her guard is an evil man who grins down at her, heat in his eyes. She escapes her bonds. An instant later a mob of drunken gangsters howl after her. She flees to the attic, diverting pursuit by a trick. But for a moment only. Only a moment.

Before adventuring goes too far, Doe and his useful friend pound up. The action climaxes in a fierce gun and fist fight, during which the forces of evil are dispersed with extreme prejudice.

After all this, Carius has escaped. Many of Doe's opponents escape, the style in endings not yet permitting the hero to gun down the villain in the final paragraphs. Still, vengeance of a sort is not usually denied. Most opponents come to horrid ends. The record of their doom is added to the final paragraphs of each story, like a sign tacked to a gate.

Carius does not die, for a wonder. He skips the country, shaken and reformed by his experience. He writes Nancy to tell her so and to bless her marriage. It is not evident that he sent any wedding present more substantial than blessings.

We have, at this point, dipped a toe into the 1930s. On every side, formidable competition looms, threatening John Doe and the *Detective Story Magazine*. Gangster magazines have appeared, their covers violent, their fiction mannered fantasy. The hardboiled school blazes in *Black Mask*, which has ignited secondary fires in *Clues* and *Detective Fiction Weekly*. Such magazines as *Scotland Yard* and *The Dragnet* offer free-wheeling mystery-adventure, strongly seasoned with fantastic elements.

You might predict that the John Doe series would follow one of these developmental lines. Instead, it ignores all trends and plunges into that most durable of fiction cliches—the struggle against a mad scientist.

It is an extended struggle. It is recorded in the final John Doe adventure, a three-part serial, "John Doe's Dilemma" (May 24 through June 7, 1930). The scientist, a fearful menace, is Dr. Gold, whose way

was the way of madness and of death. He surrounded himself with hypnotized servitors whose brains and souls were possessed and dominated by their master. His sluggish exterior cloaked an intellect of tremendous force, guided by a will of steel and hampered by no scruples with regard to human happiness, or even with regard to the wanton taking of human life.[32]

Dr. Gold is modeled after your neighborhood Gila Monster. He is a short-legged barrel of a brute, his eyes tiny and dull. Waves of—call it apprehension—radiate from him. He is one of the fiendish scientist tribe, although an extreme example of that curious folk. His mind works slowly, sluggishly, but he is brilliant, brilliant. His specialty is brain.

Dr. Gold: "This boy you speak of is of no value to himself or to the world. He is a white rat. I desire to use him for my experiments into the localization of special abilities, in the cerebral cortex! My discoveries one day will change the basic conceptions of brain physiology of the structure of the cerebrospinal system. But I must have my white rats."[33]

That means he likes to cut open the head and look at the inside.

Gold discovers that John Doe and Molly are in the same city. He owes them something—particularly Molly, who stuck him with his own hypodermic needle several years back. At the same time, a rare batch of master criminals, headed by that grim fiend, Wolf Renault, itch to come to grips with Doe. They have an idea where he may be found.

Meanwhile, Mr. Doe and lady have retired from the great game. They have rented a little cottage. Dale has set himself up in business, complete with an office, a flapper secretary, and a concealed escape exit— for one never knows, do one?

He will need it. Dr. Gold has learned all about Dale. That information came while the doctor was busy snaffeling up Wolf's outfit, man by man, and reducing them to zombies, drugged and thickly hypnotized. Itching to convert Doe to the same condition, he appears at the office.

The thrust fails. Instead, Doe captures Gold, although not for long. Gold escapes and captures Molly and before you know it, she is strapped down tight in a laboratory glowing weirdly in dancing violet light, the man-made zombies lurching, Dr. Gold's dull eyes glinting with satisfaction.

Subsequent parts of the serial feature action/excitement/thrills at levels of high, mad play. On roars the story—foul villain, lovely heroine in peril, the hero agonized. Violent action in Gold's lair at the center of the swamp. Trapped in the passageway by flooding waters. Deadly zombies. The murderous hunchback, Cole, befriended by John Doe. Molly cuts through iron links with a razor blade. Alone in the deadly dissecting room. Doe captured, escapes. Cole captured, escapes.

Molly escapes.

Gunfire in the blackness, Terror. All is lost. And yet...

Gold again escapes. New zombies. Gold attacks. In the reek of gunpowder, the hunchback's icy face. Blood pools on gray cement. Gold, in fear, fleeing, swamp mud sucking at his feet. And so they capture him.

John Doe lies dying, struck down by your treacherous shot. Fever gnaws his brain.

Molly in torment, her lovely face ridged white. If Gold will save Doe, Gold may go free.

The Doctor leers and administers to Doe. Saves him. And grinning leaves.

To die, shot down.

A zombie did it, claims hunchback Cole. Doubtful. No matter. The killing is explored no further. It was a breach of faith. Gold had done as promised, and in the 1920s the word of honor pledged was never violated.

Over now. Cole leaves. The crooks creep away. All silent in the underground Hell palace. Doe is recovering. It is the end of the adventures. They have reformed for good, Dale and Molly Worthington. John Doe is fulfilled, done, complete, will walk no more.

John Doe: "Thus pass the glories of the world and all its memories fade! Sit down beside me, sweetheart, and let me hold you tight! I want to remember that we still have each other left!"[34]

The bathos is rich as onion vapor. He does not much sound as if he is ready to retire. The abundant life of criminal joy is past. Nothing but hours and days and years of sterile honesty face them. The poor fellow!

Through John Doe, the criminal hero tradition of the 1920s was modified to meet the rigors of the next decade. The change was hardly that self conscious. Who knew, then, the coming rigors. It was evident, however, that fiction styles were changing, that after a violent decade lead characters need not be so squeamish about firearms, that millionaires were not indispensable to the cast of characters. That the hero shone even brighter against intelligent opposition. That a modern story included gangsters, snarling hordes of them, eager to kill. That a scene of extended violence neatly capped a long narrative. That women need not be treated as incapable objects but as individuals competent in a crisis and able to raise Holy Ned on their own. That a wider palate of human feelings could be used without affecting the tempo of the fiction; indeed, that emotion could intensify the drama. And that the hero required some stronger motivation for his acts than boredom.

The John Doe series is one of many series in which these changes worked. In few others can these changes be seen as clearly. At the beginning stands the conventional, bright young man of crime; at the end stands the hard-eyed fighter. Behind John Doe, calm 1920s' sunlight. Ahead, Depression grimness—the slam of pistols, hoodlums blue of chin, struggle against intolerable odds.

Doe stands between the decades, a character racked by transition. It is only a single step now to The Shadow.

AFTERWORD

Those readers unhypnotized by the bland irrelevance of these pages may crave sterner fare. Their minds ache for piercing social summations, at the very least; their hearts yearn for intellectual integrations knitting these fleeting threads to a Single Unified Field Theory. Which theory, we may assume, would analyze today's agonizing inadequacies in terms of yesterday's fallacious psychosocietal paradigms, and, in the course of that analysis, trot out many newly sawn phrases to replace old, amid an atmosphere of severe awareness.

Alas for integrating paradigms. To dress these pages in such ceremonial robes is equivalent to dressing the cat in doll's clothing. This does little for cat or clothing, although it has been observed to produce great satisfaction in the heart of the dresser.

Stern analysis is incidental to our main quest. We seek a milder road, following through early mystery-adventure fiction such themes and narrative conventions as are demonstrated by series characters. Criminally-oriented series characters, to be sure.

All magazines used crime stories—stories about criminals—the emphasis placed on the crime, not the detection. No large numbers of these stories were published each month. But there were enough to tweak readers' imaginations and jab their enthusiasm. The crime story that developed over a period of years was no simple thing. It was complex as a coral reef. It included several story types and many differing kinds of criminals.

The Oriental emperors of evil barely classify as criminals. As representatives of the Yellow Peril, they are revolutionists, war makers, their eyes glittering green stones. Their purpose is the overthrow of Western Civilization, followed naturally by world conquest. Fu Manchu stands tall among them. Most crime emperors after him retained that purpose. They would rather crush England and the United States than watch a roomfull of dancing girls. They employ advanced technology and magic (no distinction being drawn between these), as they mobilize Asian hordes, as they scheme, as they commit all manner of crimes. Although these crimes seem piddling stuff when compared to their lofty aims.

The master criminal has no such broad aim. He scorns the abstract. Cash is his goal. He manipulates armies of underlings and spends as lavishly as he steals. The proper master criminal treats his massive crimes as games. These are a means of demonstrating his intellectual superiority—this is the essential motivation of Black Star and Rafferty and, initially, the Gray Phantom.

To ease the reader's conscience, every crime is justified. Somehow. In some way. Although, admittedly, the reasoning is usually as thin as the girl advertising diet cola.

We are assured that these gigantic thefts are quite proper. For don't you agree that society is corrupt, as is the law, as are all the rich people, profiteers and scoundrels to a man. It is a moral obligation to steal from the wicked rich, particularly since part of the spoils is donated to charity. And no robbery involves bloodshed—which demonstrates the moral sensitivity of the thief. What a misfortune that this superior individual is marooned in a society so petty that his talents can only flower in this manner. But if you can't be a senior executive, you must become a master criminal.

Often the master criminal seeks to reform, the consequence of love or boredom. In older works of fiction, the reformed criminal sought to make restitution for his crimes, *a la* Cleek and the Lone Wolf. Such later figures as the Gray Phantom merely retired from active crime, retaining all its fruits.

Reform is no velvet road. Those retiring from crime are constantly threatened by their past—a signed confession, a rival gang leader, a discarded mistress. Their past forever nibbles at their present. Still, we can forgive them much. Their will to reform excuses all past excesses. We can easily forgive Blue Jean Billy and the White Rook, naughty as they have been, for they now try to be good. They have become valued members of society, requiring not even a day's correction in prison, and they frequently aid society by battling criminals. Real criminals; low, mean, sordid criminals. The type that never reform.

Certain series criminals rarely reform, either. These are the professionals, the street crooks, thugs, fences, and con men who pursue their careers through the decades, skillfully balancing between public outrage and acceptance. The fundamental stuff of their lives—that they steal from people—is concealed by a thick glaze of humor. So Big-nose Charlie and Thubway Tham are amusing fellows, amiable to a fault. Mr. Clackworthy often fails under laughable circumstances or gives up his spoils for humanitarian reasons.

If humor does not conceal the grime, then elaborate justifications soften the crimes to mere pranks. Big Scar was unjustly treated and has found honest men more corrupt than cons. Sanderson preys upon exceedingly unpleasant people who deserve punishment. In any case, the crime is against personal property. The victim deserves to be punished by losing his property. It will teach him to be righteous.

A final group of criminals are not criminals at all but social benefactors. Some pretend to be criminals while they investigate or avenge otherwise uncorrectable wrongs. Others commit a limited series of crimes, intent on correcting a personal wrong. A very few, eager to assure equal justice, set themselves up as judge, jury, and executioner, purifying society by selective murder. They only perform this helpful service when a perfectly terrible individual is immune to the Law's correction.

Justice figures are in the minority. While many criminal heroes carry weapons, few use them. Black Star and the Crimson Clown specialized in the gas gun, a convenient device. Others rely on nerve pressures or knockout drops. Not until a decade of newspaper headlines had brutalized national tastes did American heroes begin to use weapons with the intent of damaging someone. The physical violence that crept into the John Doe series was only a prelude to the violence which would explode through the 1930s pulp magazines.

It was violence made acceptable by a flow of beautiful reasons. Violence was a means of administering justice in a society unwilling or unable to defend itself and its members. Gangsters swarmed the alley, inhuman, rapacious horrors, unchecked by restraint. How far they are from the tuxedo-clad hordes of Black Star. Every gangster has a machine gun and sprays it busily. Faced by these warped figures, the hero must defend himself, and so the exciting chapters fly by.

Similar, if less violent, imperatives lie behind the Four-Square Jane-Thunderbolt-Avenging Twins stories. Here, too, the lead characters must defend themselves from predatory forces unchecked by usual social mechanisms. They are morally obligated to take action on their own behalf. It is a position forced upon them by the same society whose functional disjunction generated the original wrong.

Woman as well as men may plunge into this active struggle. Feminine criminals were no strangers to the dime novels. The pulp magazines introduced them more cautiously. At first women were exquisitely fragile objects to be saved or menaced, as required by the plot. Soon enough their role expanded. Boston Betty plundered the city, Blue Jean Billy the ocean, while various McCulley heroines either encouraged costumed crime or planned it. Crime and bad company affected neither their looks nor their morals. They were as sexless as plastic dolls. Not till the late 1920s, with the appearance of Molly Worthington in John Doe and The Flame in the Race Williams *Black Mask* novelettes, did the feminine criminal begin demonstrating the emotions and vulnerabilities afflicting women in the less sterile world outside the magazines. As their capacity for feeling expanded, so did their active role in the story. Molly Worthington functions brilliantly in John Doe's absence. And if she is captured at least as often as less capable women, and faces considerably more sexual danger, she is able to rescue herself. She can think her way out of danger as adroitly as any male lead. Her decisions influence the course of the narrative. She is no longer a passive decoration, even in high heels and skirts.

As women's conventional role in crime fiction slowly changed, other conventions were in the process of hardening. The criminal hero story is the detective story turned inside out. Most of the same character relationships appear. The ghosts of Holmes and Watson show transparent behind Mr. Clackworthy and the Early Bird, or Sheik and Simp, or the Thunderbolt and Saggs.

Frequently the hero's Watson is a reformed criminal, inept, slow-witted, intensely loyal. Later variations improved his ability, while retaining his criminal background.

Both characters are pursued by a non-too-scrupulous detective, a device used in the Jesse James dime novels. This convention moved directly into the pulps, appearing in the Ravenswood and Rafferty series, and most of the Johnston McCulley series. In both the Thubway Tham and Scarlet Fox series, the character of the officer was softened. His function remained the same—to endanger the hero's plans and liberty, adding suspense to other plot complications.

In such series as the Gray Phantom, the Picaroon, and the Crimson Clown, the criminal hero has a friendly relationship with the pursuing officer, who may or may not suspect the identity of his quarry. Most of these officers have a built-in-dumb spot to permit the relationship to continue. Later, as the alternate identity criminal hero was superseded by the alternate identity justice figure, the convention was continued unchanged. It is a basic device in such 1930s series as The Shadow, The Spider, and Captain Satan.

The alternate identity hero continues lines laid down in the dime novels and explored through such early series as Colonel Clay, Cleek, and Jimmie Dale. At first, the alternate identity was a matter of disguise, continued during the 1920s by such excellences as the Picaroon and the Gray Phantom. Costumes—another dime novel device—were used by McCulley for Zorro (1919) and afterward for his long string of criminal heroes. The device continued into the 1930 magazines, where it raged unchecked until it fell into the comic books.

Alternate identities required considerable paraphernalia—costumes, disguise materials, chemicals, tools, shelves for stolen property. All items hard to explain if discovered by the police. Jimmie Dale stored these artifacts in a rented room; the Picaroon used an old house. Whatever its form, the residence mid-way between one identity and another proved an exceedingly useful device. Through the years it was augmented to include garages, aircraft hangers, and docks for all the vehicles required in chasing back and forth, baffling the police and punishing crime.

Other characters, unfettered by secret identities, built themselves wonderful hideouts. In these secure places, the hunted man could pull off his shoes and pour a highball, surrounded on every side by evidences of his skill and taste. Rafferty enjoyed a cave; Fu Manchu and Mr. Chang preferred luxurious rooms, richly ornamented, bung-full of secret doors and traps for the unwary. These glorious places became a convention in themselves. For the next fifty years, master criminals would weave plots amid crushing luxury, symbol of their power, clear indication that crime can be made to pay handsomely, no matter what the threadbare honest may believe.

Of devils and smoky imps, thieves and rascals, we have had a sufficiency. We have seen a grand parade of villains, world conquerors, con men, bored young safe crackers, hard-eyed Oriental killers. They made their way through twenty years of popular magazine fiction.

During the same period, an even more scintillating parade—larger, more varied, longer remembered—had flowed on and on through the magazines. It was an unquenchable stream of lucid men and women who penetrated, at a glance, those enigmas posed by the people from the dark side. They were extraordinary people. Some were official investigators. Others sold intellectual penetration by the day. Many were simple folk with a gift, amateurs like you and me.

After Sherlock Holmes, a reeling tumble of imitators burst into print. It was Holmes large, Holmes small. Holmes in official dress. Holmes as the unblooded amateur.

Immediately they began to differentiate. General types formed. The enthusiasm of the dime novels folded into Holmes' intellectual sleight-of-hand. For every crook story, six stories were published featuring men of genius, women of unearthly beauty and penetration.

The spark flared in them all. Perception, that searing jewel, glared and blazed. Internal psychological need drove them to understand and on the screen of their minds, faint clues built elaborate images of crimes past, emotions vanished.

They are investigating masters. They are geniuses, the people we will meet in the next volume of *Yesterday's Faces*.

Notes

Evocation

[1]For those unenthused by obscure references, the voices of the Evocation are, respectively, Sherlock Holmes, Chick Carter and Nick Carter, Nayland Smith and Doctor Petrie, Craig Kennedy and Walter Jameson, and The Shadow and Harry Vincent.

CHAPTER I: Emperors of Evil

[1]This story is included in *The Wrath of Fu Manchu*, NY: DAW Books (1976).

[2]Robert Howard's novel *Skullface* features a direct copy of Fu Manchu. The novel was first published as a three-part serial in *Weird Tales*, October through December 1929, and was reprinted in *Famous Fantastic Mysteries*, December 1952.

[3]Barbara W. Tuchman, *The Zimmermann Telegram*, NY: McMillan (1950), p. 25.

[4]John D. Squires provided this information in the "Letters" column of *Xenophile* #17 (September 1975), p. 61.

[5]William Vivian Butler, *The Durable Desperados*, London: MacMillan (1973), p. 46.

[6]Tuchman, *op cit.*, p. 64. Chapter 4 contains a fascinating account of Germany's aspirations and manipulations in Mexico during the early 1900s, and discusses the role of the Hearst press in elaborating the myth of a potential Japanese-Mexican invasion of the United States.

[7]Richard H. Dillon, *The Hatchet Men*, NY: Ballentine Books (1972), p. 65.

[8]St. Clair McKelway, "Tong Leader," *True Tales from the Annuals of Crime and Rascality*, NY: Random House, no date, 2nd printing, pp. 52-53.

[9]Dillon, *op. cit.*, pp. 130-132.

[10]A.E. Apple, "No. 13 Ching Street, Chinatown," *Detective Story Magazine*, Vol. CVIII, No. 5, (March 23, 1929). pp. 1-2.

[11]H. Irving Hancock, "Li Shoon's Deadliest Mission," *Detective Story Magazine*, Vol. IV, No. 5 (September 5, 1916), p. 27.

[12]A. E. Apple, "Mr. Chang's Blackmail Horde," *Detective Story Magazine*, Vol. LXXXIV, No. 4 (June 12, 1926), p. 5.

[13] *Ibid*, p. 8.

[14]A. E. Apple, "Mr. Chang," *Detective Story Magazine*, Vol. XXVI, No. 2 (September 9, 1919), p. 7.

[15]Bill Pronzini, *Gun In Cheek,* NY: Coward, McCann, & Geoghegan (1982), pp. 142-146. Mr. Apple's literary transgressions are extensive. As Pronzini points out, his ear for dialogue was faulty, his sense of situation flawed, and his style unencumbered by grace. These technical infelicities failed to damp his sense of parody. As the series matured and its content thinned, like hair on an old scalp, the element of parody increased all out of proportion. The final stories are one long grimace at the convention of the crime master and the Oriental fiend.

[16]D. C. Hubbard, "Popular Detective Story Writers: A. E. Apple," *Detective Story Magazine,* Vol. CI, No. 2 (May 12, 1928), pp. 122-123.

[17]The earliest date of Mr. Chang's reappearance that has come to light, so far, is the October 25, 1924, "Mr. Chang, Man-Trapper." Earlier stories are certainly possible. Mr. Chang also appears, although unnamed, in a bit part in "Sweet Plunder," a three-part serial, September 7 through 21, 1920, in *Detective Story.*

[18]A. E. Apple, *Mr. Chang of Scotland Yard.* NY: Chelsea House (1926), p. 255. This book includes the novelettes, "Mr. Chang of Scotland Yard" and "The Glittering Lady," which have been run together to form an apparent novel.

CHAPTER II—*Crime Extraordinary*

[1]Pierre Souvestre and Marcel Allain, *A Nest of Spies,* NY: Brentano's (1918), The passages quoted are from pp. 274-277.

[2]Robert Sampson, *The Night Master.* Chicago: Pulp Press (1982). The origins of the mystery figure are examined in detail in Chapter III of this book.

[3] Quentin Reynolds, *The Fiction Factory.* New York: Random House (1955), p. 173.

[4] *Ibid,* p. 176.

[5]John Mack Stone (pseudonym for Johnston McCulley), "Rogue For A Day," *Detective Story Magazine,* Vol. 2, No. 5 (March 5, 1916), p. 3.

[6] *Ibid,* p. 13.

[7]Chelsea House, the imprint under which Street & Smith republished fiction from its magazines as inexpensive books, issued *The Black Star* (1921)—later reprinted by Grosset in 1925—*Black Star's Campaign* (1924), and *Black Star's Return* (1926).

[8]"Black Star On the Air" gives every evidence to having been written years before its publication in *Detective Story,* possible as a sequel to the 1921 "Black Star Comes Back."

[9]Johnston McCulley, "The Spider's Den," *Detective Story Magazine,* Vol. XIV, No. 1 (April 16, 1918), p. 10.

[10] *Ibid,* p. 5.

[11]McCulley, "The Spider's Reward," *Detective Story Magazine,* Vol. XXIII, No. 1 (April 29, 1919), p. 90.

[12]A. Conan Doyle, "The Final Problem," *The Memoirs of Sherlock Holmes,* contained in *The Complete Sherlock Holmes,* NY: Garden City (1938), p. 544.

[13]A. E. Apple, "Rafferty, Master Rogue," *Detective Story Magazine,* Vol. XCV, No. 6 (October 1, 1927), p. 2.

[14] *Ibid,* pp. 5-6.

[15] *Ibid,* p. 7.

[16]A. E. Apple, "Rafferty's Phantom Plunder," *Detective Story Magazine,* Vol. CXII, No. 4 (August 31, 1929), p. 44.

[17]Apple, "Rafferty and the Chinese Eight," *Detective Story Magazine*, Vol. CXII, No. 6 (September 14, 1929), p. 11.

CHAPTER III—The Wicked Brotherhood

[1]The Jeff Peters stories were written specifically for book publication and were not first published in magazines.

[2]Eugene Current-Garcia, *O. Henry*, Twayne Pub (1965), p. 52.

[3]Campbell MacCulloch, "Brokers and Bankers," *Peoples Short Story Magazine*, Vol. III, No 4 (October 1907), p. 741.

[4] *Ibid*, p. 738.

[5]D. C. Hubbard, "Popular Detective Story Writers: Christopher B. Booth," *Detective Story Magazine*, Vol. CIII, No. 4 (August 18, 1928), p. 113-114.

[6]John A. Hogan, "The Mission That Succeeded," *The Edgar Wallace Society Newsletter 48* (November 1980), p. 3. When the Elegant Edward stories were assembled into the book, the original publication sequence was scrambled. The discussion in the text follows the sequence provided by John Hogan: and by Christopher Lowder, *Edgar Wallace Newsletter* No. 26 (June 1975), p. 4.

[7]Charles W. Tyler, "Big-Nose Charlie's Florida Front," *Detective Story Magazine*, Vol. C, No. 1 (March 24, 1928), p. 44.

[8]Tham's later appearances were more scattered. Occasional stories have been reported in *Popular Detective* and *Famous Detective*, although these have not been confirmed.

[9]Johnston McCulley, "Thubway Tham's Ides of March," *Detective Story Magazine*, Vol. C, No. 1 (March 24, 1928), p. 76.

[10]Harold Brainard Hersey, *Pulpwood Editor*, Greenwood Press (1974), p. 139.

[11] *Ibid*, p. 138.

[12]Henry Leverage, "The Old Clam," *Flynn's Weekly*, Vol. XIX, No. 3 (October 30, 1926), p. 406.

[13]Leverage, "The New Warden," *Flynn's Weekly*, Vol. XIX, No. 6 (November 20, 1926), p. 905.

[14]D. C. Hubbard, "Popular Detective Story Writers: John Jay Chichester," *Detective Story Magazine*, Vol. C, No. 1 (March 24, 1928), pp. 133-134. The quotation is attributed to Chichester, although it may have been retouched for Hubbard's article.

[15] *Ibid*, p. 134. The prison practices of sixty years ago may have been casual enough to permit conversation between prisoners and walk-in visitors, improbable as this seems. That these conversations gave Chichester insight and "authenticity" may be possible, although no high concentration of either seeped into his prose.

[16]John Jay Chichester, "Helpless Hands" (part 2 of 3-part serial), *Detective Story Magazine*, Vol. LXXXIX, No. 5 (January 15, 1927), p. 56.

[17]D. C. Hubbard, "Popular Detective Story Writers: Roland Krebs," *Detective Story Magazine*, Vol. CXIX No. 5 (June 28, 1930), pp. 111-112.

[18]Anonymous, "Headquarters Chat," *Detective Story Magazine*, Vol. CXXXV, No. 1 (April 2, 1932), p. 141. In response to a reader's query, the editor states that Krebs is working in advertising.

[19]Roland Krebs, "Reward—500 Smackers," *Detective Story Magazine*, Vol. CXIX, No. 5 (June 28, 1930), p. 88.

[20]D. C. Hubbard, "Popular Detective Story Writers: Arthur Mallory," *Detective Story Magazine*, Vol. CI, No. 5 (June 2, 1928), pp. 102-104.

[21]Robert Sampson, "The Death Givers," *Yesterday's Faces, Vol. 1: Glory Figures*. Bowling Green Popular Press (1983). This chapter contains a detailed account of the Just Men series.

CHAPTER IV: *Four From Wallace*

[1]Ellery Queen, Introduction to "The Adventure of the Steel Bonds," *The Great Women Detectives and Criminals* (retitling of *The Female of the Species*). NY: Blue Ribbon Books, 1946, p. 369.

[2]John A. Hogan, "The Mission That Succeeded," Edgar Wallace Society Newsletter 48 (November 1980), p. 4. This article discusses Edgar Wallace series fiction originally published in the newspapers, *The Sunday Post* and *The Weekly News*. Mr. Hogan's findings are of particular interest because they trace, for the first time, the original publication of stories which, in whole or part, comprise such books as *Four Square Jane*, *The Mixer*, *The Brigand*, *The Black*, *The Iron Grip*, *The Adventures of Heine*, *Elegant Edward*, and *Tam O'The Scouts*.

[3]Similar keys were used in the Nick Carter and Cleek series about ten years before. Apparently based on actual devices, their primary use was to speed up the story.

[4]Edgar Wallace, *Four Square Jane*, The Reader's Library. London: undated, pps. 57-58.

[5] *Ibid*, p. 59.

[6]Edgar Wallace, "The Outwitting of Pony Nelson," *The Mixer*, London: John Long, Ltd., 1927, second impression, p. 19.

[7]The figure of the Dude, the Beau, the Fop, has been a familiar literary target since the early 1700s, and was mercilessly set upon in the works of Addison, Steele, and Pope.

[8]The tangled history of The Brigand series was unraveled by John A. Hogan in two articles published in the *Edgar Wallace Newsletter:* "Seek And You Will Find," Newsletter 26 (June 1975), p. 3; and "Some Bits And Pieces," Newsletter 54 (May 1982), p. 4. Following publication of *The Brigand* in 1927, four stories from the series, that had originally been published in *The Novel Magazine*, were reprinted in the September 6, 1932, *Weldon's Ladies Journal (Special Fiction Supplement)*. Additional stories were also reprinted in the 1935, *The Thriller*. Still later, two stories about Captain Hex were reprinted in the *Edgar Wallace Mystery Magazine*, December 1966 and February 1967.

[9]Edgar Wallace, "A Matter of Nerve," *The Brigand*, London: Hodder and Stoughton (undated but issued 1927), p. 1.

[10]Wallace, "On Getting An Introduction," *The Brigand*, p. 48.

[11]Wallace, "The Lady In Grey," *The Brigand*, pps. 187-188.

[12]Hogan, "The Mission That Succeeded," Newsletter 48, p. 3.

[13]Wallace, *The Mixer*, p. 12.

[14] *Ibid*, p. 19.

[15] *Loc. cit.*

[16]Butler, *op. cit.*, p. 94.

[17]Wallace, *The Mixer*, p. 142.

[18] *Ibid*, p. 283.

[19]The quoted material is from Wallace's *The Gaunt Stranger*, London: Hodder and Stoughton, undated (1925).

[20]Ibid, p. 318.

[21]Edgar Wallace, *The Ringer*, London: Pan Books (1948), "Dedication."

[22] *The Gaunt Stranger* begins: "Flanders Lane, Deptford, is narrow and dingy.' The revised *The Ringer* begins: "The Assistant Commissioner of Police pressed a bell on his table...." It should be noted that the most readily available edition of *The Ringer* in the United States (1926) is a retitling of *The Gaunt Stranger*.

[23]Wallace, *The Ringer* (Pan), p. 223.

[24]Wallace, "The Blackmail Boomerang," *The Ringer Returns*, NY: Crime Club (1931), p. 104.

[25] *Ibid.*, "The Obliging Cobbler," p. 277.

[26] *Ibid.*, "The Case of the Home Secretary," p. 29.

CHAPTER V—In Name Only

[1]Johnston McCulley, "Master and Man," *Detective Story Magazine*, Vol. XXXI, No. 4 (May 4, 1920), p. 1.

[2] *Ibid*, p. 22.

[3]McCulley, "The Kidnapped Midas," *Detective Story Magazine*, Vol. XXXII, No. 6 (June 29, 1920), p. 63.

[4]McCulley, "The Big Six," *Detective Story Magazine*, Vol. XXXIV, No. 4 (September 7, 1920), p. 11.

[5] *Ibid*, p. 5.

[6]McCulley, "The Thunderbolt's Engagement," *Detective Story Magazine*, Vol. XLII, No. 2 (July 30, 1921), p. 25.

[7]Johnston McCulley, *The Avenging Twins*, NY: Chelsea House (1927), p. 32.

[8]Sampson, *op. cit.*, Chapter V, "Alias the Gray Seal," pp. 132-161. In this chapter, The Toscin's role in the Jimmie Dale series is examined in detail.

[9]McCulley, *op, cit.*, pp. 83-84.

[10]E. R. Hagemann, *A Comprehensive Index to Black Mask, 1920-1951*. The Popular Press (1982), p. 37.

[11]Eustace Hale Ball, *The Scarlet Fox*, NY: Grosset & Dunlap (1927), p. 161.

[12] *Ibid*, p. 178.

[13] *Ibid*, p. 44.

[14]Hugh Kahler, "The White Rook's Pawn," *Detective Story Magazine*, Vol, XVIII, No. 1 (October 1, 1918), p. 35.

[15]Charles W. Tyler, *Quality Bill's Girl*, NY: Chelsea House (1925), pp. 21-23.

[16]D. C. Hubbard, "Popular Detective Story Writers: Charles W. Tyler," *Detective Story Magazine*, Vol,. CXI, No. 4 (July 20, 1929), pp. 106-107.

[17]Tyler, "Blue Jean Billy Plays Fair," *Detective Story Magazine*, Vol. CXV, No. 6 (January 18, 1930), p. 2.

[18]Tyler, "Sea Law and Blue Jean Billy," *Detective Story Magazine*, Vol. CXXXI, No. 5 (November 14, 1931), p. 58.

[19]Hugh Kahler, "The Joker's Last Card," *Detective Story Magazine*, Vol. XXVII, No. 1 (October 14, 1919), p. 16.

[20]Herman Landon, "Seven Signs," *Detective Story Magazine*, Vol. XI, No. 2 (December 18, 1917), pp. 3-4.

²¹ *Ibid*, p. 4.

²² *Ibid*, p. 37.

²³ *Ibid*, p. 39.

²⁴Landon, "Gray Terror," *Detective Story Magazine*, Vol. XXIII, No. 4 (May 20, 1919), pp. 7-8.

²⁵Landon, "The Gray Phantom Goes It Alone," *Detective Story Magazine*, Vol. XXVIII, No. 1 (November 25, 1919), p. 39.

²⁶ *Ibid*, p. 41.

²⁷Landon, *The Gray Phantom's Return*, NY: A. L. Burt (1922), p. 22.

²⁸ *Ibid, p. 21.*

²⁹The Gray Phantom novels were initially published by G. H. Watt, rather than by Street & Smith's Chelsea House. As far as is known, the earliest Gray Phantom stories from his master criminal period were never reprinted.

³⁰The Gray Phantom's imposture is seen through in about half an hour. The Duke disguise is the most formal one donned by the Phantom, who was more usually content with a false beard or a change of clothing and a cringing attitude. Disguise, he believed, is a matter of blending into the background. In this matter, the Gray Phantom and Vance's Lone Wolf share compatible views.

³¹Leslie Gordon Barnard, "Drowned To Win," *Detective Story Magazine*, Vol. CX, No. 6 (June 22, 1929).

³²Barnard, "The Pond Lily," *Detective Story Magazine*, Vol. CXVI, No. 3 (February 8,. 1930), p. 38.

³³Sampson, *op. cit.*, Chapter IV. "Rogues and Bent Heroes," pp. 98-100. This chapter discusses a few of the early bent heroes whose activities, even before Jimmie Dale, established the type in popular magazine fiction.

CHAPTER VI—Still More Rogues and Bent Heroes

¹The Picaroon's first cards are written in a disguised hand. Later they are engraved. You wonder what printer did that job for him—and why the police couldn't follow out the clue.

²Herman Landon, "The Benevolent Picaroon," *Detective Story Magazine*, Vol. XLI, No. 6 (July 16, 1921), p. 5.

³ *Loc. cit.*

⁴ *Ibid*, p. 20.

⁵Landon, "Picaroon's Crystal Gazer," *Detective Story Magazine*, Vol. CXV, No. 5 (January 11, 1930).

⁶The name, The Picaroon, reappeared in 1954, attached to a brand new character, Ludovic Saxon. He strongly resembles a renovated Bulldog Drummond. The old and new Picaroons share nothing in common but their sobriquet.

⁷Butler, *op. cit.*, p. 74. *The Durable Desperadoes*, that vivacious book, is packed with accounts of England's brightest bent and slightly criminal heroes, their authors, and the publications in which they appeared. An indispensable volume. It contains a spirited detailing of Blackshirt's life and times. The Blackshirt books are not in print in the United States, although early volumes are reasonably available through used book channels.

[8]Blackshirt's ability to melt into darkness illustrates the hazard of attempting to establish clear lines of influence between series characters. The convention may be obvious and it is possible to specify the contributing characters chronologically. It is another matter to identify the real influence on a given character. For instance, Blackshirt's garb was suggested to Jeffries when his mother, dressed in black, abruptly appeared from the twilight. In the case of the 1930s Shadow, a black-garbed figure of the night, the convention is that of the mystery figure. The specific influence, however, was dual: first, the figure of Dracula as portrayed in the stage play; second, that technique of stage magic in which all lights are briefly turned out, permitting one of the magician's assistants, dressed in black, to cross the stage secretly. Neither influence is obvious. The incautious commentator will tumble into error by citing the more obvious, if incorrect, lines of influence which apparently lead from Fantomas to Blackshirt to The Shadow.

[9]Bruce Graeme, *Blackshirt*, NY: Grosset & Dunlap (1925), p. 13.

[10] *Ibid*, pp. 14-15.

[11] *Ibid*, pp. 80-81.

[12]William Vivian Butler, *op. cit.*, pp. 192-193.

[13]Johnston McCulley, "The Man in Purple," *Detective Story Magazine*, Vol. XLIII, No. 5 (October 1, 1921), p. 7.

[14]McCulley, "The Man in Purple Meets a Man in Blue," *Detective Story Magazine*, Vol. XLIV, No. 4 (November 5, 1921), p. 42.

[15]McCulley, "The Man in Purple," p. 9.

[16]McCulley, "The Man in Purple Meets a Man in Blue," p. 50.

[17]McCulley, "The Man in Purple," p. 1.

[18]This Announcement of the first Crimson Clown novelette appeared a week before the story in *Detective Story Magazine*, Vol. LXXXV, No. 4 (July 24, 1926), p. 2.

[19]The group of quotations has been drawn from "The Crimson Clown Cornered," *Detective Story Magazine*, Vol. LXXXVI, No. 2 (August 21, 1926).

[20]McCulley, "The Crimson Clown," *Detective Story Magazine*, Vol. LXXXV, No. 5 (July 31, 1926), p. 12.

[21]McCulley, "The Crimson Clown Is Cornered," p. 33.

[22] *Ibid*, p. 39.

[23] *Ibid*, p. 42.

[24] *Ibid*, p. 58.

[25] *Ibid*, p. 42.

[26]Leo Margulies, editor, *Master Mystery Stories*, NY: Hampton (1945). In this collection of mystery-adventure fiction from the mid-1940 Standard publications, "The Crimson Clown's Return" was reprinted under the title of "The Crimson Clown."

[27]The character type persists. The television season which began September 1978 included a brief series titled *Sword of Justice*. This featured a black clad, thoroughly updated justice figure, Jack Cole. He was a wealthy playboy framed into prison by crooks, came out seeking revenge, filled with a need to fight untouchable crime for the sake of justice. His symbol is a three-pip playing card—one pip for each year he served in prison—which he leaves at the scene of his generally bloodless exploits. He is assisted by a humorous friend, Hector Ramirez, who knows the Sword's secret. And he is inadvertently aided by the federal agent, Arthur Woods, who babbles out all the necessary plot background and never understands what Jack Cole is doing at the scene of so many violent incidents.

[28]Paul Ellsworth Triem, "Enter—John Doe," *Detective Story Magazine*, Vol. CI, No. 6 (June 9, 1928), p. 4.

[29] *Loc, cit.*

[30]Triem, "John Doe's Dilemma,(Part I), *Detective Story Magazine*, Vol. CXVIII, No. 6 (May 24, 1930), p. 15.

[31]Triem, "Fugitive Finger Prints," *Detective Story Magazine*, Vol. CXVI, No. 2 (February 1, 1930), pp. 119-120.

[32]Triem, "Dilemma," p. 13.

[33] *Ibid*, p. 33.

[34]Triem, "Dilemma" (Part 3), Vol. CXIX, No. 2 (June 7, 1930), p. 89.

SELECTED BIBLIOGRAPHY

Apple, A. E. *Mr Chang of Scotland Yard*. NY: Chelsea House, 1926.

———— *Mr. Chang's Crime Ray*. NY: Chelsea House, 1928.

Ball, Eustace Hale. *The Scarlet Fox*. NY: Grosset & Dunlap, 1927.

Blackbeard, Bill. "Foreshadowings," *Xenophile* #17, September 1975, pp. 6-7, 59-60. Includes discussion of Blackshirt.

———— "The Information Center," *Xenophile* #30, March 1977, p. 139. Letter discussing McCulley's Spider.

Booth, Christopher B. *Mr. Clackworthy*. NY: Chelsea House, 1926.

———— *Mr. Clackworthy, Con Man*. Chelsea House, 1928.

Butler, William Vivian. *The Durable Desperadoes*. London Ltd: MacMillan, 1973.

Chichester, John Jay. *Rogues of Fortune*. NY: Chelsea House, 1929.

———— *Sanderson: Master Rogue*. NY: Chelsea House, 1929.

———— *Sanderson's Diamond Loot*. NY: Chelsea House, 1935

———— *The Silent Cracksman*. *NY: Chelsea House, 1929*.

Current-Garcia, Eugene. *O. Henry*. Twayne Pub., 1965.

Dillon, Richard H. *The Hatchet Men*. NY: Ballentine Books, 1972.

Graeme, Bruce. *Blackshirt*. NY: Grosset & Dunlap, 1925.

———— *Blackshirt Again*. London: Hutchinson, 1951.

The Return of Blackshirt. London: Harrap, 1931.

Hagemann, E. R. *A Comprehensive Index to Black Mask, 1920-1951*. The Popular Press, 1982.

Henry, O. (pseudo for William Sidney Porter). *The Gentle Grafter* in *The Complete Works of O. Henry*. NY: Garden City, 1937.

Hersey, Harold Brainerd. *Pulpwood Editor*. Westport: Greenwood Press, 1974.

Hogan, John A. "The Mission That Succeeded," *Edgar Wallace Society Newsletter 48*, November 1980, p. 4.

———— "Seek and You Will Find," *Edgar Wallace Society Newsletter 26*, June 1975, p. 3.

———— "Some Bits and Pieces," Edgar Wallace Society Newsletter 54, May 1982, p. 4.

Howard, Robert. *Skull-Face Omnibus*. Jersey: Spearman, 1974.

Hubbard, D. C. "Popular Detective Story Writers: A. E. Apple," *Detective Story Magazine*, Vol. CI, No. 2, May 12, 1928, pp. 122-123.

———— "Popular Detective Story Writers: Christopher B. Booth," *Detective Story Magazine*, Vol. CIII, No. 4, August 18, 1928, pp. 113-114.

———— "Popular Detective Story Writers: John Jay Chichester," *Detective Story Magazine*, Vol. C, No. 1, March 24, 1928, pp. 133-134.

_____ "Popular Detective Story Writers: Roland Krebs," *Detective Story Magazine*, Vol. CXIX, No. 5, June 28, 1930, pp. 111-112.

_____ "Popular Detective Story Writers: Arthur Mallory," *Detective Story Magazine*, Vol. CI, No. 5, June 2, 1928, pp. 102-104.

_____ "Popular Detective Story Writers: Charles W. Tyler," *Detective Story Magazine*, Vol. CXI, No. 4, July 20, 1929, pp. 106-107.

Kahler, Hugh McNair. *The White Rook*. NY: Chelsea House, 1927.

Landon, Herman. *Gray Magic* (retitling of "The Human Pawn"). NY: A. L. Burt. 1925.

_____ *The Gray Phantom* (retitling of "The Gray Phantom's Romance"). NY: W. J. Watt, 1921.

_____ *The Gray Phantom's Return* (retitling of "The Gray Phantom's Defense"). NY: A. L. Burt, 1922.

_____ *Gray Terror* (retitling of "Human Pawn"). NY: A. L. Burt, 1925.

_____ *The Green Shadow*, NY: Dial, 1928.

_____ *Hands Unseen* (retitling of "The Gray Phantom Madness"). NY: Watt, 1924.

_____ *Picaroon In Pursuit*. London: Cassell, 1935.

_____ *The Picaroon, Knight Errant*. London: Cassell, 1933.

_____ The Picaroon Resumes Practice, London: Cassell, 1935.

_____ *Trailing the Picaroon*. London: Cassell, 1935.

Lowder, Christopher, "Odds and Ends: No. 4, 'Elegant Edward,' " *Edgar Wallace Society Newsletter 26*, June 1975, p. 4.

McCulley, Johnston. *Alias the Thunderbolt*, NY: Chelsea House, 1927.

_____ *The Avenging Twins*. NY: Chelsea House, 1927.

_____ *The Avenging Twins Collect*. NY: Chelsea House, 1927

_____ *The Black Star*. NY: Chelsea House, 1921.

_____ *Black Star's Campaign*. NY: Chelsea House, 1924.

_____ *Black Star's Return*. NY: Chelsea House, 1926.

_____ *The Crimson Clown*. NY: Chelsea House, 1928.

_____ *The Crimson Clown Again*. London, Cassell, 1928.

_____ *The Spider's Den*. NY: Chelsea House, 1925.

_____ *The Spider's Debt*. NY: Chelsea House, 1930.

_____ *The Spider's Fury*. NY: Chelsea House, 1930.

_____ *The Thunderbolt's Jest*. NY: Chelsea House, 1927.

McKelway, St. Clair, "Tong Leader," *True Tales from the Annals of Crime and Rascality*. NY: Random House, 2nd printing, no date.

Margulies, Leo. *Master Mystery Stories*. NY: Hampton, 1945.

Pronzini, Bill, *Gun In Cheek*. NY: Coward, McCann & Geoghegan, 1982.

Queen, Ellery (editor). "Introduction" to "The Adventure of the Steel Bonds," *The Great Woman Detectives and Criminals* (retitling of *The Female of the Species*). NY: Blue Ribbon, 1946.

Reynolds, Quentin, *The Fiction Factory*, NY: Random House, 1955.

Rohmer, Sax (pseudo for Arthur Henry Sarsfield Ward). *Daughter of Fu Manchu*. NY: Doubleday, Doran & Co., 1931.

_____ *Emperor Fu Manchu*. NY: Pyramid Books, 1976.

_____ *The Insidious Dr. Fu Manchu*. NY: Pyramid Books, 1970.

_____ *The Mask of Fu Manchu*. NY: Pyramid Books, 1966.

_____ *The Shadow of Fu Manchu*. NY: Pyramid Books, 1970.

―――― *The Wrath of Fu Manchu.* NY: DAW Books, 1976.

Sampson, Robert. *The Night Master.* Chicago: Pulp Press, 1982.

―――― *Yesterday's Faces, Vol. 1: Glory Figures.* The Popular Press, 1983.

Souvestre, Pierre, and Allain, Marcel. *The Long Arm of Fantomes.* NY: Macaulay, 1924.

―――― *A Nest of Spies.* NY: Brentano's, 1918.

Triem, Paul Ellsworth. *Alias John Doe.* NY: Chelsea House, 1930.

Tuchman, Barbara W. *The Zimmermann Telegram.* NY: McMillan, 1950.

Tyler, Charles W. *Blue Jean Billy.* NY: Chelsea House, 1926.

―――― *Quality Bill's Girl.* NY: Chelsea House, 1925.

Wallace, Edgar. *The Brigand.* London: Hodder & Stoughton, undated (1927).

―――― *Elegant Edward.* London: Readers Library, undated (1928).

―――― *Four Square Jane.* London: Readers Library, undated (1929).

―――― *The Gaunt Stranger.* London: Hodder & Stoughton, undated (1925).

―――― *The Mixer,* London: John Long (2nd impression), 1927.

―――― *The Ringer.* NY: Doubleday & Doran, 1926.

―――― *The Ringer.* London: Pan Books, 1951 (reprint) (revised edition).

―――― *The Ringer Returns.* NY: Crime Club, 1931.

MAGAZINE APPEARANCES OF SELECTED SERIES CHARACTERS

The following lists are not complete. That they are provided at all is because even partial references are better than none. Additional information and corrections would be appreciated. Thanks go to Dave Arends and Fred Siehl for their work in developing much of this information.

The Avenging Twins by Johnston McCulley in *Detective Story Magazine:*

1923	May 12	The Avenging Twins
	Jun 16	The Avenging Twins Try It Again
	through	(3-part serial)
	Jun 30	
	Aug 25	The Avenging Twins' Third Trick
	through	(3-part serial)
	Sept 8	
	Nov 10	Pearls of Great Price
1924	Feb 23	The Avenging Twins' Fifth Victim
	Apr 5	The Avenging Twins' Last Blow
	through	(2-part serial)
	Apr 12	
1925	Oct 17	The Avenging Twins Return
1926	May 22	The Avenging Twins Collect

Big-Nose Charlie by Charles W. Tyler
NOTE: The name was written both as Big-Nose Charlie and Big-nose Charlie. In these listings, it is abbreviated as "BNC"

in *Detective Story Magazine:*

1917	Apr 5	BNC's Get Away
	Sept 11	BNC Works Alone
	Oct 2	BNC and the Simple Life
	Dec 25	BNC on the Mountain Division (novel)
1918	Jan 29	BNC, Bad Man
	Apr 16	BNC, "On the Cross"
1919	Mar 25	BNC Rolls His Own
	Sept 2	BNC and Human Clay
	Nov 18	BNC and Any Old Port
	Dec 16	BNC At Home
1920	Feb 24	BNC and the Promised Land
	Apr 6	BNC and Deuces Low
	Aug 17	BNC and the Double Cross
1921	Jan 22	BNC in the City of Culture
	Apr 16	BNC At the Policeman's Ball
	June 4	BNC At the Auto Show
	Aug 27	BNC's Dog Helps Out
	Dec 10	BNC Gets an Interview
1922	Apr 1	BNC on the **Barbary Coast**
	Oct 14	BNC and the Tout
1923	Feb 24	BNC Gets His Match
	May 5	BNC Sits on the World
1924	Mar 8	BNC Enters the City of Angels
	Jun 21	BNC Meets Some Home Folks
	Oct 11	BNC, Hijacker
	Oct 25	BNC On the Painted Plain
	Dec 20	BNC, Alias Santa Claus
1925	Mar 28	BNC Hops Off
	Aug 15	BNC and Madey-line
	Sept 5	BNC Finds a Brother
	Oct 24	BNC Leaves His Card
1926	Feb 13	BNC At the Opera
	Apr 17	BNC and His Jenny
1927	Jun 11	BNC and the Merry Widow
1928	Jan 6	BNC, Goober Grabber

	Jan 21	BNC's Color Blind
	Mar 24	BNC's Florida Front
	Jun 9	BNC in the Magic City
1929	July 20	BNC in New Orleans
1931	Jan 10	BNC's Ha-Ha
	Aug 15	BNC, Racketeer
	Nov 21	BNC At the Races
1932	Feb 13	BNC's Safe

Big-Scar Guffman by Henry Leverage in *Flynn's*

1925	Jan 10	The Warden's Watch

in *Flynn's Weekly*

1926	Oct 30	The Old Clam
	Nov 13	Delayed Justice
	Nov 20	The New Warden
	Dec 4	Liberty for Sale
1927	Jan 8	The Man Inside

in *Flynn's Weekly Detective Fiction*

	Aug 13	The Tomato-Can Vag

in *Detective Story Magazine*

	Aug 20	What Goes Up
	Sept 10	Buzzards At Bay
	Oct 1	The Gold Room
	Nov 5	The Crooked Cross
	Nov 19	Seven Grains and Chinese Cribs
1928	Aug 4	Homemade Kick
	Sept 1	The Man Who Couldn't Squeal
	Oct 6	Big Scar's Prison Break
1929	Jan 5	Shot With Gold
	Feb 2	Menacing Bill
	May 4	Hot Wires
	June 22	Too Cheap

in *Black Mask*

| 1928 | Mar | The Clue Upstairs |

in *Complete Detective Novel Magazine*

| 1929 | July | The Snapshot |
| *1931* | June | Electric Ballots |

Black Star by Johnson McCulley
in *Detective Story Magazine:*

1916	Mar 5	*Rogue For a Day
	Jun 20	*Black Star's Defiance
	Oct 5	**Black Star's Subterfuge
	Nov 5	**Black Star's Revenge
	Dec 20	***Black Star's Masquerade
1917	Feb 5 & 20	Black Star's Mistake (2-part serial)
	Oct 2	Black Star's Return
	Oct 23	Black Star's Rebuke
	Nov 27	Black Star's Serenade
	Dec 11	Black Star's Raid
1918	Jan 29	Black Star's Hobby
	Feb 26	The Defeat of Black Star (on cover, title is given as "Black Star's Defeat")
1919	Jan 14 thru Feb 18	Black Star's Campaign (6-part serial)
1921	Jan 8 thru Jan 22	Black Star Comes Back (3-part serial)
1928	Mar 3 thru Mar 17	Black Star on the Air (3-part serial)
1930	Nov 1 thru Nov 15	Black Star Back—and How (3-part serial)

in *Best Detective Magazine*

1930	June	Rogue for a Day (signed John Mack Stone)

*Story is signed John Mack Stone
**Story is signed John Mack Stone (Johnston McCulley)
***Story is signed Johnson McCulley (John Mack Stone)

Blue Jean Billy by Charles W. Tyler
in *S&S Detective Story Magazine:*

1918	Mar 26	*Raggedy Ann
	Jul 16	Raiders from Raggedy Ann
1919	Mar 11	*Nix's Mate
	Oct 7	*The Haunt of Raggedy Ann
1921	Jun 25	**Blue Jean Billy at Fiddler's Reach
1922	Aug 19	**Highway Woman of the Sea
1925	Apr 4	Blue Jean Billy, Sky Pirate
	Aug 22	Blue Jean Billy and the Lone Survivor
1926	Nov 6	Blue Jean Billy, Waif of the Sea
1930	Jan 18	Blue Jean Billy Plays Fair
1931	Nov 14	Sea Law and Blue Jean Billy

in *Best Detective:*

1937	Mar	Sky Pirate *Included in *Quality Bill's Girl* **Included in *Blue Jean Billy*

Boston Betty by Anna Alice Chapin
in *Detective Story Magazine*

1918		
	Jan 29	With Alibi's Aid
	Mar 26	The Dog in the Machine
	Apr 23	"Baby Jane's" Revenge
1919	Jun 10	Alibi on the Board Walk

Mr. Chang by A. E. Apple *in Detective Story Magazine*

1919	Sept 9	Mr. Chang
1920	Sept 21	Sweet Plunder
	thru	(3-part serial; Mr. Chang appears in a walk-on part,
	Oct 5	but is not identified by name)
1924	Oct 25	Mr. Chang, Man Trapper
	Nov 22	Mr. Chang's Hush Money
	Dec 13	Wanted for Murder
1925	Jan 3	Mr. Chang of Scotland Yard
	Feb 28	Mr. Chang and the Treasure Trove
	May 16	The Glittering Lady
	June 6	Mr. Chang, Hangman
	June 27	Mr. Chang Meets Mr. Jap
	July 18	The Murderer's Graveyard
	Sept 5	Mr. Chang Calls on Uncle Sam
	Oct 3	Mr. Chang Turns to Dope
	Nov 28	Mr. Chang and the Murder Expert
1926	Jan 9	Mr. Chang, Detective
	Feb 13	Mr. Chang Strikes for Diamonds
	Apr 3	Mr. Chang and the Chinese Merchants
	June 12	Mr. Chang's Blackmail Horde
	Sept 25	Mr. Chang's Coffin
	Oct 30	Mr. Chang and the Counterfeiters
	Nov 13	Mr. Chang Takes the Bait
	Dec 4	The Trapping of Mr. Chang
1927	Jan 15	Mr. Chang's Revenge
	Feb 5	Mr. Chang, Raider
	Feb 19	Mr. Chang Deals In Snow
	Apr 9	Mr. Chang and the Crime Ray
	May 28	The End of Mr. Chang
1930	Nov 15	Mr. Chang, Tortured
	Dec 27	Mr. Chang's Tong War
1931	Jan 31	Mr. Chang vs Rafferty
	Feb 28	Mr. Chang Cages Rafferty
	May 23	Mr. Chang Meets the Devil

in *Best Detective Magazine*

1933	Apr	The Evil Mr. Chang
	July	Mr. Chang Turns to Dope
	Nov	Mr. Chang. Hangman

1934	Mar	Mr. Chang's Blackmail Horde
	June	Mr. Chang and the Treasure Trunk
	Sept	Mr. Chang of Scotland Yard
	Nov	Mr. Chang, Detective
1935	Jan	Mr. Chang and the Chinese Merchants
	Mar	Mr. Chang's Hush Money
	May	Mr. Chang, Counterfeiter
	Jul	Mr. Chang, Wanted for Murder
	Sept	Mr. Chang Meets Uncle Sam
	Dec	Mr. Chang Strikes for Diamonds
1936	Apr	The Murderer's Graveyard

Amos Clackworthy by Christopher Booth in *Detective Story Magazine*

1920	Feb 3/10/17	The Feminine Touch
	Mar 2	*Moonshine Preferred
	Mar 9	*The Million-Dollar Air Bag
	Mar 16	Mr. Sackett Sees Red
	Mar 23	Blasted Reputations
	Mar 30	A Modern Lazarus
	Apr 20	*The Knock-out
	Apr 27	*Painful Extraction
	May 4	*Family History Capitalized
	May 11	The Comeback
	Sept 28	Mr. Clackworthy Stakes a Friend

* Not confirmed as Clackworthy.

	Oct 19	Mr. C. Tells the Truth
	Nov 30	Mr. C. to the Rescue
	Dec 11	Mr. C.'s Cool Million
	Dec 18	Mr. C. Gets $20,000 a Word
	Dec 25	Amos Clackworthy, Alias S. Claus
1921	Jan 29	Mr. C. Plays Sleuth
	Feb 26	Mr. C. Sells Short
	Apr 2	Mr. C. Collects
	Apr 23	Mr. C. Studies Politics
	Jul 16	Mr. C. Digs a Hole
	Aug 13	Mr. C. Within the Law
	Aug 27	Mr. C. Goes to Jail
	Sept 24	Mr. C. Revives a Town

	Nov 5	Mr. C. Deals With a Fence
	Dec 3	Mr. C. Goes In for Art
	Dec 10	Mr. C. Gets Stung
	Dec 17	Mr. C. Turns Chemist
	Dec 24	Mr. C.'s St. Nicholas Company
	Dec 31	Mr. C., Mineralogist
1922	Jan 14	Mr. C. Forgets His Tonic
	Jan 21	When Mr. C. Needed a Bracer
	Jan 28	Mr. C. and the Auto Rim
	Feb 4	Mr. C. Profits By the Drama
	Feb 18	Thubway Tham and Mr. Clackworthy (by Johnston McCulley)
	Mar 4	Mr. Clackworthy and Thubway Tham (by Christopher Booth)
	Mar 11	Mr. C.'s Pipe Dream
	Mar 25	Mr. C. Sells a Gold Brick
	Mar 27	Mr. C. Puts Water to Work
	Jun 3	Clackworthy Coddles a Contract
	July 15	Mr. C. At Atlantic City
	July 29	Mr. C. and the Blue Canary
	Oct 7	Mr. C.'s Pot of Gold
1923	Jan 13	Mr. C. Moves to the Country
	June 30	Mr. C. Takes a Dip in Rye
1924	Apr 19	Mr. C. Tips a Teapot
	Oct 4	Mr. C. Turns to the Law
1925	Nov 7	Mr. C. Sheds a Tear
1926	Dec 25	Mr. C's Christmas Present
1928	Jul 14	Mr. C. in Florida
1929	Mar 23	Mr. C. On the Air
1930	June 14	Mr. C's Return
	Sept 27	Mr. C. Pays a Debt

in *Best Detective*

1933	May	Mr. C. Pays His Income Tax
	June	C. Coddles a Contract
	Oct	Mr. C., Mineralogist
1934	Mar	Mr. C. Takes a Dip in Rye
	Apr	Mr. C. Revives a Town
	June	Mr. C. Sheds a Tear

	Jul	Mr. C. Studies Politics
	Dec	Mr. C. and Thubway Tham
1935	Mar	Mr. C. Moves to the Country
1937	Jan	Mr. Sackett Sees Red
	May	Mr. C. Tips a Teapot

The Crimson Clown by Johnston McCulley in *Detective Story Magazine*

1926	July 31	The Crimson Clown
	Aug 21	The Crimson Clown is Cornered
	Sept 4	The Crimson Clown's Competitors
	Sept 18	The Crimson Clown Pursues Himself
1927	Apr 23	The Crimson Clown's Dumb Friend
	June 18	The Crimson Clown's Treasure Hunt
	Oct 29	The Crimson Clown's Blackmail Trail
	Dec 24	The Crimson Clown's Double
1928	Feb 18	The Crimson Clown's
	Sept 29	The Crimson Clown's Matinee
	Nov 3	The Crimson Clown Scores With a Snore
	Nov 11	Thubway Tham Meets the Crimson Clown
	thru	(5-part serial)
	Dec 9	
1929	May 25	The Crimson Clown Faces Murder
1930	Oct 18	The Crimson Clown's Return
	Nov 29	The Crimson Clown—Avenger
1931	May 2	The Crimson Clown's Threat
	May 16	The Crimson Clown's Romance

in *Best Detective Magazine*

1936	Sept	The Crimson Clown

in *Popular Detective*

1944	Oct	The Crimson Clown's Return

Mr. John Doe by Paul Ellsworth Triem in *Detective Story Magazine*

1928	June 9	Enter—Mr. Doe
	June 23	John Doe's Prisoner
	Aug 18	John Doe's Crimson Catch
	Oct 13	John Doe's Golden Gift
	Nov 17	John Doe Kidnapped

	Dec 15	John Doe's Straight Jacket

1929	Mar 9	John Doe's Funeral
	May 4	John Doe's Dummy
	June 8	John Doe Strikes from Ambush
	Aug 3	Black Magic
	Sept 28	John Doe's Third Degree
	Oct 26	John Doe's Plant
	Dec 14	John Doe's Flying Loot

1930	Feb 1	Fugitive Finger Prints
	Apr 5	John Doe's Killing
	May 24	John Doe's Dilemma
	thru	(3-part serial)
	June 7	

Barton Edgeworth by Scott Campbell in Detective Story Magazine:

1917		(Under series title, "Exploits of Barton Edgeworth")
	July 5	I-Saved By the Dead
	July 20	II-Doubles and Quits
	Aug 5	III-Worked in Clay
	Aug 20	IV-The Stolen Teller
	Sept 4	V-Unexpected Loot
	Sept 11	VI-The Kellogg Torpedo
	Sept 25	VII-Without Collateral
	Oct 9	VIII-Sham Chivalry
	Oct 23	IX-Silhouette or Shadow?

The Gray Phantom by Herman Landon in Detective Story Magazine

1917	Dec 18	Seven Signs

1919	May 20	Gray Terror
	Nov 25	The Gray Phanton Goes It Alone

1920	June 1	The Gray Phantom's Defense
	thru	(6-part serial)
	July 6	

1921	Jan 15	The Gray Phantom's Romance
	thru	(5-part serial)
	Feb 12	
	April 2	The Gray Phantom's Guests
	Oct 15	The Gray Phantom's Surrender

1922	Sept 30 thru Nov 11	Human Pawn (7-part serial)
1923	May 26 thru June 30	The Gray Phantom's Madness (6-part serial)
1924	Aug 30 thru Oct 4	The Speaking Fog (6-part serial)

The Joker by Hugh Kahler in *Detective Story Magazine*

1919	July 8	Left By the Joker
	Aug 12	With the Help of the Warden
	Sept 16	A Deal In Silence
	Oct 14	The Joker's Last Card

Li Shoon by H. Irving Hancock *in Detective Story Magazine*

1916	Aug 5	Under the Ban of Li Shoon
	Sept 5	Li Shoon's Deadliest Mission
1917	Jan 5	Li Shoon's Nine Lives

Pat the Piper by Joseph Harrington *in Flynn's*

1927	Mar 5	An Up-To-Date Cavalier
	Mar 12	The Piper Pays
	Mar 19	The Piper's Name
	Mar 26	The Piper's Partner
	Apr 2	So the Papers Said
	Apr 9	The Rose Diamond Necklace
	Apr 16	The End of the Piper

Mr. Philibus by Leslie Gordon Barnard in *Detective Fiction Weekly*

| 1928 | Dec 22 | Mr. Philibus' Christmas Eve |

in *Detective Story Magazine*

| 1929 | May 4 | Mr. Philibus Cries for the Moon |

	June 22	Drowned To Win
	Jul 20	Mr. Philibus' Romance
	Aug 3	Mr. Philibus Goes Ratting
1930	Feb 8	The Pond Lily
	Feb 22	Mr. Philibus Inspects Bobbies
	Mar 22	Mr. Philibus Shaves
	June 14	Mr. Philibus—Thousand-Dollar Man
	June 21	Don't Trust the Ladies
	Dec 20	Mr. Philibus' Chilly Romance
1931	Jan 31	Fugitive Lady
	Feb 7	Mr. Philibus—Rescuer
1932	Mar 12	Mr. Philibus' Unwanted Partner
1935	Aug 25	Winner Take All

The Benevolent Picaroon by Herman Landon in *Detective Story Magazine*

1921	July 16	The Benevolent Picaroon
	Aug 13	The Picaroon and the Girl
	Sept 17	The Picaroon and the Snare
	Dec 3	The Picaroon and the Steel Link
	Dec 24	The Picaroon Discovers Christmas
1922	Feb 11	The Picaroon and the Black Bag
	Feb 25	The Picaroon's Wager
	June 3	The Picaroon's Jest
	June 24	A Hundred Dollars a Day
	Nov 18	The Picaroon and the Jade Earrings
	Dec 16	The Picaroon Framed
1923	Apr 14	The Picaroon and the Silver Slipper
	Sept 1	The Picaroon's Exit
1924	July 5 thru July 12	The Picaroon Turns Detective (2-part serial)
	Nov 15 thru Nov 29	The House of Mirrors (3-part serial)
1925	Aug 8	The Screaming Statue
	Dec 19	The Picaroon Seeks an Alibi
1926	July 3	The Picaroon and the Pearls

	Sept 11	The Picaroon and the Pawn Ticket
	Nov 27	The Green Shadow (6-part serial)
	thru	
	Jan 1,1927	
1928	May 5	Picaroon—Peacock Avenger
	July 14	The Man in the Cage
	Dec 29	The Silent Watch (3-part serial)
	thru	
	Jan 12,1929	
1929	Oct 26	The Picaroon's Bargain
	Dec 28	The Picaroon's Crystal Gazer (3-part serial)
	thru	
	Jan 11,1930	
1930	Jan 25	The Picaroon's Iron Band (3-part serial)
	thru	
	Feb 8	
	June 28	The Million Dollar Cane
1931	Jan 3	The Picaroon Handcuffed (4-part serial)
	thru	
	Jan 24	
	July 25	The Picaroon Fights for A Idol
1932	Feb 6	Tools of Madness

Rafferty by A. E. Apple *in Detective Story Magazine:*

1927	Oct 1	Rafferty, Master Rogue
	Oct 22	The Diamond Pirate
	Nov 26	Rafferty Steals a Harem
	Dec 17	Rafferty Pursues Art
1928	Jan 14	Rafferty's Raid on the Law
	Feb 4	A Trap for Rafferty
	Apr 14	Rafferty Gets Locked Up
	May 12	Rafferty Loots Chinatown
	Sept 22	Rafferty-Detective Kidnapper
	Oct 20	Tied to His Enemy
	Nov 10	Rafferty, Gentleman Jailbird
	Dec 22	Rafferty and the Hush Money King
1929	Jan 19	Rafferty Invents a New Crime
	Feb 16	Rafferty and the Count of Five
	Aug 31	Rafferty's Phantom Plunder

	Sept 14	Rafferty and the Chinese Eight
	Oct 12	Rafferty Robs Himself
	Nov 30	Rafferty Joins the Police
1930	Nov 1	Rafferty Steals 200 Dicks
1931	Jan 31	Mr. Chang vs Rafferty
	Feb 28	Mr. Chang Cages Rafferty

Red Raven by Scott Campbell in *Detective Story Magazine*

1915		(First Series: *The Red Raven Stories*)
	Nov 20	A String of Beads
	Dec 5	Plot and Counter-Plot
	Dec 20	The Inner Wheel
1916	Jan 5	With Malice Aforethought
	Jan 20	Prison Bars
	Feb 5	Gold Plate
	Feb 20	A Sin That Saved
	Mar 5	A Chance Clew
	Mar 20	The Closing Net
		(Second Series: *The Return of*
		Red Raven)
	Dec 5	The Opening Wedge
	Dec 20	The Lure of the Lady
1917	Jan 5	The Absconder
	Jan 20	At His Own Game
	Feb 5	When Tides Meet
	Feb 20	Coals of Fire
	Mar 5	The Corruption Fund
	Mar 20	On Thin Ice
	Apr 5	But For Her
	Apr 20	The Green Curtain (final story)

The Ringer by Edgar Wallace in *Detective Story Magazine* (NOTE: The title in parenthesis is that used for book publication).

1925	Apr 18	The Ringer (6-part serial)
	thru	
	May 23	
1928	May 26	The Ringer and the Brute
	June 2	The Ringer to the Rescue (The Case of the
		Home Secretary)
	June 9	X and The Ringer
		(The Escape of Mr. Bliss)

June16	Blackmail and The Ringer (The Blackmail Boomerang)	
June 23	The Ringer and the Vamp (The Complete Vampire)	
June 30	The Ringer and the Nose	
July 7	The Ringer and the Cop	
July 21	The Ringer Wring (The Obliging Cobbler)	
Aug 4	The Ringer and the Outcast (The Fortune of Forgery)	

in *Detective Fiction Weekly*

1928	Dec 22	The Ringer's Christmas Party (Miss Brown's 7000

in Dime Mystery

1933	Aug	The Man with the Red Beard
	Sept	Ringer's Trap
	Oct	The Murderer of Many Names
	Dec	The Slave-Maker

Sanderson by John Jay Chichester in *Detective Story Magazine*

1925	Jan 17	All But His Hands (first of series)
	Aug 29	The Crimson Witness
1926	Feb 20	The Tear Trap
	May 15	The Unwilling Cracksman
	July 10	Sinking Safety
1927	Jan 8 thru Jan 22	Helpless Hands (3-part serial)
	Jul 30	Broken Bars
	Aug 20 Sept 3	The Deadly Door (3-part serial)
1928	June 30	King and Queen of Diamonds
1929	Apr 20	The Unconscious Accomplice
	June 1	Sanderson's Rejected "Moll"
	July 6	Sanderson Handcuffed
	Sept 21	Sanderson's Revenge
	Dec 21	Sanderson's "Queer"

1930	Aug 23	Sanderson Does London
	Nov 22	Sanderson Takes To the Sea
1931	June 13	Tears For Sanderson (2-part serial)
	and 20	
	Oct 31	Desperate Rogues
1932	Dec 19	"Two-Three"—Free (3-part serial)
	thru	
	Jan 2	

in *Best Detective Magazine*

1936	Feb	All But His Hands
	May	Collared
1937	June	Dots In the Dark

Sheik and Simpson by Roland Krebs in *Detective Story Magazine.*

1927	June 23	The Perfect Misfit
	Nov 12	Candy Kidding
	Dec 3	The Shirt Trail
	Dec 10	Lucky Star
	Dec 31	The Stuck-Up Man
1928	Jan 21	Sweet Music
	Feb 11	The Cut-Up
	Mar 3	The Children's Hour
	Mar 24	Culture Pays
	Mar 31	Amateur Night
	Apr 28	Cupid's Night Off
	Jun 2	The Devil To Pay
	Jun 16	Sheik's Last Word
	Jul 14	A Scrambled Egg
	Aug 11	Fiddle Fooled
	Aug 25	Handle With Gloves
	Sept 8	Flying Time!
	Oct 6	Too Nice To Rob
	Oct 27	The Seal of Trouble
	Nov 3	Dressed To Rob
1929	Jan 12	Walking Crime
	Jan 19	Every Pore A Picture
	Feb 2	Close To the Vest
	Apr 13	Greedy Guys
	Apr 27	The Catch in It
	May 4	Diving High and Dry

	June 1	Here's How
	June 22	Sheik's Mice
	July 13	Simp's Ps-eye-chology
	July 27	Bright Dummy
	Aug 10	Big Feet and Little Feet
	Nov 2	A Chased Kisser
1930	Jan 4	Beauty's Ghost
	Jan 18	Pick-Up and Knock-Down
	Jun 28	Reward—500 Smackers

The Spider by Johnston McCulley in *Detective Story Magazine*

1918	Apr 16	The Spider's Den
	May 21	The Spider's Sign
	Jul 2	Into The Spider's Jaws
	Jul 23	The Shekel of Shame
	Aug 13	The Turquoise Elephant
	Sept 10	The Spider's Venom
	Sept 24	The Spider's Debt
	Oct 22	The Spider's Wrath
	Dec 17	The Spider's Command
1919	Apr 8	The Spider's Strain
	Apr 29	The Spider's Reward

Thubway Tham by Johnston McCulley in *Detective Story Magazine*

NOTE: The abbreviation "TT" stands for Thubway Tham in the following listing.

1918	June 4	Thubway Tham (first appearance)
	June 11	TT's Rival
	Jul 9	TT's Romance
	Jul 30	TT's Act of Mercy
	Oct 29	TT's Income Tax
	Nov 19	TT's Inthane Moment
	Nov 26	TT's Thanksgiving Dinner
	Dec 3	TT's Double
	Dec 24	TT's Merry Christmas
	Dec 31	TT's Understudy
1919	Jan 7	TT's Triumph
	Mar 4	TT and Elevated Elmer
	Mar 25	TT's Baggage Check
	Apr 1	TT, Philanthropist
	Apr 15	TT's Inthuranthe

	Apr 22	TT's Holdup
	May 27	TT's Bank Account
	Jun 10	TT's Vacation
	Jul 8	TT's Gloriouth Fourth
	Jul 15	TT's Flivver
	Oct 7	TT, Fashion Plate
	Oct 21	TT's Inthult
	Nov 25	TT's Preth Agent
1920	Jan 6	TT Rides In Style
	Jan 27	TT's Darkest Day
	Mar 20	TT's Thympathy
	Apr 13	TT's Birthday
	May 25	TT's Four Queens
	Jun 1	TT's Tenth of Honor
	Jun 15	TT In the Movies
	Jul 27	TT's Tobacco Heart
	Aug 24	TT, Optimitht
	Oct 5	TT's Revenge
	Dec 25	TT Playth Thanta Clauth
1921	Feb 12	TT Getth Bail
	Mar 12	TT's Operation
	Apr 30	TT's Legathy
	May 28	TT's Fithing Trip
	Jun 11	TT, Delegate
	Jun 18	TT Meetth a Girl
	Aug 6	TT and Cupid
	Aug 20	TT's Engagement
	Oct 15	TT's Dithilluthionment
	Oct 29	TT Goes to the Ratheth
	Nov 12	TT's Hoodoo Roll
1922	Feb 11	TT Reformth
	Feb 18	Thubway Tham and Mr. Clackworthy (by Johnston McCulley)
	Mar 4	Mr. Clackworthy and Thubway Tham (by Christopher Booth)
	Apr 1	TT, April Fool
	Jul 1	TT's Dog
	Sept 30	TT's Apprentithe
	Oct 21	TT's Honethty
	Nov 25	TT's Better Half
	Dec 23	TT's Chrithtmath Thpirit
1923	Jan 20	TT'th Buthinethth Thlump
	Feb 10	TT'th Jury Thervithe
	Mar 10	TT'th Honetht Hundred

	Oct 27	TT Dons a Dinner Jacket
	Nov 17	TT's Thure Thing
1924	Mar 8	TT Gets A Mud Pack
	Mar 22	TT'th Thcoop
	Jul 26	TT Consults a Doctor
	Sept 13	TT's Brother in Affliction
	Nov 1	TT, Hero
	Nov 29	TT's Tough Day
	Dec 27	TT's Word of Honor
1925	Apr 11	Simon Trapp and TT (by Roy W. Hinds)
	Jun 13	TT Meets Elevated Elmer
	Jun 27	TT and Simon Trapp's Trap (by Johnston McCulley)
	Jul 4	TT's Underground Loyalty
	Aug 29	TT' Croth-word Puthle
	Sept 12	TT Plays
	Oct 24	TT's Labor of Love
	Nov 28	Get Your Hair Cut
1926	Feb 13	TT and the Con Man
	Mar 27	TT, Good Thamaritan
	Apr 10	TT Tunes In
	Apr 17	TT's Red Wallet
	Jul 3	TT's Skyrocket
	Aug 7	TT's Monkey Pal
	Oct 9	TT's Pupil
	Dec 25	TT's Chrithmath Tree
1927	Oct 8	TT Steals A Base
	Nov 12	TT and the Rube
	Nov 26	TT's Puzzling Leather
1928	Feb 25	TT, Patriot
	Mar 24	TT's Ides of March
	Mar 31	TT Shakes a Star
	May 5	TT's Terror
	June 23	TT's Tender Heart
	July 28	TT's New Thuit
	Sept 8	TT's New Thought
	Nov 11 thru Dec 8	TT Meets the Crimson Clown (5-part serial)
1930	Aug 23	TT's Female Petht
	Sept 27	TT Loveth Dogth

	Nov 22	TT—Kidnapper
	Dec 6	TT on the Air
	Dec 13	TT's Ignoble Patht
1933	Dec 10	TT and Nira
1937	Dec	TT—Vox Pop
1938	Jan	TT's Old Coin

in *Best Detective Magazine*

1929	Nov	TT's Rival
1930	March	TT's Romance
	Apr	TT's April Fool
	May	TT's Act of Mercy
	June	TT's Inthane Moment
	July	TT's Double
	Aug	TT's Understudy
	Sept	TT and Elevated Elmer
	Oct	TT's Baggage Check
	Nov	TT's Inthuranthe
	Dec	TT's Bank Account
1931	Jan	TT's Vacation
	Feb	TT's Flivver
	Apr	TT's Fishing Trip
	May	TT's Preth Agent
	June	TT's Darkest Day
	July	TT's Revenge
	Aug	TT's Curiothity
	Oct	TT's Jealouthy
	Nov	TT's Thanksgiving Dinner
	Dec	TT's Thenthe of Honor
1932	Jan	TT's Merry Christmas
	Feb	TT's Four Queens
	Mar	TT's Better Thelf
	Apr	TT, Delegate
	June	TT Reformth
	July	TT's Income Tax
	Nov	TT's Jury Thervithe
1933	May	TT Consults a Doctor
	June	TT's Apprentithe

| | Aug | TT's Honethy |
| | Oct | TT's Buthineth Thlump |

1934	Jan	TT's Thcoop
	Feb	TT's Crothword Puthle
	Mar	TT's Tough Day
	Apr	TT's Honetht Hundred
	May	TT's Word of Honor
	June	TT Tunes In
	July	TT's Skyrocket
	Aug	TT's Monkey Pal
	Sept	TT's Dog
	Nov	TT Meeth Elevated Elmer
	Dec	Mr. Clackworthy and Thubway Tham (story signed Christopher Booth)

1935	Jan	TT and Simon Trapp
	Feb	TT's Pupil
	Mar	TT Plays
	Apr	TT's Labor of Love
	May	TT and the Con Man
	June	TT's Underground Loyalty
	July	TT's Red Wallet
	Sept	TT's Puzzling Leather
	Oct	TT's Ides of March
	Nov	TT and the Rube
	Dec	TT Steals a Base

1936	Jan	TT's Tender Heart
	Feb	TT, Patriot
	Mar	TT Shakes a Star
	Apr	TT's Terror
	May	TT's New Thuit
	June	TT's New Thought
	Jul	TT's Female Petht

in Clues

1937	Oct	TT's Jewelry Haul
	Nov	TT—Model
	Dec	TT Buys Buttons

in Black Book Detective

| *1948* | Sept | TT's Deed of Mercy |
| | Nov | TT's Perfect Day |

1949   March   TT's Quiz Program

in *Detective Fiction Weekly*

1937   May 29   TT Meets a Racket

in *Detective Story Annual*

1943   TT—Framed

The Thunderbolt by Johnston McCulley *in Detective Story Magazine*

1920   May 4   *Master and Man
                    Jun 29   *The Kidnapped Midas
                    Sept 7   *The Big Six
                    Dec 11   **The Thunderbolt Collects

1921   June 4   **The Thunderbolt's Jest
                    July 30   **The Thunderbolt's Engagement

*   Included in *Alias The Thunderbolt*.
** Included in *The Thunderbolt's Jest*.

Simon Trapp by Roy W. Hinds

NOTE: The abbreviation "ST" stands for Simon Trapp in the following
listing.
in *Detective Story Magazine:*

1921   Jan 8   Full of Tricks
                    Mar 5   And They Called In the Police
                    July 9   Where They Make 'Em
                    Jul 30   A Burglar for a Lady
                    Aug 13   Forging His Own
                    Aug 20   Simon Trapp and the Irony of Mercy
                    Sept 3   What He Taught Best
                    Sept 17   Justice Uncovers Her Eyes
                    Nov 5   A "Cellar Plant"
                    Dec 10   The Snitch
                    Dec 17   An Old Man's Chance
                    Dec 31   Diamond Bait

1922   Jan 28   ST Views the Tombs
                    Feb 11   ST Pays a Doctor's Bill
                    Feb 18   Inside of a Book

	Feb 25	Not a Killer
	Mar 4	ST's Birthday Party
	Mar 11	White Blackmail
	Mar 18	ST, Reformer
	Apr 8	Set to Jazz
	Apr 29	A Message to Solitary
	May 20	ST To the Rescue
	May 27	ST, Bootlegger
	Jul 8	ST's Race Horse
	Jul 22	Six Feet Deep
	Oct 28	ST Finds a "Zebra"
	Nov 11	ST's Detective Agency
	Dec 2	ST's Prize Pupil
	Dec 16	ST Goes to Sing-Sing
	Dec 23	The Christmas Crust
	Dec 30	The "Sprinklers"
1923	Jan 6	ST Frisked
	Jan 13	Cupid Below the Dead Line
	Jan 20	ST's Insurance Club for Burglars
	Jan 27	ST and the Loft King
1924	May 24	ST Returns
	Jun 14	When Honest Men Fall Out
	Jun 21	ST Kidnapped
	Jun 28	ST's Button Gang
	Jul 5	ST Balks At Blackmail
	Aug 16	The Soup Sisters
	Aug 23	Three Old Men
	Sept 6	ST's Clean Sweep
	Sept 13	ST Brings Midnight Cheer
	Sept 20	ST Starts a College
	Sept 27	ST Hires a Detective
	Oct 4	ST Goes Fishing
	Nov 15	ST's Clipping Box
	Nov 29	Two Back Numbers
	Dec 6	ST's Locksmith
	Dec 13	Burned Fingers
	Dec 20	Yuletide on Broome Street
1925	Jan 3	ST Opens a Bank
	Mar 7	ST's Helping Hand
	Mar 14	ST's Huckleberries
	Apr 11	ST and Thubway Tham
	Apr 18	ST Goes Out On a Job
	May 9	ST's Double-jointed Burglary
	Jun 27	Thubway Tham and ST's Trap
	Sept 5	ST Broadcasts

	Oct 3	ST and the Swinger
	Oct 31	ST Takes a Bus Ride
1926	Jan 2	ST Issues a Parole
	Mar 6	One Locked Door
1927	Jul 9	ST Padlocked
	Dec 10	ST's Nest Egg
1928	May 5	ST's Big Laugh
	May 12	ST Makes a Hero
1929	Feb 16	ST's "Sumpin Nice"
	Feb 23	ST's Red Money
	Mar 30	ST Buys a Voice
	Apr 20	ST's Square Guys
1930	Sept 20	St's Fancy "Murder"

in *Best Detective Magazine*

1933	May	ST Goes to Sing-Sing
	June	St Pays a Doctor's Bill
	Oct	ST's Locksmith
1934	Jan	ST's Detective Agency
	Feb	ST Balks At Blackmail
	Mar	ST's Prize Fight
	May	ST Finds a Zebra
	Aug	ST's Clipping Box
	Sept	ST Hires a Detective
	Dec	ST Opens a Bank
1935	Jan	Thubway Tham and Simon Trapp
	Feb	ST's Clean Sweep
	May	When Honest Men Fall Out
	Aug	ST's Button Gang
	Sept	Burned Fingers
1936	Jul	ST Kidnapped
1937	Feb	Six Feet Deep
	Aug	ST Starts a College

Wallace, Edgar. The following list, although incomplete, is provided as a beginning toward identifying the novels of Edgar Wallace serialized in the American pulp magazines. Much of this information was originally developed by John Hogan in his pursuit of the ultimate Edgar Wallace collection. Several of the titles were altered by the magazine editors: both English and American book titles are cited where there is a significant difference.

"The Arranways Mystery," *Cosmopolitan*, 5-part serial, September 1931 through January 1932. (Published as *The Coat of Arms*.)

"Blind Men," *Detective Story Magazine*, 5-part serial, May 7 through June 4, 1921. (Published as *The Dark Eyes of London*.)

"Blue Hand," *People's Magazine*, 6-part serial, April 1 through June 15, 1923.

"The Book Of All Power," *Star Novels Quarterly*, Spring 1933.

"The Children of the Poor," *Detective Story Magazine*, 6-part serial, September 1 through October 6, 1928. (Published in US as *Gunman's Bluff*.)

"The Clew of the Silver Key," *Detective Story Magazine*, 6-part serial, September 20 through October 25, 1930.

"The Counterfeiter," *Detective Story Magazine*, 6-part serial, September 3 through October 8, 1927. (Published England as *The Forger*; in US as *The Clever One*.)

"The Daffodil Enigma," *The Popular Magazine*, 4-part serial, Sept. 7 through Oct. 20, 1920.

"The Devastating Angel," *Detective Story Magazine*, 5-part serial, March 18 through April 15, 1922. (Published as *The Angel of Terror*.)

"The Door With Seven Locks," *Flynn's*, 4-part serial, November 28 through December 19, 1925.

"The Feathered Serpent," *Flynn's*, 4-part serial, May 7 through 28, 1927.

"Flat 2," *Detective Story Magazine*, 2-part serial, January 27 and February 3, 1923. Also in *Best Detective Magazine*, short novel, January 1930.

"The Flying Squad," *Detective Story Magazine*, 6-part serial, November 3 through December 8, 1928.

"The Gallows Hand," *Detective Story Magazine*, 6-part serial, November 14 through December 19, 1925. (Published as *The Terrible People*.)

"The Girl From Scotland Yard," *Detective Story Magazine*, 5-part serial, April 24 through May 22, 1926.

"The Green Ribbon," *Detective Fiction Weekly*, 4-part serial, January 18 through February 8, 1930.

"The Hairy Arm," *Detective Story Magazine*, 5-part serial, February 9 through March 8, 1924. (Published as *The Avenger*.)

"His Devoted Squealer," *Detective Story Magazine*, 5-part serial, August 29 through September 26, 1931. (Published as *The Man At the Carlton*.)

"Jack o' Judgement," *Detective Story Magazine*, 6-part serial, March 9 through April 13, 1920.

"The Joker," *Flynn's Weekly*, 4-part serial, October 23 through November 13, 1926. (Published US as *The Colossus*.)

"The Lone House Mystery," *Detective Story Magazine*, 3-part serial, September 28 through October 12, 1929.

"The Man Who Knew," *Popular Magazine*, 3-part serial, January 7 through February 7, 1918.

"The Million Dollar Story", *Popular Magazine*, novel, March 7, 1920.

"The Missing Million," *Popular Magazine*, 5-part serial, June 20 through August 20, 1923.

"On the Spot," *Detective Story Magazine*, 6-part serial, April 25 through May 23, 1931.

"The Ringer," *Detective Story Magazine*, 6-part serial, April 18 through May 23, 1925. (Published England as *The Gaunt Stranger*.)

"Scotland Yard's Yankee Dick," *Detective Story Magazine*, 5-part serial, April 16 through May 14, 1932. (Published as *When the Gangs Came To London*.)

"Silver Steel," *Detective Story Magazine*, 6-part serial, January 24 through February 28, 1931. (Published as *The Devil Man*.)

"Sinister Halls," *Detective Story Magazine*, 6-part serial, December 10, 1927, through January 14, 1928. (Published as *The Double*.)

"The Sinister Man," *Detective Story Magazine*, 6-part serial, May 24 through June 28, 1924.

"Sins of the Mothers," *Flynn's*, 5-part serial, February 7 through March 7, 1925. (Published as *The Strange Countess*.)

"The Squealer," *The Popular Magazine*, 4-part serial, August 7 through September 20, 1925. Also in *Detective Story Magazine*, 4-part serial, February 19 through March 12, 1927.

"Stamped In Gold," *Detective Story Magazine*, novel, November 4, 1919. (Published as *The Golden Hades*.)

"Terror Keep," *Detective Story Magazine*, 5-part serial, November 6 through December 4, 1926.

"The Three Just Men," *Short Stories*, 4-part serial, April 10 through May 25, 1925.

"The Three Oaks Mystery," *Short Stories*, novelette, November 10, 1921. Also in *Star Novels Quarterly*, novelette, 1932.

"The Traitor's Gate," *Detective Story Magazine*, 5-part serial, June 5 through July 3, 1926.

"The Twister," *Detective Story Magazine*, novelette, April 28, 1928.

"The Valley of Ghosts," *The Popular Magazine*, 4-part serial, July 20 through September 7, 1922.

"White Face," *Cosmopolitan*, 5-part serial, October 1930 through February 1931.

"The Yellow Snake," *Short Stories*, novel, June 25, 1926. Also, *Great Detective Stories*, abridged novel, March 1933.

WHITE ROOK (by Hugh Kahler) in *S&S Detective Story Magazine:*

1918	Oct 1	White Rook's Pawn
	Nov 5	The Rook's Defense
	Nov 26	White Rook's Secret
	Dec 31	The White Rook's Mate
1919	Feb 4	Thirty-Three

in *Best Detective Magazine*

1930	July	White Rook's Pawn
	Oct	The Rook's Defense
1931	Jun	The White Rook's Mate

Index

A

Adventure, 13, 138
Alcott, Louisa May, 126
Aletha, 134, 135, 136
Alias the Thunderbolt, 131
Alibi, 75
Allain, Marcel, 27
alternate identity, 190, 220, 222
Amateur Cracksman, The, 86
Angel Esquire, 107, 108
Anstruther, John (pseudo for
    Edgar Wallace), 111-112
Apple, A.E., 17, 18, 20, 21,
    25, 52, 56, 57, 59, 225n
Arends, Dave, 235
Argosy, 17, 38, 80, 152
Argosy All-Story Weekly, 37, 81, 103
Avenger, The, 40, 59
Avenging Twins, The, 103, 132-137, 213,
    220, 235
Avenging Twins, The, 133
Avenging Twins Collect, The, 133

B

Ball, Eustace Hale, 139
Barnard, Leslie Gordon, 174
bent heroes, 2, 180, 187, 190,
    191, 212
Best Detective Stories, 40, 104,
    150, 207
Big-nose Charlie, 72-74, 96, 112,
    156, 220, 235-237
Big-scar Guffman, 81-86, 96, 123,
    220, 237-238
Black Bat, The, 37, 146
Black Book Detective, 76
Black Mask, xi, 61, 82, 137-138,
    142, 215, 220
Black Star, 25, 36-45, 52, 58, 127,

195, 199, 206, 220, 238-239
Blackshirt, 188-195, 229n, 230n
Blackshirt Again, 192
Blackwell, Frank, 36, 199
Blake, Sexton, 9
Bliss, Insp., 118-119, 120, 121
Blodgett, Peter, 87, 88
Blue Book, 61
Blue Jean Billy Race, 151-156, 214,
    220, 221, 239
Blue Jean Billy, 153
Booth, Christopher, 65
Boston Betty, 74-76, 221, 239
Bradley, Det., 56-57
Brady, Peter, 140, 141, 142
Brannigan, Charlie, 67-68, 96
Bray, Enfield (See White Rook)
Bride of Fu Manchu, 7, 8
Brigand, The, 108, 109-111, 115
Bronson-Howard, George, 108
Broph, 197, 199
Butler, William Vivian, 104, 224n

C

Calwood, Betty, 136
Campbell, Scott (pseudo for F.W.
    Davis), 36, 69
Caniff, Milton, 13
Captain Hex, 108-109, 227n
Captain Satan, 222
Carrick, Donald, 15-16
Carter, Chick, 70, 224n
Carter, Nick, 11, 16, 32, 35,
    36, 59, 70, 81, 106, 143, 144
    172, 187, 214, 224n, 227n
Castle, Irene, 9
Chang, Mr., 17-25, 59-60, 223,
    225n, 240-241
Chapin, Anna Alice, 74

Charteris, Leslie, 116
Chichester, John Jay, 86, 91, 226n
chinatown, 9, 10, 11, 13
Clackworthy, Amos, 64-67, 220, 222, 241-243
Clark, Barton, 86-89, 91
Cleek, xi, 165, 190, 197, 204, 220, 227n
Clifford, Patricia (See Pat the Piper)
Clue of the New Pin, The, 29
Clues, xi, 61, 76, 81, 104, 171, 215
Collier's, 6, 150
Collinson, Peter (pseudo for Dashiell Hammett), 138
Colonel Clay, x, 27, 69, 116
Confidence Man, The, 63
costume tradition, 37, 127, 195, 197, 200 220
Craddock, Det., 76, 77, 79
Craig, Anthony, 210-212
Craig, Leila, 149, 150
criminal heroes: cracksmen, 146, 189-190; limited, 143, 179-180, 220; professional, 2, 85; reform, 146, 172, 220
Crimson Clown, The, 37, 40, 127, 195, 199-208, 213, 243
Crimson Clown, The, 200
Crimson Clown Again, The, 200
crook fiction, 36, 61, 71, 79, 81, 83, 85, 96, 103, 223
Culligore, Lt., 166, 168, 170
Curran, Connie, 70, 71

D
Dale, Jimmie, 11, 80, 81, 134, 146, 147, 148, 172, 183, 187, 189, 190, 209, 214, 222
Dale, Martin (See The Picaroon)
Daly, Carroll John, 138
Daughter of Fu Manchu, The, 4, 5
Davis, Frederick, W., 32, 69
Dawes, Peter, 100, 102, 103
Decker, Adam, 87, 88, 90
Detective Fiction Weekly, 76, 104, 174, 215
Detective Story Magazine, xi, 35-36, 39, 43, 52, 61, 65, 74, 81, 83, 92,

103, 117, 132, 137, 150, 152, 154, 174, 179, 182, 196, 209, 215
Detective Tales, xi, 61
devices: gas guns, 40, 204, 221; keys, 100, 227n; sleeping gas, 40, 221
Dime Mystery Book, 104
dime novels, 10, 11, 14, 35, 36, 63, 126, 220
disguise, 27, 171-172, 184, 187, 229n
Disney, Walt, 38
Doc Savage, 40, 134
Doc Savage Magazine, 40, 59, 134
Doe, John, 209-217, 243-244
Donler, Dave, 200, 201, 203
Dorrance, Sylvia, 15-16
Dracula, 230n
Dragnet, The, 215
Drummon, Bulldog, 229n
Du Maurier, Sir Gerald, 118
Dulla, 161, 162
Dunn, Bobbie, 191, 192
Durable Desperadoes, The 104, 229n

E
Early, James, 65
Edgar Wallace Newsletter, 226n, 227n
Edgeworth, Barton, 69-71, 96, 244
Elegant Edward, 68, 96
Eliot, T.S., 193
Emperor Fu Manchu, 4
emperors of crime, 1, 2, 13, 25, 219
Everhard, Don, 138

F
Fah Lo Suee, 5, 6, 7
Famous Fantastic Mysteries, 224n
Fandor, Jerome, 29
Fantomas, 25, 27-30, 37, 116 126, 230n
Fitzgerald, Scott, 193
Flame, The, 220
Flatchley, John (See Thunderbolt)
Flynn's Weekly, xi, 61, 80, 81, 83, 103, 172-173, 179
Four Square Jane, 98-103, 107, 108, 124, 220
Four Square Jane, 99, 103, 107, 108
Fu Manchu, 4-8, 219, 222, 224n

G

G-Men, 171
gangsters, 217, 220
Gaunt Stranger, The, 117-118, 119,
    227n, 228n
Gentle Grafter, The, 63, 64
Gibson, Walter, 30
Glidden, Joe, 32, 33, 34
Gold, Dr., 216-217
Golden Book, 104
Golden Scorpion, 5
Gonzales, Leon, 118
Graeme, Bruce (pseudo for Graham
    Montague Jeffries), 188, 193-194
Graeme, Roderic (pseudo for Roderic
    Jefferies), 188, 194
Gray, Douglas, 36
Gray Ghost, 159
Gray, Phantom, The, 158-172, 187,
    220, 229n, 244-245
Gray Terror, 169
Green Shadow, The, 185
Griff, Milton, 133, 134, 135

H

Hammett, Dashiell, 83, 138
Hancock, H. Irving, 14
Hands Unseen, 169
Hardwick, Helen, 164, 167, 168,
    170, 171
Harrington, Joseph, 143
Harrison, Keith, 36
Hayler, Betty, 196, 198
Heine, Herr, 52, 55-56, 59
Hemingway, Ernest, 193
Henry, O., 63
Hersey, Harold, 81, 82
Hinds, Roy, 80
Hogan, John A., 226n, 227n, 259
Holmes, Sherlock, 14, 33, 51, 220
    223, 224n
Howard, Robert, 224n
Hubbard, C.D., 19
Huckleberry Finn, 63
Hutchison, Don, xiii

I

Insidious Dr. Fu Manchu, The, 4, 5, 8

J

Jack O'Judgement, 29
James, Jesse, x, 222
Jameson, Walter, 224n
Johnson, Roland, 172
Joker, The, 26, 156-158, 245
Jungle Stories, 104
Just Men, 96, 104, 116,
    118, 121, 227n
justice figure, 37, 96, 126,
    220, 230n
Juve, 27, 29

K

Kahler, Hugh, 147, 150, 157-158
Kelsey, Clyde, 70
Kennedy, Craig, 224n
Krebs, Roland, 92, 226n
Krook, Karl B., 94-95

L

Landon, Herman, 158, 172
Lantana, Eugene, 20, 21
Larimer, Agnes, 127, 131
Leith, Lester, 86, 109
Leverage, Henry, 81-82
Ling, Dr., 21, 22, 24
Li Shoon, 14-17, 245
Lisle, Basil, 173-174
Lone Wolf, xi, 53, 165, 189,
    190, 209, 220, 229n
Lonsdell, Daniel, 75
Lowder, Christopher, 226n
Lupin, Arsene, xi, 27, 197

M

MacCulloch, Campbell, 63
Mallory, Arthur, 94-95
Man in Purple, The, 37, 127,
    195-199, 200
Mander, Inspector, 120-121
Mansar, Vera, 110, 111
Margulies, Leo, 230n
master criminals, 2, 25, 26, 45,
    60-61, 159, 162, 220
Master Mystery Stories, 230n
McCulley, Johnston, 37, 46, 76, 126,
    127, 132, 172, 188, 195,
    199, 200, 220

Melville, Herman, 63, 68
Milton, Cora Ann, 116-117, 119, 121
Milton, Henry Arthur (See The Ringer)
Mr. Chang of Scotland Yard, 17
Mr. Chang's Crime Ray, 17
Mr. Clackworthy, 64
Mr. Clackworthy, Con Man, 64
Mixer, The, 108, 111-116
Moonstone, The, 161
Moriarty, Prof., 6, 25, 51, 56
Motor Cracksman, The, 172-174
Movie Action Stories, 158
Mrs. Raffles, 99
Muggs, 38-44
mystery figure, 28, 29, 126-127
Mystery Magazine, xi
Mystery Stories, xi

N
New Magazine, 188
New York Weekly, 32
Newton, Anthony, 108-111
Nick Carter Stories, 35
Nick Carter Weekly, 11, 12
Nolan, Paddy, 30, 33, 34, 35
Norry, 108
Novel Magazine, The, 109, 227n

O
Operator 5, 9
Oppenheim, E. Phillips, 145
Orczy, Emmuska, 126
Oriental, menace, 13, 14

P
Packard, Frank, 183
Pat the Piper, 103, 143-145, 245
People's Magazine, 61, 63, 147, 152
Peter the Brazen, 13, 17
Peters, Jeff, 63, 226n
Petrie, Dr., 7, 8, 224n
Phantom Detective, The, 121, 171
Philibus, Mr., 174-179, 245, 246
Picaroon, Benevolent, The, 159,
    182-188, 220, 222, 229n, 246-247
Picaroon, Knight Errant, The, 185
Picaroon Resumes Practice, The, 185
Pimpernel, Scarlet, The, 126
Popular Detective, 200, 207, 226n

Popular Magazine, The, 32, 35, 61,
    65, 80, 103, 108, 175
pressure points, 48, 134
Pringle, Romney, 69
Prison Stories, 81
Pronzini, Bill, 225n
Prouse, Delton (See Crimson Clown)

Q
Quality Bill, 151, 153
Quality Bill's Girl, 153
Quartz, Dr., x, 1
Queen, Ellery, 99, 179

R
Radner, Martin, 128, 129, 130
Rafferty, 24, 25, 52-60, 220,
    223, 247-248
Raffles, x, 31, 44, 56, 86, 91,
    92, 93-94, 146, 188, 189
Raffles, A. J., Mrs., 99
Railroad Stories, 72
Ravenswood, 25, 30-35, 69, 222, 248
Real Detective Tales, xi
Reeder, J. G., 104, 105, 107, 121
Reeve, A. B., 14
Return of Blackshirt, The, 191
Ringer, The, 116-121, 248-249
Ringer, The, 117
Ringer Returns, The, 117
Robertson, Stewart, 67
Robin Hood, 52, 94, 166
Rodney, Silvia, 47, 48, 49
Rohmer, Sax (See A.H.S. Ward), 14
Romance of Elaine, The, 14
Ryan, Hot-dog, 178, 179

S
Saggs, 128-129, 131
Saint, The, 86, 109, 116, 121
Sanderson, Maxwell, 86-91, 96,
    220, 249-250
Saturday Evening Post, 81
Saxon, Ludovic, 229n
Scallywags, The, 111-112
Scarlet Fox, The, 137-143, 222
Scotland Yard, 125, 215
Secret Agent X, 40, 171
Shadow, The, 30, 126, 197, 217,

222, 224n, 230n
Shadow Magazine, The, 13, 171, 188
Sheik, 92-94, 96, 222, 250-251
Shiel, M.P., 9, 13
Shores, Arlin, 155
Short Stories, 9, 61, 80, 104
Si Fan, 5, 15
Siehl, Dave, 235
Simpson, Mr., 63-64
Simpson, Simp, 92, 93
Smart Set, 137
Smith, Anthony, 108, 111-115
Smith, E. Graham (pseudo for Edgar Wallace), 109
Smith, Nayland, 4, 7, 224n
Souvestre, Pierre, 27
Spider, The, 25, 46-51, 251; novels about, 46
Spider, The, 13, 171
Staegal, Richard (See Man in Purple)
Stillington, Agnes, 114, 115
Stone, John Mack (pseudo for Johnston McCulley), 40, 225n, 239
Summers, Capt., 184, 185, 186, 187
Sunday Post, The, 68, 108, 111
Sword of Justice, 230n

T
Thriller, The, 227n
Thubway Tham, 37, 66, 76-79, 220, 226n, 251-256
Thunderbolt, The, 37, 103, 124-132, 195, 200, 220, 256
Thunderbolt's Jest, The 131
tongs, 10, 11
Topical Times, 111
Toscin, The, 134, 144, 228n
trademarks, 146
Trapp, Simon, 79-81, 256-258
Trent, Anthony, 26, 166
Triem, Paul Ellsworth, 210
Tyler, Charles W., 72, 151, 152, 156

U
Union Jack, 9

V

Valentine, Jimmy, 165
Vanardy, Cuthbert (See Gray Phantom)
Verbeck, Roger, 38-44
Verrell, Anthony, 194
Verrell, Richard (See Blackshirt)
Vidcoq, 55
Villette, Phiphi, 140, 141, 143
Vincent, Harry, 224n

W
Wallace, Edgar, 29, 37, 68, 96, 97, 98, 103-104, 111, 145, 227n, 259-260
Wallace, Robert, 121
Ward, Arthur Henry Sarsfield, 4
Warwick, John, 47-50
Weekly News, 99
Weird Tales, 224n
Weisinger, Mort, 19
Wendell, Faustina, 40, 43
Wentworth, Richard, 86, 129, 188
West, 38
White Rook, The, 26, 146-150 158, 220, 260-261
Wild West Weekly, 80
Wilhelm, Kaiser, 8
Williams, B. Church, 11
Williams, Race, 220
Worthington, Dale (See John Doe)
Worthington, Molly, 210, 212, 213, 214, 215, 216, 217, 220
Wrath of Fu Manchu, The, 4, 7, 224n
Wu Fang, 14

X
Xenophile, 224n

Y
Yat, Doctor, 22
Yellow Label, The, 35
Yellow Peril, 4, 8-9, 14
Young, Gordon, 138

Z
Zorro, 37, 38, 46, 127, 146, 199, 220